The Essential Chaplin

THE
Essential Chaplin

PERSPECTIVES ON THE LIFE AND
ART OF THE GREAT COMEDIAN

Edited with an Introduction by

RICHARD SCHICKEL

Ivan R. Dee
CHICAGO

www.ivanrdee.com

Library of Congress Cataloging-in-Publication Data:
Schickel, Richard.
    The essential Chaplin : perspectives on the life and art of the great comedian / Richard Schickel.
        p. cm.
    ISBN-13: 978-1-56663-682-7 (cloth : alk. paper)
    ISBN-10: 1-56663-682-5 (cloth : alk. paper)
    ISBN-13: 978-1-56663-701-5 (pbk. : alk. paper)
    ISBN-10: 1-56663-701-5 (pbk. : alk. paper)
    1. Chaplin, Charlie, 1889-1977. I. Title.
PN2287.C5S35 2006
791.4302'8092—dc22   200503725

Contents

CHAPLINESQUE

We make our meek adjustments,
Contented with such random consolations
As the wind deposits
In slithered and too ample pockets.

For we can still love the world, who find
A famished kitten on the step, and know
Recesses for it from the fury of the street,
Or warm torn elbow coverts.

We will sidestep, and to the final smirk
Dally the doom of that inevitable thumb
That slowly chafes its puckered index toward us,
Facing the dull squint with what innocence
And what surprise!

And yet these fine collapses are not lies
More than the pirouettes of any pliant cane;
Our obsequies are, in a way, no enterprise.
We can evade you, and all else but the heart:
What blame to us if the heart live on.

The game enforces smirks; but we have seen
The moon in lonely alleys make
A grail of laughter of an empty ash can,
And through all sound of gaiety and quest
Have heard a kitten in the wilderness.

—HART CRANE

The Essential Chaplin

Introduction:
The Tramp Transformed

Charlie Chaplin needed the movies. And, as it happened, the movies needed him. This mutual dependency was not, however, immediately clear to either party when Mack Sennett began releasing Chaplin's first primitive one-reelers and split reels early in 1914. The comedian was, at age twenty-five, a youthful veteran of the English music halls, plucked from one of Fred Karno's comedy companies, then touring the United States. He was a headliner with Karno but an underpaid one. He was also tired of the road. So what he mainly saw in Sennett's contract was better money ($150 per week) and a chance to settle down in pleasant Los Angeles for a year's stay. It is impossible to imagine him thinking that his gifts were uniquely suited to film or that he would necessarily linger long in the movies.

As for the movies, they were even younger than Chaplin, about a decade old as a narrative art form and just beginning to attain feature length (Griffith would make *The Birth of a Nation* in this very year), but still mainly wedded to a length of one reel, still for the most part distributed via nickelodeons and very reluctantly starting to embrace the star system, which would be a major engine of their transformation from profitable fad to major American industry. As important to Chaplin's story, movies were not at this point generally regarded as an art form—or even as a potential art form.

They were, of course, wildly popular, but, generally speaking, with all the wrong people—immigrants and the working class mainly. The middle class did occasionally drop in at the flickers, but chiefly as a guilty pleasure. Or when the newspapers reported the release of something extraordinary: a passion play, for example, or Sarah Bernhardt

3

starring awkwardly in Queen Elizabeth, or one of the historical spectacles then being imported from Italy.

The great exception to this indifference to quotidian moviemaking was D. W. Griffith, failed stage actor and playwright, who sensed the potential of the medium and from 1908 onward directed some four hundred increasingly ambitious one-reelers, many of them truncated adaptations of famous plays, novels, and even poems as well as original slices of urban life, realistic and melodramatic in tone. People began to notice and talk and write about his work. Then, in the years after World War I, other films (*The Cabinet of Dr. Caligari*) and other filmmakers (Sergei Eisenstein and the other Soviet masters of the epic) began attracting a certain amount of high critical attention. In those years Chaplin was very much of this ilk. And we were haltingly on the way to our present situation—film archives, film schools, cinema studies—an academic interest in film that is now more intense than that of the general public or the general-interest publications that are supposed to serve it.

The premise of this anthology—the primary aim of which is to gather the most interesting writing about Charles Chaplin from commentators whose primary concern was not movie reviewing—is that this activity was a necessary step on the movies' road to respectability, to its recognition as a legitimate art form with its own grammar and narrative tropes. The likes of T. S, Eliot, Sigmund Freud, and George Bernard Shaw all commented upon Chaplin approvingly (though not at essay length), and that approval reflects the intense interest in Chaplin among the intellectual and artistic communities at large. Some—but not all—of this writing was a bit desperate in its search for analogies between the traditional expressive forms and this new one. Especially in the first years of Chaplin's fame, his critics failed to isolate and analyze film's unique ways of telling a story or Chaplin's instinctive mastery of the form. Still, in a certain sense, in certain circles of the commentaria, he became the new medium's most important test case, the repository of the high artistic hopes of the small, slightly beleaguered group whose passion for the new medium was boundless.

In time that interest would have an effect on Chaplin's work—and not always for the better. It would turn his head and turn him away from his best vein, since intellectually, at least, he was a rather simple man whose genius—and I use that word advisedly—was not for literary, political, or socio-psychological expression. He would eventually over-reach himself in part because of his attempt to satisfy the expectations of his more literate admirers, some of whom would finally turn against him. It is a secondary premise of this book that in tracing the course of their affections and disaffections we can, metaphorically, observe the often tormented relationship between the higher cinephile community and the more serious filmmaking community. Filmmakers relish the attentions of cinephiles but are not—certainly in the United States—an intellectual group, except in their self-delusory moments.

2.

A tiny, passionate literature of film had begun to take root before Chaplin's arrival on screen. The movie trade press, in those days, took the movies with great critical seriousness, very soberly attending each new technological and aesthetic advance of the new medium. Its reviewers are now forgotten, but their work was filled with aspirations for the movies and, one suspects, for themselves as the first commentators to make film a subject worthy of thoughtful discourse. Then, in 1915, Vachel Lindsay, the populist poet, published what may be the first book-length study of the movies, *The Art of the Moving Picture*. There was something wild and wooly about his prose, which to the modern reader is often unconsciously comic. But his work was widely read and discussed (though he spoke only briefly and unenthusiastically about Chaplin). A year later Hugo Munsterberg brought out *The Film: A Psychological Study*, very Germanic in its taxonomic humorlessness but still something to be reckoned with.

In this period Francis Hackett, novelist and biographer, began writing sensible and attentive movie reviews in *The New Republic*, and by the early 1920s most serious publications were reviewing movies on a regular and by no means patronizing basis. Robert E. Sherwood, soon to be a famous playwright, was one such critic. So was Robert Benchley, later a beloved comic bumbler in the movies. Perhaps most important among these figures was Gilbert Seldes, who was the first multimedia critic, writing about all the popular arts—film, of course, but also vaudeville, Broadway revues, pop music, comic strips—arguing in lively, unpretentious prose for their expressive vitality, their importance in shaping the American sensibility at the beginning of the modern media age.

All these critics quickly began to pay particular attention to the works of Charles Spencer Chaplin. He was, in fact, a godsend to them. That's what I mean about the movies needing him as much as he needed the movies. For here was an inordinately gifted and popular star whose skills could be linked to the long tradition of clowning, traceable to the commedia dell'arte or even, if you liked, to Aristophanes (Seldes was the author of a modern version of the *Lysistrata*), who nevertheless owed his worldwide fame to the newest of all the media. His theatrical experience prior to the movies may have been no more distinguished than that of such other stars as Mary Pickford and Douglas Fairbanks (who came to film a year after Chaplin and became his best friend). But you could make something elevated, and, just as important, reassuring to the middlebrow audience, out of Chaplin's links to the great comic tradition. They were given leave not just to like him but to respect him—and the movies as well.

In a matter of a couple of years the early critics were in full appreciative cry, and with their aid Chaplin achieved a stardom unprecedented in the movies' short history. A case can be made that he was, from about 1917 or '18 through the late 1930s, the most famous man in the world. There were other famous people around, of course, and for the first time the mass media—film, radio, popular magazines, and newspapers—had the technology to apply a relentless scrutiny to the public's favorites. But no one—sports star, politician, author—commanded for so many years the avid gaze of the multitudes. Others came and went, but Chaplin abided, in ever-growing prosperity, at the top of the heap.

But we are getting ahead of our story. Chaplin's first success was an authentically populist one. It was the general public, not the artistic and intellectual communities, that first singled him out of the Sennett crowd. The not-so-hot Sennett movies tend to be narratively ramshackle, and though Chaplin found the rudiments of the costume and makeup that would stamp him forever in his second film, *Kid Auto Races at Venice* (which is one of his better Sennett releases), he appeared in a variety of other guises during that year and was often enough quite unsympathetic, not to say mean-spirited. One suspects that his delicacy had something to do with the notice that was taken of him. Sennett's comedians were, on the whole, rather large men, given to rather crude comic activities. Chaplin was slight of build, graceful in his movements, and—at least in this bustling context—subtle in his responses to comic predicaments. He appears to have instinctively grasped the essence of movie performance, which is that the camera must be, and can be, trusted to direct our attention to the small, telling gesture or expression, that you don't necessarily have to do a pratfall or a skid turn to claim its regard. Chaplin mastered the broad basic grammar of silent comedy, but it was often his minimalism at the center of the Sennett frenzy that caught the audience's eye. This was especially so when he began writing and directing his own work, about four months after his first Sennett film was released.

The first prominent person outside the trade press to write appreciatively of Chaplin was Minnie Maddern Fiske. Forgotten now, she was, in her rather long day—her career lasted from the 1870s until 1930—generally thought to be one of the great American actresses. She too was a minimalist, famous for commanding the audience's attention by standing stock still on the stage for twenty minutes, or turning her back on it to deliver an important speech. In 1916 she wrote that much of Chaplin's work was vulgar, but she observed that vulgarity had been essential to comic art from the its beginnings (she was probably the first writer to evoke the spirit of Aristophanes and Plautus in considering Chaplin). More important, she noticed the precision of his technique, asserted amidst the "primitive and meaningless" hubbub of his first films. She predicted for this "extraordinary artist," with his "serious, wistful face," that he would "attain the artistic stature to which he seems entitled."

3.

It seems likely that Chaplin read Mrs. Fiske's article; it was, according to David Robinson's extremely good biography of him, widely commented upon at the time. And, indeed, a few months later she was back in print, defending Chaplin against a drama critic's slighting deprecation of him. Robinson discovered, in this period, all sorts of flattering mentions of him in the nonmovie critical press; his name appeared in a Los Angeles review of Paul Dukas's *The Sorcerer's Apprentice*, Haywood Broun mentioned him in a review of a Broadway show, Benchley drew a broad comparison between him and Falstaff. By 1917 the playwright Henry O'Higgins, writing in *The New Republic*, was observing that Chaplin's style was becoming "more delicate and finished" all the time while noting a bourgeois backlash against him as a "moral menace," to borrow a phrase from a Brooklyn reformer who was concerned with the effect of Chaplin's occasional anarchism on young people. In the end O'Higgins, writing very much in the populist spirit animating the American left at that time, more or less dismissed the intellectual swells and their learned commentary on Chaplin. His success, was, O'Higgins said, an excellent example "of how the popular eye can recognize such a talent without the aid of the pundits of culture and even in spite of their anathemas."

We must imagine Chaplin, in these years, as too busy to pay more than glancing attention to the culturati. In all of movie history no one's rise was ever more meteoric than his. A year after his Sennett debut, he signed with Essanay for $1,250 a week. A year after that he was with Mutual at $10,000 a week (with a $150,000 signing bonus). In 1917 he signed a million-dollar contract with First National—and began building his very own studio. A couple years after that his partial ownership of United Artists guaranteed him full ownership and total artistic control of all his films. In the four years between his 1914 debut and his initial First National production he made sixty-one of the eighty-two films he created over the course of a very long career—all of which he did the hard way.

By this I mean he could not write out a scenario and then direct himself doing whatever it called for. The comic sequences that are his glories had to be created live on his stages, with Chaplin inventing every bit of business for himself and the other actors, then trying them out with everyone on their feet, varying their bits, their interactions—adding and subtracting to their ideas, often enough abandoning them completely. He was famous for making multiple takes—sometimes as many as eighty of them—just to get one portion of a sequence right. And when inspiration failed to flow, Chaplin would simply shut down the set, idling his cast and crew who were nevertheless kept on salary. It was an expensive way of working, though since these were silent films, it was easier to do than it was later when sound production more or less doubled both the costs and complexity of shooting. But for Chaplin it was the only possible way of working. To put the point simply, his working method was that of a choreographer, not that of a movie director.

For—and this is the most significant thing about him—his was essentially a kinetic genius. He had little formal education, and though he was a devout autodidact his literary intelligence by no means functioned at the genius level. It was in motion—the ability to convey emotion in seemingly heedless, thoughtless, purely instinctive action—that his unique gift resided. And never mind that the improvisatory impression he conveyed was almost always the result of relentless and agonizing experiment. It was the impression of heedlessness that counted.

In the teens of the twentieth century Chaplin was a man possessed—by this new medium so perfectly suited to his gifts, by the need to explore and expand his relationship to it. There was nothing to trammel his energies. He had a brief taste of his stardom's power when he journeyed to New York to sign his Mutual contract and was astonished by the crowds that jammed the stations wherever his train stopped. But, isolated in Los Angeles, a long way—five days by rail—from the population centers of the East, the rumble and roar of his fans was muffled by distance. He might read some of the press's comments about his work, but it is hard to imagine him being more than bemused by it. He had time, of course, for his extraordinarily busy romantic life and to be something of a man about town in Los Angeles, seen frequently at premieres and sporting events. But LA's provincial and brainless life in no way interfered with his creative activities.

Doubtless there are artists in other field who have had periods as fecund as Chaplin enjoyed in the years immediately after he left Sennett—periods in which almost everything they touched turned out brilliantly. Generally these artists, like Chaplin, were obsessively exploring new ways of seeing—one thinks of Matisse's fauve period or Picasso's embrace of Cubism—but it is also generally true that their immediate reward was controversy and critical contempt. Chaplin's reward was the opposite.

Most of the writing about Chaplin rather missed the main points of his work. The reviewers, like the best moviemakers, were desperate to assert film's claims as an art form; that's why they were so assiduous about tracing Chaplin's roots back into theatrical history. Meanwhile filmmakers were doing something comparable in their choice of material. Griffith in particular—but many others as well—thought that by making movie adaptations of the literary works that had enjoyed enormous popularity in the genteel parlor culture of the late nineteenth and early twentieth centuries the new medium could, in effect, co-opt that culture, bring it out of the house and into the theaters, which were growing ever more ornate and comfortable. This strategy worked. Never mind that much of what they adapted to the screen was sentimental and melodramatic, not necessarily the best the older culture offered. Never mind that the silent screen's inability to reproduce dialogue—intertitles were never an adequate substitute for the spoken word—often fatally flawed their enterprise, essentially reducing complex literary works to their narrative outlines. People approved the effort; it bespoke a noble and uplifting attempt to move the movies away from their low-life beginnings.

No one seemed to notice that Chaplin, for all his sublimity, stood outside this effort. His sensibility remained as Victorian in outlook as Griffith's, but he didn't do adaptations. And, in this period, he didn't inflate his material. His films remained short—three or four reels, less than an hour in running time—and they were very austerely realized. He was at heart a frugal soul, ever the poor lad who worried about losing his money. So, for example, his street scenes always seem rather underpopulated, his restaurants somewhat lacking in customers. Even his World War I trenches in *Shoulder Arms* are not exactly teeming with soldiers. He understood, instinctively, that the camera had nothing more interesting to look at than himself. So what he did, primarily, was establish an arena in which he along with one or two foils could move with unfettered comic grace before a camera that was pretty much anchored in the middle distance passively observing the actors, generally in full frame, largely uninterrupted by close-ups or medium shots or editing for editing's sake. He had said when he left Keystone that all he needed to make a movie was a park, a cop, a pretty girl, and, of course, himself, comically embroiled with the other elements of his little scenario. Through the years he would add other characters to the mix, but essentially that remained his aesthetic through his last silent film, the great *City Lights* of 1931.

In the 1920s a few complaints—they were never many and didn't interfere with his huge popular success—began creeping into the press that Chaplin was cinematically "old-fashioned." You will read herein the likes of Stark Young, as early as 1922, urging him on to finer, more ambitious things—*Lilliom*, perhaps, or *Peer Gynt*, or *He Who Gets Slapped*. This represented a fundamental misunderstanding of Chaplin, world-class solipsist that he was; everything he produced had to be handcrafted, and the hands doing the crafting had to be his alone. Unlike the other great comedians of his era, he did not employ gag men. Virtually every idea he explored in his films was his. So far as we can tell, he could not be influenced by developments elsewhere in cinema; he had no interest in films of "crowd splendor" (to borrow Vachel Lindsay's quaint phrase) or in Eisensteinian montage or in the expressionism that was Germany's great contribution to the intellectual stir surrounding film in the twenties. His greatest rival, Buster Keaton, was much more attentive to settings, to the camera's potential for delightful tricks, to the comic possibilities of major disaster—train wrecks, cyclones, rock slides—than Chaplin, and in time his reputation as a filmmaker would come to exceed Chaplin's among cineastes and cinephiles, though his popularity with the general public never approached Chaplin's.

But Chaplin was, in these years, spectacularly right about the nature of his gifts and the best way of presenting them to the public. There is an unimprovable perfection to many of the short films he made after leaving Sennett. Sometimes his gags were quite brief and simple. I think, for example, of a moment when he must move something like a dozen bentwood chairs from one place to another. He keeps piling them on his back until, suddenly, Chaplin has turned himself into a human hedgehog. Or there's *One A.M.*, the entire one-reel running time of which is devoted to a spifflicated Chaplin trying to mount a set of stairs in order to get to his bedroom. You cannot imagine the malevolence of that staircase, its ability to thwart Chaplin's every attempt to accomplish his simple goal. Then there's *The Pawnshop*, which contains an immortal sequence in which a customer offers an alarm clock as surety for a loan to the clerk, played by Chaplin. He submits the thing to what amounts to a full-scale medical examination. Then, whimsically, he begins to regard it as a can of tuna, which he prizes open with a can opener. All along, he never changes expression—he's just a man doing his job in a setting that is almost stark in its simplicity—a counter, a shelf behind it, one other actor (the customer) shot almost entirely from behind. That he wrecks the object of his attentions, in the process reducing the customer to a quivering mass of puzzled protoplasm, goes entirely unnoticed by a Chaplin intently caught up in the implacable logic of his gags. I've never seen another comedian get so much out of so simple a situation.

On the other hand, there are things like *The Rink*, in which Chaplin's great heavy-set foil, Eric Campbell, is intent on seducing the object of Chaplin's affections, the sublimely good-natured Edna Purviance. The film consists largely of Chaplin and Campbell contending for the girl on roller skates. The contrast between Campbell's bulk and Chaplin's slightness is inherently funny. But Chaplin's inventiveness in eluding the bigger man's potentially crushing grip is mind-bending. Again, until you see it you cannot imagine how many ways he can invent to frustrate Campbell. At one point in the action Chaplin's cane is converted into a drill, which he spins into Campbell's capacious stomach, keeping him at a distance sufficient to prevent his flailing arms from locking around Chaplin.

This film is considerably more complicated from a directorial point of view than the others, involving more (and more complex) movement in a much larger space. But like them, it is rich in visual puns—the cane as drill is a good example—which were one of Chaplin's great strengths in his early days. Such moments belie the notion that he was unaware of, or indifferent to, cinema's unique expressive possibilities. He instinctively understood that you could not, for instance, do the clock gag on a stage—it would be very largely lost to the balcony or, for that matter, to the back rows of the orchestra. The intimacy of the camera, its ability to reveal the pun in, as it were, the wink of its closely peering eye, permits the joke to work—no matter where we happen to be sitting.

4.

At around the time Chaplin began working for First National, the question of consciousness began to intervene in his work. His production pace had already begun to slow—almost from the beginning of his career, his inability to satisfy his producers' release schedule as he searched for comic perfection bedeviled his relationship with his backers. This problem was not entirely of his own making. At this point in time it was becoming impossible, especially for an artist of Chaplin's stature, to prosper making short films—exhalations of a single comic breath. Feature length required something more than a park, a cop, a girl, and a man in baggy pants. Longer films required narratives of greater complexity.

And, since he was nothing if not ambitious, Chaplin himself needed to expand his horizons. Which says nothing about the ever-heightening expectations of his fans, both among the literati and among ordinary moviegoers. There is about his early short films an air of careless rapture. The newness of the movies, the freshness of the California landscape, with Los Angeles just a sketch of the megalopolis it was to become, seems to have lifted the weight of his grim past from him. These movies were just little behavioral anecdotes. They did not have to mean, they had only to be.

But longer films required backstory, some sense of a man's—even a humble tramp's—place in the universe, some sense of how he regarded the people with whom he shared that universe. And here Chaplin's personal history belied the good cheer, the sheer delight, of his early films. He had to face up to—and draw upon—a grim past he had, for a few years, escaped.

5.

He had been born into relative comfort. His father, Charles Chaplin, Sr., had been a singer and headliner in the English music halls of the late nineteenth century, and his mother, Hannah, had performed successfully in them as well. But the father was an alcoholic who deserted his family and died out of work and in poverty when Chaplin was fourteen. Nominally he was in the care of his mother, whom he adored. In his memoirs he speaks of her standing at the window of one or the other of their bed-sitters, describing the odd gaits and behaviors of passersby, which Chaplin would then satirically replicate, eliciting gales of laughter from her. But when Chaplin was seven years old she began succumbing, with increasing regularity, to bouts of mental illness, and from that time onward she was in and out of mental institutions. And Chaplin himself began his childhood career as a ward of the state, resident in a variety of schools for orphaned and abandoned children. David Robinson estimates that such education as he acquired in these years amounted to no more than the fourth grade level. He was essentially parentless, an orphan in fact, if not in name, from the time he was six years old.

His childhood has often been described as Dickensian, which it surely was—just as the more complex artistic products he derived from it were also Dickensian in their combinations of grotesque characters, melodramatic incident, alternations of terror and sentiment. But the main thing we have to understand about Chaplin's youth was how lonely it must have been, how surviving on these streets made him into the radically self-sufficient man he became. Aside from his half-brother Sidney, a sailor who returned from the sea and became Charlie's only true intimate when he was fifteen, he essentially lived by his own wits. As far as we can tell, he made no close or lasting friends in those years or, for that matter, anytime in his later years. He had many acquaintances and many colleagues, some of whom he worked with for years, but these relationships were not—Fairbanks aside—close. We do not gain the impression that they had any influence on his art or thought. Everything he accomplished was the product of his own almost completely self-referential imaginings, slightly tinctured by the cultural climate in which he existed as a child.

There is a hidden and tragic story to these years. The piece by Stephen M. Weissman, reprinted here, persuasively argues that Hannah Chaplin's insanity must have been the result of syphilis. None of Chaplin's biographers mention this diagnosis, very likely because none of Hannah's doctors definitely mentioned it in their written reports. In those days, as Weissman observes, the disease was known as "the great mimic," since its symptoms were so often mistaken for those of other, less lethal, less socially unacceptable illnesses.

It's impossible to imagine the very young Charlie knowing immediately what was ailing his mother. But he was a smart street kid, and he must soon have discovered her secret and come to the hushed and reluctant understanding that her illness was the result of an occasional career as a prostitute. In any event we know that Chaplin kept his distance from her until her death in 1928. He supported her when he began earning money and later brought her to America and bought her a little house in Los Angeles where she was cared for by nurse-companions. But he rarely visited her or mentioned her to others.

Once, surely, he had loved her. Surely he continued to do so in his way. But he must also have seen her as his great betrayer—not merely because she could not support him, but because one of her ways of trying to do so was so shameful. His later work shows a powerful interest in women who, like his mother, stand on the brink of poverty and thus on the brink of the temptation to sell themselves to men. This interest was, of course, heightened by the plays and novels of the late Victorian and early Edwardian era, where that theme was common. But Chaplin had reason to know, at firsthand, the cost of succumbing to temptation. In the very last film of his career, *The Countess from Hong Kong* in 1967, he was still exploring this situation.

But he was equally concerned with its obverse. When he was not thinking about "fallen" women and the virgin-whore dichotomy, he was thinking about innocence and purity, "the Victorian cult of the child," as social historians of the era call it. Whether it is Jackie Coogan in *The Kid* or the flower girl in *City Lights*, Chaplin's character will do anything to protect their purity against society's impositions. The Tramp will somehow rescue them because their fates are so intimately bound up with his own.

For the Tramp, though wonderfully inventive in his ability to escape the law and the social conventions it upheld, was himself an imperiled innocent. His character was—no other word for it—infantile, pre-moral, maybe even prelapsarian. Like a child, his ideas of how the adult world actually worked were primitive and rather mechanistic. In a certain sense, Chaplin was always reinventing the wheel, and he was frequently bedeviled when his wheel didn't spin the way he thought it should. This was one of the great sources of his visual punning. If, to take a very modest example, a couple of lengths of welded pipe looked to him like binoculars, it was a source of puzzlement and frustration for him when he looked through them and they didn't bring distant objects closer to his view. But more significant was his child-like relationship to authority. The sources of its power were always mysterious—and arbitrary—to him. It was usually, in one way or another, the adult looming over the wayward kid, and no more than any other child could he discern why—brute strength aside—its impositions had to be obeyed. But, like a child, he reserved the right to sly rebellion—the kick in the policeman's pants, the source of which was undetectable to the distracted guardian of the law.

This figure of his lived in a nominally real world. It wasn't, of course, but (unlike a commedia dell'arte character) his settings were not abstract. They looked enough like the world his audience inhabited so that an illusion of reality—and a direct identification with his character—could be sustained. He did not hide the fact that his Tramp had his roots in his own desperate London childhood, and people naturally noticed this autobiographical element in his work. "[H]e always plays only himself as he was in his dismal youth," Freud wrote, thinking Chaplin an "exceptionally simple and transparent case" of the artist whose achievements were "intimately bound up with their childhood memories, impressions, repressions and disappointments." But there was a little bit more to the matter than that.

As we've already observed, Chaplin's early, shorter films have about them an almost giddy playfulness (however painstaking their construction might have been) that remains palpable to this day. It was if, under the California sun, working in an industry that was not yet hidebound by rules, he was finally enjoying the pleasures he had never known in his grim London boyhood. He was like a child on a long summer vacation, utterly absorbed in the games he's playing— the essence of a kid at play is that he is completely committed to the fantasies he's living within, the world well lost. But Chaplin had, of course, an advantage denied childen: he was blessed with free will. If something went radically wrong for the Tramp, he could simply hit the road as the camera irised in on his jauntily waddling figure—no questions asked, no responsibilities nagging at him.

We must remember that he was in his early twenties at the time, young enough so that the memories of his harsh early years were still painfully fresh, but also young enough to believe that his present success predicted a future even more promising. Why should it not be? He was playing out for an enraptured audience a near-perfect fantasy. To be a child and yet to be able to escape all the punishments, all the dreary learning experiences, inherent in that condition is to be in a state of regressive bliss. It is childhood without tears, childhood in which pathos is only a temporary and surmountable inconvenience. In effect, Chaplin was able to live on the screen within a child's version of paradise. And in his greatest version of this paradise, *The Kid*, he was, in effect, able to be his own idealized parent.

That is to say that the perfectly beautiful and stunningly gifted little boy, Jackie Coogan—the only true co-star Chaplin ever permitted to arise in his presence—played a version of Chaplin as a boy while Chaplin himself played the father figure—benign, indulgent, and, above all, fiercely protective—he must have dreamed of having when he was roughly Coogan's age. When the child is abducted from him by the soulless organs of the state, Chaplin permits himself the one unambiguously heroic sequence in his entire canon. The child, begging piteously not to be taken from the Tramp, is carried off in the orphanage's open truck through a cityscape that is clearly meant to be more London than Los Angeles. Chaplin gives pursuit over the tenement rooftops, risking life and limb to rescue the lad, in a sequence that is much more suspenseful than it is comic, finally dropping into the truck, beating the attending official nearly senseless, scaring off the truck's driver with his protective fury, and embracing the Kid heedlessly.

It is a terrific sequence—made with simple eloquence and elegance (let no one doubt that when he was of a mind to be, Chaplin could be a master filmmaker)—as well as, if you will, a statement of principle. This is innocence with muscle, innocence asserting itself without tricks or slyness. It is also possibly the greatest love scene Chaplin ever filmed.

Those scenes always gave Chaplin trouble. "The history of bisexuality in the movies begins with Chaplin," David Thomson writes, and I do not disagree with him. Once or twice Chaplin was quite fetching in drag. And there were many moments when his response to trouble or to simple masculine intrusions on his privacy was simpering and "feminine" in the very old-fashioned definition of the term. This does not, I hasten to add, indicate a streak of latent homosexuality in him. In the tradition of clowning there is a very strong element of bisexuality. Or perhaps one should call it a sort of anti-sexuality. But Thomson

is right to see something less than straightforward in Chaplin's relationships with women. He is never the aggressor with them; he never
makes his admiration or his needs known to them in an open—one almost wrote healthy—way. He tends to idealize them, to see them as
more girlish than womanly, and to moon over them from afar.

Of all his on-screen love objects, it seems to me that Edna Purviance brought out the best in him. In life she was a simple, straightforward, no-nonsense kind of girl, whom Chaplin discovered working
in the Essanay office and made her his lover, on screen and off. There
was nothing ethereal about her, or about Chaplin's treatment of her
in their films. You believed, watching them work together on screen,
that their real-life relationship was easy and, just possibly, kind of
fun—very much in the spirit of Chaplin's sunny early movie days, so
little shadowed by his past. Much later, when Paulette Goddard was
his lover, wife, and co-star, something equally natural attended their
relationship. As far as we were allowed to see, there was more of pal-
ship than passion in these romantic transactions, nothing that was
openly sexy in them.

This opens up a paradox, for Chaplin was a notorious and invet-
erate womanizer. Literally thousands of women passed through his
bedroom. Yet most of them were teenage girls—jailbait, not to put too
fine a point on it. Some have argued that the great unconsummated
love of his life was just such a girl, the beautiful Hetty Kelly, whom he
met early in his theatrical career and whom he idealized from afar for
years (she died in the flu epidemic of 1918). I suppose this unattained
dream woman may have permanently bent his sexuality.

But it seems to me equally likely that Chaplin simply mistrusted
more experienced women, women like his mother, who were capable
of terrible betrayals. As he perhaps saw it, a fresh young woman, smit-
ten by a first love for an older man, was incapable of that kind of behavior. In any event, these girls most closely matched the Victorian
ideal of childish innocence that was so important to him. Just why the
destruction of that innocence was such a compelling need for him—
and for others like him (D. W. Griffith offered another example)—is
another, perhaps unanswerable question. It must have something to
do with taking possession of that innocence, being the male force that
gently, wisely (as the male sees it) brings it to worldliness. At which

point, of course, the male loses interest in the very "goods" he has "damaged."

To me it is interesting that in the one film in which Chaplin addressed these issues in detail, *A Woman of Paris*, he appears unrecognizably only in an uncredited bit part. Released in 1923, it received excellent reviews and did no business, precisely because of Chaplin's absence from it. Be that as it may, it offers a mature Purviance as the title character, introduced as an innocent country girl, Marie, who finds herself alone in the French capital because her equally innocent artist-lover, with whom she was running away from home, has been detained by the sudden death of his father. She becomes the kept woman of an elegant boulevardier (superbly played by Adolph Menjou) and endures the suicide of her first love after he finds her, so profoundly changed, in Paris. After that tragedy, she magically reverts to her lost innocence, becoming in the film's final sequence the chaste guardian of, yes, orphans. The film was much praised at the time for its "sophistication," so unlike Chaplin's other works in its portrayal of rather sexy high life. But it also represents, in the fate he devised for Marie, wish-fulfillment of a much simpler order. The values it finally upholds are, for a jazz-age film, the old-fashioned opposite of sophisticated.

A Woman of Paris brought out the best in him directorially, but it became a signpost on a road not taken by Chaplin. He followed it instead with what are commonly regarded as his two best "pure" comedies of feature length—*The Gold Rush* (1925) and *The Circus* (1928). The former is, in a sense, epic autobiography. What is the film's Klondike but Hollywood as Chaplin first encountered it—a place where an innocent little fellow can strike it rich? And what is Georgia Hale's "dance hall girl" but one of those tricky grown-up women, alternately teasing and indifferent (and perhaps no better than she should be), who haunted Chaplin's darker imaginings. Nevertheless it is the one Chaplin feature with an unambiguously happy ending (he emerges from the adventure with millions in his pockets and the woman on his arm), and it contains some of his greatest comic inventions—most notably the roll dance and the scene in which the starving Chaplin and Mack Swain boil a shoe and try to eat it. People immediately recognized the film for the comic masterpiece it was, the

great achievement Chaplin had been striving for since he began making features. In it, certainly, he achieves an almost perfect balance between the comic, the pathetic, the melodramatic, and the spectacular
that feature production demanded.

Yet, perhaps perversely, I prefer *The Circus*. Of all Chaplin's
longer films, it is the most purely and perfectly comedic. Its romantic
elements—he's in love with the bareback rider who is also the abused
daughter of the circus's enigmatically cruel owner—are quite perfunctory. It concentrates instead on a masterful orchestration of brilliantly extended comic set pieces, climaxed by the great sequence in
which Chaplin tries to walk a high wire while assailed by a troupe of
malevolent monkeys. The film was well enough received at the time,
and it came close to making the case that one could make a (relatively
short) feature that was essentially all laughs all the time. But Chaplin
himself was distracted by a messy divorce at the time, a studio fire
burned down his main set—the circus tent, and reviewers implied
that compared to *The Gold Rush*, this was a "minor" work. He did not
disown it, but, on the other hand, in his autobiography he refers to it
only in a single passing sentence.

Intricate as its gagging is—and it was never more so in any of his
pictures—it perhaps seemed a sort of half-step backward to him, not
the giant step forward he wanted to make. And would make with *City
Lights* three years later. It is the film in which the romantic yearnings
of this isolated man emphatically burst forth. The blind flower girl is
unquestionably a version of "blind" Hetty Kelly. For the film he went
so far as to reproduce the park fence where he used to meet Hetty, and
stationed the blind flower girl whom he chastely adores at that fence
for most of their encounters. His Tramp is, of course, a version of
Chaplin as he once was, a man with no obvious prospects. Finally, his
desire to find the money to pay for the operation that will restore her
sight is an obvious symbolization of Chaplin's need to prove himself
to Hetty.

It seems to me that *City Lights* is emotionally Chaplin's most
nakedly autobiographical film; it is suffused with might-have-been
sadness and, at its end, with an ambiguous attempt to fictionally set
right what in reality could never be. If, in life he had been able to do
for Hetty what the Tramp does for the flower girl, we can imagine

things working out for Chaplin in quite a different way. He would surely have prospered theatrically—he was too gifted not to—but perhaps in a purely local, English way, not as a world figure. But having no binding ties, and having been steeled in adversity, he was free to make his own very different destiny. And to make himself his only reliable reference point as he confronted the problems that his art, his life, presented to him.

6.

None of this would have been clear to someone viewing *City Lights* in 1931. By then everyone knew of Chaplin's harsh beginnings, but Hetty's rejection was unknown. So was the fact that Chaplin's first return to Europe in 1921 was heavily motivated by his desire to reconcile with her (he learned of her death when he was on his way to her). What people at the time saw was simply a wonderful romance, shot through with some of his most inventive comic turns—in some ways his most perfectly balanced film. But they also saw it more as an exercise in conventional, as opposed to heartfelt, sentiment. They had no way of knowing its subjective importance to Chaplin.

He had now gone as far as he could reasonably go with his particular blend of comedy and romance. He needed to make statements of more self-evident social "importance." There were reasons beyond the demands of his own ego for doing so. There was the vast social trauma of worldwide depression to take into account. There was the coming of sound to movies, which threatened the foundations of his aesthetic more seriously than it did that of any other film performer. There was the ever growing complexity of his relationship to his audience that had to be reckoned with.

On this last point let me use myself as a case in point. Members of my own and later moviegoing generations had to approach Chaplin from the wrong end of his career. A re-release version of *The Gold Rush* aside, the movies of his that I had seen in my most impressionable moviegoing years were his later ones—*The Great Dictator, Monsieur Verdoux, Limelight,* all of them in one way or another unsatisfying. To put the point more rawly, they were mostly unfunny. They made it difficult to understand what our parents, or his early critics, had seen in him. His best work had been accomplished during the impressionable years of earlier generations, and it required for my generation a large act of imagination to recapture the simple rapture of the relationship between them and Chaplin. "Yes, but . . ." one tended to say. What we knew of him—his troubles with the courts and the politicians (which made us sympathetic to him, but in a rather dispassionate way) and his exile in Switzerland—seemed to be marked by a bitterness that we could not entirely understand. It was a great fuss about something that, with the passing years, seemed rather trivial.

I began to engage with him in a more fully sympathetic way in 2002 when I began producing *Charlie*, my documentary film about him. This began to happen when I was studying some film he did not make—newsreel footage of his first return to England and Europe in 1921. This material is astonishing, for the crowds that surrounded him from the moment he stepped off the boat train in London till the day he left for home are huge and essentially uncontrolled. One might have thought that his friends, Douglas Fairbanks and Mary Pickford, who had encountered similar mass hysteria on their European wedding trip a year earlier, might have warned him of what awaited him, but either they did not speak of the matter or he ignored them. In any case, aside from a few distinctly overmatched policemen, no one was attending to crowd control. Indeed, Chaplin's entourage for the trip consisted of a valet-secretary and one lone press agent, and there is no evidence that temporary help was hired along the way to help manage his near-riotous public.

This naiveté on Chaplin's part was compounded of several factors. One was that in provincial Los Angeles he was a familiar figure, part of the local landscape, and thus able to move about quite freely. Another was that he underestimated the impact of his movies on Europe. He knew, of course, that they were popular there, but his royalty statements did not reflect the pent-up passions of this audience. He likely imagined that Europeans would be more sensitive to his need for privacy than rough-and-ready America was. Nor could he see that the comparative rarity of his overseas visits lent a near-uncontrollable need to the public's desire to see and touch him.

A part of him surely reveled in this attention, particularly in England, which he had last seen as a humble, near anonymous music hall performer. But another part of him must have been alienated by the crowds. It is the most common of celebrity complaints: the more famous you become, the less able you are to get in touch with the roots of your art. "You can't look out if everyone is looking in," Clint Eastwood recently said to me, and that's a serious problem for actors who need to be able to study human behavior from an anonymous vantage point. Chaplin always did his best to do so. For example, on this trip, as on every subsequent visit to London, he made a point of visiting the South End haunts of his childhood, to experience its streets as he had experienced them as a child, an adolescent, a young man. It was on this trip, too, that he was introduced to the Parisian demimonde which led directly to A Woman of Paris.

But still. . . . The lonely young man was now, perhaps, an even lonelier adult. More important, he was an adult who was getting his first glimpse of his own power—"the looming mad politician of the century, the demon tramp," David Thomson calls him in one of those great phrases the only flaw of which is its inaccuracy. He must surely have seen in the mob hysteria surrounding him his own potential power to lead the crowd, bend it to his will.

This did not happen of an instant in 1921, if it occurred to him at all. What he did very clearly see was that, as if in compensation for the popular hubbub he caused, his status as the first artist of an exciting new medium entitled him to the company of similarly exalted figures in other fields, which filled his ego with something like childlike delight. Better still, these encounters with the elite could be managed quietly, without the intrusions of the crowd. So if H. G. Wells, to take just one example of many, asked him to his country house for a weekend, he was flattered by the invitation, by the opportunity for intimate congress with one of the world's most famous intellects. In time he would meet Gandhi, hobnob with Winston Churchill, invite Albert Einstein to accompany him to one of his premieres.

At one time it was easy for me to see all of this as having a bad effect on Chaplin's art. But now I am far less certain of that. He (or Fairbanks or Pickford) were improvising in a void. There was simply no precedent for the way the new mass media amplified their fame, no history they could look to for guidance in dealing with this problem. I now think of Chaplin much more sympathetically; he did better with the issues of celebrity than anyone had any right to expect of him. He never placed layer upon layer of functionaries between himself and the importunate world. He did his best to move freely about in it (aided, of course, by the fact that when he was not wearing his Tramp outfit he did not look a bit like the Little Fellow). Finally, he resisted, for a very long time, the temptation to instruct his public. In general, of course, his Tramp elicited sympathy for the wretched of the earth. But the Tramp was never himself wretched. He was gallant and plucky and romantic and hopeful, and the distant dream he pursued was bourgeois contentment, not revolution.

In my early years as a movie critic I reacted badly to that. A lot of people did at that time. They—we—were in the process of rediscovering the much cooler art of Buster Keaton and to it we compared Chaplin's work disadvantageously. But working on my film I found myself less certain on this point. Women are present in Keaton's work, of course, but they are treated perfunctorily in it, often enough as pests, interfering with the star's attempts at intricately heroic action. Chaplin, as we've already noted, was much more romantically aware of them. He might not get the girl in the end, or the final fade-out might be ambiguous, but still there was that tremulous yearning about him that began to seem to me much more moving than it had originally appeared.

Woody Allen once spoke to me on this point. He feels that for all of Keaton's technical brilliance as a filmmaker (considerably higher than Chaplin's), Chaplin is both the more profound—and funnier—comedian. His skills as an actor are higher than Keaton's, but, more to the point, particularly in City Lights, "he said more about love than so many purportedly serious investigations of the subject in books or films" did. Allen conceded that when "anyone tries to be sentimental or moving, and they fail at it . . . you want to wring their necks," but when Chaplin succeeded in that mode, as he did in City Lights, it becomes "a finer achievement, a deeper achievement, than all of the moments in the Keaton films and many of the [other] moments in Chaplin's films."

But Chaplin had taken that strain as far as he could in City Lights. And, besides, the effects of the Great Depression began to haunt him. He had always been acutely conscious of the fact that he had become

an inordinately wealthy man by playing the humblest of human beings. It was a slightly bitter irony to him, and now the notion that his
celebrity might sweeten it attracted him. There is an almost divine
hubris in this idea. Yet, there was—from his egocentric point of
view—a decent justification for his ambitions. What was the point, after all, of being the world's leading celebrity if you could not use the
power of that position to do good on a grand scale? These were tacitly
encouraged by his friend Winston Churchill when he wrote about
Chaplin in this period. And there were in the 1930s rumors that he
was contemplating films about Napoleon and even Christ. He seems
actually to have written an unpublished book-length tract about socio-
economic reform.

But there were two problems with this ambition. The first was that
his genius was, as we have seen, not the least bit literary or intellectual. He was a consumer of big ideas, not a creator of them—still essentially that bright, lonely, absorbent slum kid, who could have his
head turned by the great minds he had access to but was not capable
of participating in a dialogue with them as an equal—even though
both sides maintained the fiction that he was.

Nor did he see that artists and intellectuals are not reliable allies of
instinctive genius. They relentlessly demand a certain self-consciousness
in the artists they favor, an ability to calculate the metaphorical meanings of their activities. They are unforgiving of highly stylized artists like
Chaplin who operate out of quite simple observational premises and
leave grand interpretations to others. The ever-treasonable clerks are
never satisfied when these artists attempt to give them what they want.
"No, no," they in effect say, "that's not what we had in mind at all." (In
this very decade of the 1930s, that portion of the intellectual community
that, in its always patronizing way, claimed to care about film, anointed
another untutored artist, Walt Disney, as Chaplin's successor, then
turned against him when, in *Fantasia*, he tried consciously to give them
what he understood they wanted. That fate has been visited on many a
filmmaker before and since.)

Beyond the dilemma of his relation to his audience, another,
more practical problem confronted Chaplin. Much as he resisted the
sound film, he knew he could not forever avoid talking pictures. Or
should we say, talking *in* pictures. He also surely sensed that dialogue

changed the whole equation of pictures. The silent film was largely, and perforce, a cinema of broad romantic and exotic adventure, a cinema that had to deal mainly in the kind of emotional expression that did not require nuanced explanations, that did not even offer a realistic portrait of the world as we daily lived in it and perceived it. So many of the silent film's greatest achievements were set in imaginary countries, acted by people whose beauty was unreal in its perfection. Many of its representations of the modern world were—as they were in Chaplin's cityscapes—rather abstract.

Sound changed that. Spoken dialogue was not "poetic" (or to be more accurate, "flowery") as intertitles had been. It was much grittier— the age of the wisecrack was upon the movies. The actors were less idealized in their looks and their playing. The stories were more cynical, more urban than they had been. In effect, low romance replaced high romance as the prevailing screen mode. It would obviously be hard for Chaplin to fit his Tramp—that dreamy, wistfully romantic figure—into this radically changed landscape.

The first thing he thought to do—and it took him five years to realize it—was *Modern Times*. Narratively it is a patchy film, almost like a compilation of several short, old-fashioned, Chaplin films, as Otis Ferguson observed. Its high point, of course, is the sequence that carries Chaplin's latest thinking, the famous factory sequence in which he, as a worker caught in a speed-up, is driven mad by his inability to tighten the bolts on some mysterious metal plates speeding past him on an assembly line. Eventually he falls onto the conveyor belt and is ground through the great gears of the plant. It is a brilliantly realized piece, and it makes its anti-capitalist point. Chaplin's figure is perhaps the most alienated laborer in the history of film. On the other hand, the equally famous eating-machine sequence wears less well. In it Chaplin is strapped to a machine that is supposed to feed him mechanically at a vast saving of time. It's funny for a while, but it's also visibly an imported comic device (and a tour de force for Chaplin). And it is an imposition on the film; we don't for a minute believe it as a valid comment on "modern times." As for the rest of the film, it has some nice stuff—Chaplin and Goddard blithely roller skating on the edge of an abyss, a funny little piece in which Chaplin is a harassed waiter trying to serve too many customers in a crowded restaurant.

But these are sequences that Chaplin might well have concocted fifteen or twenty years earlier. They have nothing to do with the movie's eponymous theme. As Ferguson says, "*Modern Times* is about the last thing they should have called the Chaplin picture." Brooks Atkinson was even more blunt: "As social philosophy it is plain that he [Chaplin] has has hardly passed his entrance examinations, his comment is so trivial."

In their response to *Modern Times* we can read a sort of indulgent disappointment. People wanted to go on loving Chaplin in the old way, and I think many of them were prepared to allow him time to find ways of expressing the large ideas they implicitly demanded of him. Indeed, in a short sequence in the film, nowhere nearly as elaborately developed as the factory scenes, Chaplin gives them what they want while brilliantly bespeaking his own best comic self.

The Little Tramp is ambling along a street when a lumber truck rumbles past him. Boards are sticking out beyond the back end of its open bed. On them is perched a red flag, intended to warn motorists that this load exceeds the truck's limits. The red flag falls off the truck. Chaplin picks it up and begins waving it at the driver to attract his attention so he can return it. As he does so, a Communist demonstration, its members shouting slogans and waving similar flags, rounds the corner and falls in behind Chaplin. Now he's innocently leading a presumptively revolutionary band. A police riot squad moves in. Heads are busted, arrests made, and Chaplin ends up in jail for disturbing the peace. In its simultaneous economy and richness, this is one of Chaplin's supreme moments, a gag as classic as any he had perpetrated twenty years earlier. I also think it perfectly symbolizes his relationship to left-wing politics—innocently supportive of communism but scarcely a devoted ideologue.

Whatever his political sympathies, aesthetically he was becoming more grumpily conservative. "Chi-chi," he would say when a cameraman suggested even a mild variation on his straight-ahead style. He did not wish to be accused of "going Hollywood." Ferguson had him dead to rights when, in his review of *Modern Times*, he wrote: "I'll take bets that if he keeps on refusing to learn any more than he learned when the movies were just learning, each successive picture he makes will seem, on release to fall short of what went before."

This is a remarkably prescient comment. Chaplin had to find some appropriate way to speak to the world, not solely through mime but with his tongue; the expectations of talking pictures Chaplin had yet to fulfill. And the grudging note that marks the praise for *Modern Times* is an acknowledgment of that fact.

7.

Everyone had noticed the physical resemblance between them, which centered on their mustaches—one comic, one strangely disquieting. Some had noted the curious coincidence of their birth—same week, same month, same year—the fact that each was the product of a poor and otherwise distressed childhood, that each had developed an un-canny ability to move the multitudes to mass adoration—though, of course, their techniques were different. Above all, Adolf Hitler and Charlie Chaplin had taken notice of one another early in their careers. They eyed each other with distaste from their peaks on the celebrity heights.

Hitler was erroneously convinced that Chaplin was a Jew—when asked directly if that was so, Chaplin offered this graceful and gallant reply: "I do not have that honor"—and the Führer banned his films in Germany as soon as he became its dictator. Even before that, brownshirts had harassed Chaplin when he visited Berlin in 1931. By the late thirties Chaplin had convinced himself that Hitler was a fit subject for satire. More than that, he felt that the Nazi leader was a menace so large that he must finally break his silence and speak di-rectly, from his heart, to this overwhelming evil.

The result was *The Great Dictator*, which as a moral act is proba-bly unsurpassed in American film history. By the time it was released, in October 1940, Hitler's armies had already swept across Europe— Chaplin was able to study film of Hitler's curious little victory dance after the French surrendered to him—but Hollywood, with the excep-tion of Warner Bros., was protecting its German market, refusing to make movies that criticized it. Indeed, the studios could barely bring themselves to acknowledge Nazism's existence. And at this stage the vast majority of Americans were isolationist, deeply fearful of becom-ing entangled in another European war. They were also anti-Semitic by a similarly large majority. Chaplin was risking much with this production, though there is no evidence that he hesitated over it.

In many respects *The Great Dictator* is a good film—certainly it is much stronger than *Modern Times* or any of Chaplin's later movies. It is the story of a sweet-souled Jewish barber who bears an uncanny resemblance to Adenoid Hynkel, dictator of Tomania. Chaplin plays both roles. The barber, suffering shell shock in the First World War, is released after fifteen years in an institution and is much put upon by Hynkel's stormtroopers (they all wear a parody of the swastika insignia, a double cross), but is well loved by Paulette Goddard's Hannah, doing a yet more feisty version of her *Modern Times* gamin. Their comedy, set in a rather-too-tidy ghetto, is traditional Chaplin, though it seems to me that in this film Chaplin's comic routines, when he's playing a variant on his Tramp character, are less extended, less lyrical than they had previously been.

His interest was much more with Hynkel. He had never attempted anything like him before, and it stirred him to some of his best work. One thinks, for example, of his hysterical speech to a mass rally of Tomania's citizenry. Technically this was fairly easy for Chaplin. Almost every comedian of his era could talk "Dutch"—long nonsense speeches featuring a few recognizable German words ("sauerkraut" or "gesundheit," for example) and a lot of gutturals. Chaplin brilliantly improvised both the speech and the comic business accompanying it on the set. It made no sense, and it is extraordinarily funny. Yet it clearly conveyed a menacing idea.

What's most interesting about this figure is that Chaplin did not make him entirely a monster. He is recognizably human—henpecked by his wife, impatient in his relationship with his chief ally, the hammy, Mussolini-like Benzino Napaloni, dictator of Bacteria (Jack Oakie), hesitant about invading neighboring Ostrich (Austria). Chaplin instinctively understood Hitler. To associates at the time he expressed admiration for the Führer as an actor, and, particularly when he was wearing his Hynkel costume, he was more than usually abrupt and demanding on the set. Backstage footage, shot by Sidney Chaplin, shows him being angry and tyrannical with his crew. Years later one of his assistants commented to David Robinson: "Of course, he had in himself some of the qualities that Hitler had. He dominated his world. He created his world. And Chaplin's world was not a democracy either. . . ." In my documentary film Andrew Sarris says that was *The Great Dictator*'s most important subtext: "There's a little bit of Hitler in all of us."

The movie is the better for that acknowledgment, never more so than in its highest moment, Chaplin's dance with the balloon globe. There are those, like Woody Allen, who find it impossibly arty—an unrooted metaphor—but I think he's wrong. It is, I think, a dance of desperate and ultimately unrequited yearning. He embraces the world, he toys with it, he thinks he possesses it—and then it explodes and Hynkel is left bent over his vast desk, sobbing. It is possible to see this as the great star's recognition of his own attempt to dominate the world, perhaps even his sense that, as he aged, as the world changed, he was doomed to frustration. But we don't need to make too much of that. The sequence is in itself quite beautiful, strangely poignant and resonant in ways that remain, to this day, wonderfully ambiguous.

And yet *The Great Dictator*, for all its felicities, ultimately fails—because Chaplin horribly botched its concluding sequence. The barber, having been mistaken for Hynkel, is obliged to make another speech at another rally. Now Chaplin had previously broken his long cinematic silence in the course of the film, both as Hynkel and as the barber. But he had not spoken at length or in any sense philosophically. Now at long last he was about to address the world. Yes, nominally, his fictional character was speaking to the fictional citizens of Tomania. But everyone in the audience knew better; this was Charles Spencer Chaplin addressing his own vast audience, summarizing what he most profoundly, desperately wanted to communicate to them about the nature of man, about the nature of the world we all shared.

There then ensued six minutes of the most awful banalities. His unexceptionable thoughts hymned a sort of liberal humanist sermon in which mankind was presented in the most idealistic light—honest toilers in the cause of peace and plenty, unsullied by prejudice, by nationalism, by a love of war and killing. The cadences were sometimes biblical as he rolled on and on in his prissy toff's voice—obviously earnest, obviously sincere, obviously under the impression that he was imparting thoughts of high originality. One imagined that the speech might have been effective—at least within the terms of this movie—at a minute or two in length. But it was as if, having abandoned his vow of silence, he could not stopper his locquacity.

David Robinson, among others, has bravely defended the Dictator's climactic speech. He says that even today there is nothing in it that is not true, not still idealistically applicable to the human condition. And in a certain sense he is correct. But the comedian-as-comedian had already implicitly said—not only in *The Great Dictator* but throughout his career—everything the comedian-as-thinker now felt compelled to say. He was like the midnight bore, droning on after the party is over, making sure we understand all the implications of what he has previously said. And we can't seem to get him out of the house, into his car, on his way home.

The reviews at the time made little of this sequence. Dilys Powell, to her credit, wrote that the speech "is so blatantly out of harmony with what has gone before as to nullify much of the effectiveness of the previous two hours." A few others echoed her, but most chose to stress the novelty and wit of what had gone before. It was, they seemed to imply, a small price to pay for the other gifts Chaplin imparted in this movie, and the public agreed with them. Much of Chaplin's worldwide audience was lost to him as a result of the war, but in the United States *The Great Dictator* achieved, on its initial release, the highest domestic grosses of any Chaplin film. Interestingly, after the war it was widely acclaimed in Europe. In my film, Milos Forman, the Czech director, remembered the delight he shared with other film students when they finally saw it. He saw the portrayal of Hynkel as absurdist—a permanently cautionary figure to a world ever tempted by the perverse and monstrous. About that he was not wrong. But perhaps Chaplin himself was not wrong when, later, the full extent of Hitler's crimes against humanity having became known, he regretted some of the film's comedy. He thought he should have made a much blacker film, or possibly not have made the picture at all. We can say that, given the world's knowledge of Hitlerian madness at the time, he did well enough and better than most—if we set aside that feeble and fatuous final speech.

8.

Chaplin was fifty-one when he released *The Great Dictator*—getting a bit old for the Tramp. The world too was aging. The open road, down which the Tramp could escape, would soon be an interstate. Indeed, the very figure of the Tramp was becoming an historical anomaly. Once these "knights of the road" had been a common feature of the American landscape, figures at once feared and envied—and Chaplin had by no means been the only such character on our stages, in our movies. Now his real life counterparts no longer appeared at our back doors, looking for work and food. Chaplin flirted with one or two ideas for reviving the Little Fellow by removing him from the contemporary landscape, but they came to nothing. As his friend Norman Lloyd, the actor, said to me, he was in middle age becoming a bit too grey, slow, and portly for the part. And, of course, in the 1940s he was much distracted by his legal troubles—a ridiculous Mann Act prosecution, his trial on statutory rape charges—by red-baiting, by his marriage to Oona O'Neill, which provided him with a previously unknown contentment that may have dimmed his passion for work.

But he was still Charlie Chaplin, a man who had often declared his belief that hard work was essential to human happiness, and a man whose legion of admirers kept asking him what he was going to do next. For something like seven years he wrote and rewrote the script for *Monsieur Verdoux*, one of those bad ideas that sometimes take obsessive hold of artists. It was Orson Welles who first proposed the notion of a script based on the legendary Henri Landru, the French bluebeard who made a career of marrying women and then killing them for their money.

You can see why the wicked Welles thought the idea was right for Chaplin, the notorious womanizer. And you can see why it appealed to Chaplin, especially in this period; he was a very brave man—it is one of the virtues I belatedly discovered in him—and the idea of making a piece sympathetic in its way to an immoralist, symbolically throwing his own dubious sexual reputation back in the face of his critics, he found irresistible.

The resulting film is, in my opinion, an unmitigated disaster. It is cold and witless and about as bad a picture as any major movie artist has ever foisted on his public. It operates out of what Chaplin must have thought was a saving sentimental premise: Verdoux, an underpaid bank functionary, commits his depredations in order to provide for his little family, which includes a sickly wife and a charmless child. But he continues with them—on principle—even after the wife and child die off-screen. In effect he is saying that if business is murder, then, logically, murder can be a business. Later, when he is caught and placed on trial, he further justifies his career as a "mass murderer" on the grounds that compared to the killings perpetrated by the state in the Atomic Age he is a mere "amateur." In the film's last sequence he heads almost jauntily to the guillotine.

We may agree with David Thomson that *Verdoux* is "by far his most interesting film," by which I suppose he means that it is his most transgressive work. Certainly the title character's prissy withdrawal from the world, his utter disregard for its moral conventions, manifests an element that was always implicit in Chaplin's previous work. But the natural elegance of the Tramp has now deteriorated into mere dandyism, and "interesting" is not a synonym for "success." It merely means, in this case, that Chaplin was making a decisive break with his past, among other things testing the premise that he could hold an audience's regard while playing an utterly unsympathetic character, hold it also not with his silences but with a relentless articulateness, not now confined to a few minutes at the end of a movie but spread all the way through it.

His writing is as bad as it was at the end of *The Great Dictator*. In that film's concluding sequence he in effect patronized his audience by dignifying their idealism. Now, though, he was exploring its darker dreams—of capitalist cruelty, of atomic annihilation. But these were not unspoken topics among his audience. More profound thinkers than Chaplin had already investigated their bitter ironies. Yet he seemed to think these banalities required extensive explanation.

Chaplin did not write a single spoken line or exchange in *Verdoux* that was truly funny. Occasionally he was sardonic, but mostly when he spoke he was pompous or oracular. He did not have the gag writer's gift for the epigrammatic shaft or dancing dialogue. He was as verbally ponderous as he had once been physically dexterous. And that says nothing of his performance. He was only fifty-eight when he released the film, but he seemed older. His voice is thin, his diction formal, his movements stiff. For the role to work it needs to be played with roguish charm; we need to see why Verdoux's victims would succumb to him. But Chaplin's Verdoux is distant, if not downright creepy, in the film. One cannot help but contrast the film to Hitchcock's *Shadow of a Doubt*, which in 1943 starred Joseph Cotten in a similar role—his easy Southern charm rendering his bluebeard plausibly ingratiating.

Verdoux became the great test case in Chaplin's relationship with the best critics. The film was received disastrously at its New York premiere, with many in the audience hissing it. The daily papers' reviews were mainly negative, and even those who had a few kind words to say about the film hedged their praise. They found it tedious, repetitive, and unfunny. The day after the premiere, a notorious press conference called by his distributor, United Artists (of which he was an owner), was packed with right-wingers whose media credentials were dubious at best. They weren't there to discuss the film but rather Chaplin's politics, which they viciously attacked. In this baying crowd, only James Agee, writing both for *Time* and *The Nation*, rose to his defense. Agee had committed to Chaplin as a child; in a remarkable instance of fan worship, he conceived of Chaplin as a surrogate father figure, replacing his own father who died when he was a boy. For him, *Verdoux* was the apex of Chaplin's career, the great film for which everything that had gone before was but preparation. His unprecedented three-part *Nation* review reprinted here—in part because it is a prime example of a critic refusing to deal with the object before his eyes but with the object his addled heart wanted it to be (a not uncommon phenomenon)—was in some measure a critique of the film's audience and its early reviewers. Agee read their response as shock—the smug bourgeois soul rattled by the film's apparent transgressions of conventional morality.

But what people really disliked about *Verdoux* was its coldness. Agee conceded it was not funny in any of the usual Chaplinesque ways. He argued instead for its high irony. And besides, how about that rowboat scene? That, he thought, was a real thigh slapper—as did many of the film's more dubious defenders. In it Chaplin is attempting to do in Martha Raye's Annabella, only to have his plans thwarted by a distant yodeler, who might possibly witness the murder, and by the coarse woman's impatience with his apparent clumsiness (she's like the back-seat driver of her own hearse). The scene, of course, echoes the famous murder in Dreiser's *An American Tragedy*, but it is only presumptively amusing—the one sustained comic invention the movie offers. It is a terribly pale and static joke— just two quarrelsome people in a tipsy boat—utterly lacking in the lyricism and inventiveness of Chaplin's best work.

In Agee's tone there is an unconvincing element of desperation, verging on the hysteric. A tone of forgiveness might have been more appropriate, both from him and from others who took a different view of the film. Other ambitious artists have failed, especially late in their careers. But if the body of their work is as great as Chaplin's was, neither passionate attack nor passionate defense is the right response to the offending work. Patience within the context of a larger gratitude is more useful and, in its way, more humane.

9.

I must confess to a certain sympathy for Chaplin in this moment. He was rich. He was happy in his new marriage. He was more than ever isolated from and resistant to contemporary filmmaking techniques from people who might, conceivably, have introduced him to a world of ideas—black, absurdist, anarchical—out of which he might have made fresh comic capital. He seems to me, at this juncture in his life, entitled to rest on his laurels. But, of course, the attacks on him helped drive him onward.

But also backward. For like a lot of aging gentlemen, his mind seemed to revert more and more to the dimmer reaches of the past. Which included the thought that he had lost his former careless ability to make people laugh. He confessed as much to Norman Lloyd, referring to a recurring dream he had of standing on a stage, doing one of his excellent old bits, receiving, as he imagined, the old laughter and applause, then looking out to discover that he was playing to an empty—and of course silent—house. He re-created that dream for his last significant film, *Limelight*.

In his consideration of *Limelight*, Walter Kerr observes that it is, once again, very much a talking picture. Chaplin's subject this time is not politics or the sociology of wealth; he is in a much more existential frame of mind. Calvero, his down-at-the heels vaudevillian, has rescued a ballet dancer, Terry (Claire Bloom), from a suicide attempt—she has become hysterically paralyzed and so cannot pursue her career. They move in together—chastely—and for at least half the picture the old boy gazes on about his relationship with the audience, about his loss of nerve when he confronts them, about the "feeling of sad dignity" that now commands his thoughts and prevents him from connecting with his own sense of humor—and theirs. Dignity, sad or otherwise, prevents him from taking the pratfalls that were once his stock in trade. In his extraordinarily acute consideration of *Limelight* (I think it's the finest piece of writing and thinking in this book), Robert Warshow makes much of the inherent coldness and egotism of all clowning, its self-referential qualities. Chaplin, he observes, has always wanted our love, sued endlessly for our affections. But he asks, what about him? Is he capable of loving us in return? Warshow rather thinks not and implies that Chaplin's retreat into "sad dignity" is a confession of that failure.

Be that as it may, this, not *Verdoux*, is Chaplin's concluding unscientific postscript, an awkward, pretentious, yet curiously touching attempt self-consciously to come to grips with the only subject that ever really interested him—his damaged self. Warshow, in the end, respects the effort while suggesting that it was all along foredoomed. But he also says: "One way or another, the movies are always forcing us outside the boundaries of art; this is one of the sources of their special power." That thought has a peculiar aptness to *Limelight*, which draws us quite directly, in ways that his other films do not, into the drama—and enigmas—of Chaplin's life.

Warshow's piece is largely (if brilliantly) speculative. But a movie is also a text, concrete and unchangeable, and in the end we must deal with that—with what is there on the screen before us. We might begin with poor Terry, she who is constantly being lectured at by the endlessly prating Calvero. At moments in the midst of his lectures we feel the poor girl might summon up the will to walk if only to escape the sound of his voice. Indeed, she does regain the ability to walk, which occurs, interestingly enough, when she forgets her own troubles long enough to give Calvero a pep talk about rescuing *his* career. Similarly, when he begins to take an interest in her, his own will to live comes back to him. These are standard sentimental movie tropes. When we cease focusing on ourselves, when we extend our concern to others, our lives become richer and we become better people. When this happens in *Limelight*, damned if our regard for Calvero doesn't warm.

Seeing it now there is also what Warshow calls an "extra-aesthetic" element, which he could not have been aware of when he wrote. Hannah Chaplin's last job was the same as Terry's. She was a "ballet girl" (really a chorus girl). It was then that she was stricken with her fatal madness. It is not at all difficult to see Terry's paralysis as a metaphor for Hannah Chaplin's insanity, since both afflictions isolate them from normal human intercourse and prevent them from pursuing normal lives and careers. The Chaplin who rescues Terry is not unlike the very young Chaplin, unable to find the steady work whose profits might at least have ameliorated the harshness of his mother's treatment. Calvero is no better off than the young Chaplin, but at least he has the experience, the wisdom, to "rescue" the crippled ballet girl, to get her back on her feet. In this wish fulfillment there is, to me at least, a poignant subtext.

Beyond this, *Limelight*'s continuing reputation rests on the famous sequence in which Chaplin and his old rival, Buster Keaton, do a comic musical duet at a benefit performance and it too deserves analysis. Chaplin is a violinist intent on giving a virtuoso performance; Keaton is his befuddled, nearsighted accompanist whose score keeps slipping off the piano. This is a Chaplin we have never seen before, demonic in his desire to wow the audience, his mad passion brilliantly highlighted by Keaton's divine obliviousness. Chaplin's need for approval is so naked that the sequence represents a coming-to-grips with himself that is, I think, astonishing—especially when we recall that it ends with Calvero succumbing to a fatal heart attack. He has given his all, he can do no more. And precisely because by this time we in the audience do not know where the real Chaplin ends and the fictional representation of him begins, this death represents an act of supreme egotism on his part. It is given to few performers to contemplate, then enact, their own demise so publicly.

Finally, I think, we are obliged to think about one shot in the death sequence. Far back in the frame, Calvero lies dying, friends and colleagues grouped around him in the mournful poses of a nineteenth-century genre painting. But in the foreground, Terry, who is also on the program, whirls past the camera in her ballet costume. Her face is without expression, she is apparently oblivious to the death of her benefactor back there in the shadows. It is a wonderfully enigmatic shot and cinematically as expressive as any Chaplin ever made. I think—in Terry's spinning motion and blank face—we are meant to see the obliviousness of youth, preoccupied with its own ambitions, indifferent to mortality (which is still, for them, a distant abstraction), oblivious even to the parental figure who has made the beginnings of success possible. It is a great shot, one of the greatest Chaplin ever made, and a perfect—and perfectly worked out—visual statement of the film's epitaph: "The glamour of limelight from which age must pass as youth enters . . ."

10.

Limelight is very far from being a masterpiece. It is not really what it claims to be about—the youth and age thing; it is about Chaplin admitting his long and—in his own mind—troubled relationship with his audience. It is also, I think, a partial response to the rejection of *Verdoux*, an open cry for sympathy from a troubled, aging, alienated artist. Still, I discern in it a way out for Chaplin—some suggestion of comic possibilities appropriate to an aging man that he might still explore. It proves that he was capable of being funny without resorting to his classic character (the flea circus bit, a variation on an ancient music hall turn, is also excellent).

That, however, was not to be. He was on the high seas, sailing to England for *Limelight*'s London premiere with his wife and their numerous brood when the U.S. attorney general announced that Chaplin, who had never become an American citizen, would be detained and questioned about his loyalty should he attempt to return to these shores. The action justifiably outraged Chaplin; he may have flirted with communism, but his description of himself as an anarchist seems somehow more accurate. In any case, after the premiere he sent Oona back to America with instructions to liquidate all their holdings. It was said she returned to England with her pockets stuffed with cash. Soon thereafter they settled in Switzerland, in the Manoir de Ban, outside Vevey, in an exile that cut Chaplin off from all his creative roots. He puttered about, rescoring some of his older films, scribbling away at screenplays and, finally, his memoir, so evocative in its account of his childhood, so stiff and guarded and, yes, sadly dignified in its account of his adult life.

Twice thereafter he gathered himself to make a movie. In 1957 there was *The King in New York*, which was, of course, talkative in its contempt for American life and culture but dismally unfunny as it launched rather lame, almost dutiful, satirical shafts at television and Cinema-Scope movies as well as the House Committee on Un-American Activities. A decade later there was *A Countess from Hong Kong*, which employed a miserable Marlon Brando and Sophia Loren as, if you can believe it, a whore who is obliged to pretend virginity in order to secure an American visa. It was based on a script he had written for Paulette Goddard more than twenty years earlier, which only proves how, early and late, this theme preoccupied him.

From time to time he would emerge from his great house to accept an award. Or to take his family on vacation trips. He was very much the disapproving bourgeois gentlemen when his kids expressed an interest in raffish show business; he preferred they think, perhaps, about the law or medicine. His unannounced retirement, extending over a quarter century, largely proved that his highest ideal was comfort, not controversy. He had at last what he most wanted—a large, stable, only mildly fractious family, at their ease in a country that was a tax haven for British citizens, and his autobiography indicates a contentment with his lot that was distressingly smug. The Tramp character became a silent spokesman for IBM. Chaplin was as far as he could get from the mean streets of his childhood, from the ambitions and contentiousness of his celebrity years. As time passed he grew increasingly dependent on Oona, almost unable to function when she was not in the room with him. He said the only thing he missed about America was Mounds bars.

As the McCarthyite fifties waned, it became clear that America would welcome the old man back with open arms at any time, so his exile became more and more self-imposed. He finally returned to accept an honorary Academy Award in 1972. His son Sidney said that he had agreed to accept the award largely because he thought the publicity would aid in the re-release of his major films, though one has to believe there was a bit more to it than that. Surely, even through the gathering clouds of senile dementia, he perceived that his adopted country wanted to make amends for the shabby way it had treated him in the fifties. But even though the world's eyes were again avidly focused on him, he seems not to have particularly cared for the attention—a first for him.

Oona was a shutterbug. She recorded hour upon hour of her family's life with her home movie camera, and it became what I think is the high point of the film I made about Chaplin. For it shows the old gentleman playing with his friends and children, doing for them in their backyard, on their terrace, on the streets of the towns they visited, the old bits that had once enchanted the world. (For example, he trips and then tips his hat to the rock that interrupted his passage.) Oona's was now the only camera interested in him, but that didn't bother Chaplin. He loved playing to it in the old uncomplicated way. Now there was no thought of being a great thinker, a great mentor to the wayward world. In this material there was great sweetness and a return, I think, to his best self.

He had, over the years, made many mistakes. He had been too radically self-reliant, and eventually he had allowed himself to become too isolated by his great fame. He had, I think unconsciously, internalized the adoration of his critics, taken their too ambitious and wrongheaded evaluations as the only useful guide for him. But having said that, we must also say this: he really was a genius. And they are ever an unworldly breed.

By the term we mean—or should mean—that they easily, instinctively, accomplish things in the arts and sciences, in music or math, that the rest of us cannot accomplish or even imagine, no matter how hard we try. But the downside to genius is that usually it is focused on a very narrow realm. And often it burns out very quickly—as it does for chess players, poets, and physicists, leaving them with long, leftover lives to kill. At that point they sometimes become tiresome, using their prestige to advance causes, ideas, or sometimes just their own inflated egos that are not as self-evidently as awesome or as elegant as their solutions to the problem that made them famous in the first place.

So it was with Chaplin. Search as one may through the history of the movies and the history of comedy, one cannot find more eloquent, richly comedic expressions of the human spirit in largely ambiguous conflict with the intractable world. This Chaplin accomplished in roughly fifteen years, after which he was left groping for the old, easy magic. Groping, alas, in public, with the world watching and commenting on his decidedly mixed efforts.

Charles Chaplin died on Christmas Day, 1977, aged eighty-eight. There was irony in the date because he loathed Christmas, recalling always the bitterness of the day when as a child he received no presents beyond, perhaps, poverty's conventional orange. Obituaries were lavish and sometimes critically complex. Or perhaps one should say that some of them were slightly befuddled, written by people who had to try to imagine what he had once meant to the world. If they had had the opportunity I had, when I was asked to make my film about him, they would, I think, have had an easier time. For the work abides. And though we live in an age where many young people refuse to see black-and-white movies simply because, well, they lack color, when the idea of movies that do not talk is a mystery and anathema to them, I have heard their laughter. Especially I have heard the laughter of children, my own grandchildren among them, because the Tramp speaks so directly and, yes, so intimately to the mysteries he, like them, is trying first to unravel, then to defeat. And we, watching with them, are transported back in time to our own half-buried states of frustration when we too were trying to master the world.

My God, one thinks, when all is said and done he did touch on something universal after all. If that statement seems perhaps too grand, surely we can agree that, given the complexity of his circumstances, the limits of his knowledge, and the power of the pressures he was under, he did very well. We can perhaps at long last, go easy on him, easier certainly than many of the writers in this book did when their expectations of him were higher than he, or anyone, could satisfy. Auden's lines, written when another difficult old bird, William Butler Yeats, died, somehow recur: "You were silly like us; your gift survived it all."

I

Five Overviews

ANDREW SARRIS

The Most Harmonious Comedian

Andrew Sarris (b. 1928) is among the most distinguished of American film critics. The first proponent of the auteur *theory in the United States, he reviewed for many years at* The Village Voice *and now writes for the* New York Observer. *A professor of film at Columbia University, his* The American Cinema: Directors and Directions, 1929–1968 *has influenced generations of cinephiles and cineastes. This essay is drawn from his magnum opus,* "You Ain't Heard Nothin' Yet," *a history of American sound movies in their classic years, published in 1998. His affection for Chaplin's work is both passionate and lifelong.*

Charles Chaplin is arguably the single most important artist produced by the cinema, certainly its most extraordinary performer and probably still its most universal icon. Ironically, Chaplin's enormous popularity has never been used against him even by his severest detractors. Never a suggestion of compromise and commercialism, despite all the money that rolled in at the box office. Quite the contrary. There has been a greater tendency to criticize Chaplin for abandoning the simpler needs of his audiences in order to pursue his own idiosyncrasies and ideologies more faithfully and more explicitly, or, worse still, in order to cater to his high-brow admirers.

Though Chaplin was never as stylistically influential as Griffith, Eisenstein, or Murnau, he was fortunate to work in a genre that did not date irrevocably with the period in which it was first presented. Even his earliest and crudest one-reel appearances from his 1914 Mack Sennett period are today treasured as classics rather than tolerated as archaeological artifacts. And all through the thirties, forties, and fifties, when most of his feature films were shrewdly withheld from public view, his comedy shorts floated around in the public domain to help perpetuate his reputation. By contrast, D. W. Griffith was struggling without much success even in the twenties to overcome the stigma of outdated Victorian melodrama. And Murnau (reborn in the Expressionism and spatial unity of Welles) and Eisenstein (renewed in the razor-sharp montage of Resnais), though not exactly outdated, remain of concern to aesthetes rather than to the public at large.

Charles Spencer Chaplin was born, as far as we know, on April 16, 1889, in London. Though the date and place of birth have been fairly well established, there is no birth record of the name Charles Chaplin from that period. Theodore Huff, Chaplin's most reliable and meticulous biographer, has suggested that Chaplin may have adopted his father's name in childhood either before or after Charles Chaplin the elder died of alcoholism in St. Thomas's Hospital. Chaplin's father was descended from an anglicized French-Jewish family, and his mother, Hannah (who performed under the stage name of Lily Harley), was reported to be of Spanish and Irish descent; having run away from home at sixteen, she was so completely cut of from her family circle that even her maiden name has remained unknown.

Alvah Bessie, a screenwriter blacklisted in the McCarthy era, has reported a conversation with Chaplin in the late forties in which the comedian explicitly denied being Jewish; though, he admitted, he had allowed the impression of his Jewishness to remain after *The Great Dictator* (1940) so as not to compromise his solidarity with the victims of Nazism. It is interesting in this respect that Chaplin's older half-brother, Sidney Chaplin, was the son of Hannah's former marriage to Sidney Hawkes, a Jewish bookmaker. But whereas Sidney Chaplin was later to be publicized as an ethnically Jewish comedian (much like Ernst Lubitsch in his early Berlin comedies), Charles Chaplin moved from the stoically English slapstick tradition of the Karno Company into the knockabout universality of the Sennett menagerie, where he evolved a stylized persona that was absorbed into every country's folklore.

The evolution of Charles Spencer Chaplin into the stylized creature known around the world as "Charlie," "Charlot," "Carlino," "Carlos," "Carlitos," had a beneficial side-effect for Chaplin's career, in that never having appeared "young" on the screen, he never seemed to age appreciably in the period of his ascendancy, which began in 1914 and ended in 1940 with *The Great Dictator*. A childhood traumatized by parental poverty, alcoholism, illness, and death had undoubtedly hastened his assumption of the role of an adult to the point of prodigious precocity. And, blessed with total mimetic recall, he was able to communicate emotionally with the troubled masses through all the convulsions of War, Revolution, Inflation, Depression, and disillusion that passed blindly across his pantomimic path. That he treated the symptoms of these convulsions instead of analyzing their causes seemed to bother him more than it did his admirers, but the gnawing intellectual insecurity of the artist may ultimately have expanded the informal dimensions of his films and enriched their emotional tone. Thus, it would seem that time is more on the side of his features than of his shorts, and that the most lasting image of Chaplin will be lyrical rather than exuberant, poignant rather than frenetic. And that the focus of his soul will shift from his floppy feet to his fierce eyes.

Chaplin, like most of the early stars, was lionized by the public long before the cultural chroniclers of the era could explain why. Although it was not until 1916 that articles on the phenomenon began to appear, the public had discovered the little fellow with the baggy pants, can, and derby before they knew his name. Chaplin's costume was thrown together accidentally for a rush appearance in a children's car event at Venice, the Los Angeles beach resort. *Kid Auto Races at Venice* (1914), Chaplin's second film, was thus the birthplace of the Tramp. By his twelfth film (*Caught in a Cabaret*, 1914), Chaplin's name was spelled correctly in the public prints. On his thirteenth

(*Caught in the Rain*, 1914), Chaplin took over the directorial reins, never to relinquish them. As Chaplin's star rose at Sennett's studio, Ford Sterling's (overstated body-oriented) fell. Max Linder, an earlier French pantomimist with a costume strikingly similar to the Tramp's, though with upper-class modifications, was soon to be completely eclipsed by Chaplin. Both Sterling and Linder attempted comebacks, Sterling with Sennett and Linder with Essanay, Chaplin's employer after Sennett and before Mutual. In each instance, Chaplin proved irreplaceable.

Although Chaplin's Keystone movies for Sennett had not yet marked a complete break between the music-hall performer for the Karno Company and the cinema's foremost clown, the Sennett flicks are fascinating today for all the tensions still evident between Chaplin's subtler inflections and the nihilistic physicality of the rest of the Keystone crashers. Within one year on the hectic Sennett schedule, Chaplin made thirty-five separate appearances in company with such comic colleagues and rivals as Mabel Normand, Hank Mann, Chester Conklin, Al St. John, Fatty Arbuckle, Ford Sterling, Edgar Kennedy, Minta Durfee, Mack Swain, Slim Summerville, Charley Chase, Marie Dressler, and even Mack Sennett himself. Chaplin is livelier but less coherent in this first year of his vocation than he will be in the years to come. He seems also more combative and misogynistic than he will seem later, but the roots of the later Monsieur Verdoux as well as of the Tramp have been firmly planted, and the cynic and the sentimentalist in him will be struggling for control well into the twenties.

From the outset Chaplin searched for a private space in which to perfect his characterization. He brawled with Sennett and director Henry Lebrman over the pacing and fragmentation of his screen image. He mistrusted montage at first to the full extent of his theatrical instincts, and it took him a long time to understand that theatrical mis-en-scène could be broken up into congruent shots on the moviola. At first, he could not believe that the movie audience would realize he was looking at a girl if he was not in fact looking at that same girl on the set. He had not yet learned that movie audiences had mastered the first rule of film grammar: to wit, that if shot A shows someone looking off into a distance, shot B represents what he is looking at seen from his point of view. But even when Chaplin became cine-matically sophisticated, he never entirely abandoned his predilection for spatial integration.

For Chaplin the director, his other self on the screen was always the supreme object of contemplation, and the style that logically fol-lowed from this assumption represents the antithesis to Eisenstein's early formulations on montage. André Bazin brilliantly analyzed this fundamental opposition between montage and the one-scene se-quence thus: "If burlesque triumphed before Griffith and montage, it is because most of the gags came out of a comedy of space, of the re-lation of man to objects and to the exterior world. Chaplin, in *The Circus*, is actually in the lion's cage, and both are enclosed in a single frame on the screen."

However, Bazin was not entirely historically accurate in lumping Chaplin and Sennett together against Griffith and montage. If any-thing, Chaplin and Griffith share many of the same Victorian tastes in the theater and in women; Edna Purviance is a sweetened ener-vated version of such vigorous Griffith virgins as Lillian Gish and Mae Marsh. By contrast, Mack Sennett's wild slapstick was closer in spirit and apparent formlessness to the anarchic and surrealistic romps across time and space to come in the works of Keaton, Vertov, Clair, Buñuel, and Vigo. By the mid-twenties, however, Sennett's inability to develop coherent characterizations made him a has-been in the movie industry. Sennett's perpetual motion machine was ultimately no match for Chaplin's myth-making, as the cinema moved irrevoca-bly from a delight with movement and energy for their own sakes to absorption in a subtler form of romantic drama. What Chaplin per-ceived and what Sennett did not was that the cinema was inherently such a dynamic medium that unbridled kinesis created only chaos. Hence, a certain amount of stasis was necessary to set off the kinesis, and a certain amount of contemplation and reflection to motivate the action. Gradually, Chaplin perceived also that the cinema was such a hypnotic medium that an audience could lose itself in a character with whom it identified, and hence never notice that nothing was happening on the purely kinetic level.

Chaplin can be said to have enjoyed his greatest cultural and com-mercial pre-eminence from 1915 to 1925, a hectic decade in which he refined and enriched his tenacious Tramp creation to the point where it became the most endearing and most enduring myth ever propagated by the motion-picture medium. Theodore Huff evoked the plastic appurtenances of this myth:

> Chaplin's costume personifies shabby gentility—the fallen aristocrat at grips with poverty. The cane is a symbol of attempted dignity, the pert moustache a sign of vanity. Although Chaplin used the same costume (with a few exceptions) for almost his entire career, or for about 25 years, it is interesting to note a slight evolution. The trousers become less baggy, the coat a little neater, and the moustache a little trimmer through the years.

It is an anomaly of film history that, whereas most of the earliest "creative" people in the field came to be dominated by the "front-office" financiers, Chaplin actually consolidated his control over his career during the very years when the pioneers were being gobbled up by the producers. The meteoric rise of his salary, year by year, provides an index to his increasing independence. After the expiration of his Sennett contract, which ran through 1914 at $150 a week, Chaplin switched over to Essanay in 1915 for $1250 a week. From Essanay, he jumped over to Mutual for a contract guaranteeing him $670,000 a year, and within two years signed a million-dollar-plus contract with First National. At this time he was not yet thirty years old, and he was already one of the most famous men in the world.

With Chaplin one can make meaningful aesthetic distinctions between his Sennett Period (1914), his Essanay Period (1915), his Mutual Period (1916–17), his First National Period (1918–22), and his United Artists Period (1923–52). In the relatively anarchic Sennett one-reelers, Chaplin functioned as the most talented member of a troupe of madcap soloists, and he was often pushed out to the periphery of the action. In his one Sennett feature, the six-reel *Tillies' Punctured Romance* (1914), Chaplin not only plays second fiddle to Marie Dressler's eponymous (and enormous) protagonist; he plays an unusually villainous variation of the Tramp as the city slicker, indeed almost a foreshadowing of Monsieur Verdoux. Torn (sometimes limb from limb) between Marie Dressler's Tillie and Mabel Normand's pert partner-in-crime, Chaplin's city slicker more than holds his own in terms of audience laughter without ever really being the focal point of attention.

The Essanay movies have often been lumped together and mingled indiscriminately with the Sennetts by the private promoters of this supposedly primitive era. Superfluous titles, sound and musical effects have been added and crucial footage subtracted, to give a misleadingly nonsensical impression of this crucial period in Chaplin's artistic evolution. Not that there are any of the Chaplin "classics" among the fifteen Essanays turned out in 1915 and 1916. Chaplin is still too close to the Sennett slapstick tradition, and he is still too busy experimenting with gags which he will later integrate more adeptly with character continuity. For example, the topsy-turvy tray-balancing routine in *Shanghaied* (1915) can be appreciated not only for its own sake but also as a dry run for a similar but seemingly more spontaneous exercise in equilibrium in *Modern Times* (1936). The real tip-off on the Essanays as transitional advances on the Sennetts is the emergence of Edna Purviance as the first of Chaplin's flowery heroines. For the first time, Chaplin had found his Victorian equivalent of what Lillian Gish and Mae Marsh signified to Griffith. After her debut in *A Night Out* (1915), Purviance appeared in no fewer than thirty-five movies, the only exception being *One A.M.* (1916), in which Chaplin did a stunning solo. Thus she became a myth in her own right as Chaplin's fantasy darling, and she began almost immediately to leaven the Sennett slapstick with a distinctively Chaplinesque sentimentality. Edna Purviance was not so much a comedienne as a leading lady, and (unlike the Sennett girls) less a professional Challenge to Chaplin than an emotional correlative.

If there is indeed a line between "primitive" Chaplin and "classic" Chaplin, it can be drawn somewhere between the Essanay and Mutual films of 1916. Certainly, the Charlie of *One A.M.*, *The Pawnshop*, *Behind the Screen*, *The Rink* (all 1916), and *Easy Street*, *The Cure*, *The Immigrant*, and *The Adventurer* (all 1917) had completely mastered the short form of cinematic farce. The sentimentality and the cruelty and the mimicry and the satire had been perfectly blended. Later, when Chaplin became more ambitious as an artist, his earlier efficiency as a comic craftsman would be remembered fondly, to his disadvantage.

Almost from the beginning of his career, Chaplin was confronted with conflicting pressures and subjected to contradictory advice. The commercial evolution of the film industry dictated feature-length films as opposed to the compact one- and two-reelers, but the more intellectual critics decried the injection of epic, romance, and sentiment into pure slapstick. At one and the same time Chaplin would be blamed for not changing the times and for changing too much from his glorious past.

Unfortunately, the eight works made by Chaplin for First National Films between 1918 and 1922 were for many years among the least accessible. Hence, there was usually a break in the critical consciousness of Chaplin between the Mutuals of 1917 and *The Gold Rush* in 1925. But it is in *A Dog's Life* (1918), *Shoulder Arms* (1918), *Sunnyside* (1919), *A Day's Pleasure* (1919), *The Kid* (1921), *The Idle Class* (1921), *Pay Day* (1922), and *The Pilgrim* (1923) that one finds the first signs of the spiritual expansion of a craft into an art, of skittish farce into comic narrative. Having adapted the suggestive principles of pantomime to the literal spectacle of cinema, Chaplin felt free to experiment with various moods and themes. Epic Existential with Canine Correlative (*A Dog's Life*), Mock Heroic (*Shoulder Arms*), Pastoral Fantasy (*Sunnyside*), Middle-Class Satire (*A Day's Pleasure*), Dickensian Romance (*The Kid*), Dualism in Class Caricature (*The Idle Class*), Desperate Poetry of Lower-Class Survival (*Pay Day*), and Religious Hypocrisy (*The Pilgrim*). It is in this period also that Chaplin's players tend to be subtler and more nuanced in their characterization. And the sight gags had never before been as logical or inventive—or since.

One of the cinema's classic sight gags can be found in *The Idle Class*, a film in which Chaplin plays a dual role, alternately the familiar Tramp and a debonairly (though no villainously) alcoholic husband. The husband is reading a letter deposited dramatically on the cocktail table. The wife is leaving the poor wretch until he stops drinking. Cut to shot of husband from the rear. His shoulders begin to heave uncontrollably, and more and more. The audience's amusement is tinged with the suspicion of a switch. Obviously, this wastrel cannot really be sobbing. Not that Chaplin is a stranger to sentiment, but he would never turn his back on the audience for a tearful collapse when his eyes are so economically emotional. Also, Chaplin has conditioned us to the relative sang-froid of the character in question. Thus we all sense that there is going to be a reversal of the conventional expectations from this situation. But what is the switch exactly, and how is it to be rendered? We are almost afraid that even Chaplin will find himself hard put to meet our demands for a suitably ironic twist. Then Chaplin turns, his shoulders still heaving, his hands occupied furiously with a cocktail shaker, his exquisite face hilariously neutral between joy and sorrow. The audience roars with collective appreciation. Chaplin has not only topped our wildest fancies; he has done so with a beautifully logical double switch, thus by-passing the cynical denial of imagined grief with a spectacular demonstration of the character's obsession with drink. We laugh not merely at the inventiveness of the gag, but at its being deftly interwoven with the narrative. Chaplin's is a triumph of both conception and execution, of both director-scenarist and actor.

Contrary to the unified field theory of aesthetics, this gag could work only in the cinema, where the screen's hypnotic light field focuses our attention on the image of the shoulders heaving first with grief and then with cocktail-shaking. On the stage, the shoulder-heaving would have been subsumed under the decor of Victorian melodrama. On the printed page, the literary expression of the effect would have become an end in itself, and the problem of establishing a visual point of view for the reader would have been almost insurmountable. Also, the gag's suspenseful ambiguity was possible only in the silent cinema where the sound of either sobs or crushed ice was impossible. This may explain why the gag was never repeated with or without variations even by Chaplin.

The Idle Class is memorable also for that breath-taking moment when Chaplin both exposes and celebrates our traditional repressions by decorously lowering an errant kilt over a male knee in an amusing parody of modesty. In a similar vein of unearthly imitation, Chaplin assumes a wheedlingly maternal pose (in the trolley car scene in *The Kid*) which derives from a merciless mimicry of motherhood as a comic mode of behavior.

Chaplin's comic *coups* were not merely accidents of inspiration and improvisation. There were endless rehearsals for even the smallest bits of business, and there was an enormous amount of footage shot from every conceivable angle. Adolphe Menjou has testified that Chaplin subjected him on occasion to as many as fifty takes to secure a suitably subtle enactment of a scene for A *Woman of Paris* (1923), one of only two films which Chaplin directed without himself in a central role, A *Countess from Hong Kong* (1967) being the other, though Chaplin makes cameo appearances in both. A *Woman of Paris* has been a "lost" film for many years, and thus its reputation has tended to outdistance its actual merit. Critic Eric Bentley defended it on its own terms as unabashed Victorian melodrama, but the conventional film historians have ventured more questionably into claims for the work's earthshaking cynicism and irony, claims which a recent exhumation of the film has shown to be wildly exaggerated. A *Woman of Paris* displays instead a very studied pattern of directorial ellipsis and understatement in the service of a sentimentality made arid by the absence of Chaplin the actor from the heart of the drama.

It is instead with *The Gold Rush* in 1925 that Chaplin arrived at his highest plateau of public acceptance, and perhaps the final moment of unclouded adulation. After *The Gold Rush*, his personal image was tarnished by a combination of marital squabbles, divorce actions, sensational gossip, political controversy, and soured idolatry. More important, Chaplin seemed to stand still technically and stylistically in an age infected by the cult of modernism and the theory of progress. Motion picture art, especially, was heralded largely as a machine art, which involved infinite expectations of "improvement" as with any gadget created by almighty science. Audiences and critics resumed their love affair with Chaplin at screenings of *The Gold Rush*, but Charlie was not longer as pre-eminent a myth as he had once been. And even his admirers soon began to worry not only about how he would meet the rising challenges of Lloyd, Keaton, Langdon, but also about where he would fit in the exploding stylistic environment of *The Last Laugh* and *Potemkin*.

The nineties view of the comic situation in the twenties tends to be considerably more complex than earlier. That is to say that if today Chaplin seems considerably less old-fashioned that he once did, Keaton and Lloyd seem considerably more humanistic and less mechanical than they were once deemed to be in comparison with

Chaplin. If anything, the startling rediscovery of Keaton has brought about an over-reaction against the relative over-familiarity (and hence alleged banality) of Chaplin. Nonetheless, though Chaplin owed a great debt to Linder, Chaplin, in turn, greatly influenced and generally anticipated every comedian of his time. Harold Lloyd, especially, was always the first to acknowledge that he had begun his career as one of the less blatant of the Chaplin imitators.

But if Chaplin survived the technological challenges he was unwilling to accept, it is because he cannily spaced out his work after *The Gold Rush*, thereby maintaining the demand by restricting the supply with *The Circus* (1928), *City Lights* (1931), *Modern Times* (1936), *The Great Dictator* (1940), *Monsieur Verdoux* (1947), *Limelight* (1952), and then in relative duress and durance vile, *A King in New York* (1957) and *A Countess from Hong Kong* (1967). The tendency nowadays is to look at Chaplin's entire career as a single slab of personal achievement, and thus to flatten out the temporal perspective by which each of his films was viewed in its own time. Thus, the oeuvre looks more sublime and less strange than it ever did in segments. *The Circus*, for example, seems to have been inexplicably under-rated in its own time. But in 1928 the big thing in movies was not the ancient art of pantomime but the then current craze for sound in the bathetic vaudevilles of Al Jolson in *The Jazz Singer* and *The Singing Fool*. By the time *City Lights* came out in 1931, audiences had become nostalgic for the lost glories of the silent screen. By 1936 everyone had adapted so completely to the sound film that Chaplin's intransigently silent mimetics in *Modern Times* seemed willful, reactionary, and technologically cowardly.

By the time of *The Great Dictator* (1940), Chaplin had begun the painful process of dissociating himself from the myth of the Tramp. But even his devastating parody of Hitler was discounted by audiences and critics on the grounds that the old comedy conventions were inadequate for the sleek new tyrannies. Only when absurdist modes of expression became the rage in the sixties and seventies could *The Great Dictator* be appreciated for the psychologically complex vision it provided through its stylized spectacles. It was only when one realized that even Chaplin was mortal that it seemed logical for him to abandon the Tramp in 1940 when he was past fifty. Chaplin himself insisted that the

Tramp could never be permitted to speak. "To talk," Chaplin reasoned, "he would have to step off his pedestal, the pedestal of the silent film."

By contrast, *City Lights* is not particularly about cities or about city life. Chaplin renders his metropolis in the scurrying grayness of the vertical figures which emphasize the black costume and sidelong gait of the Tramp as he turns corners to confront the adventures of the scenario. Chaplin's technique soundly emphasizes the spectacle of the Tramp turning the corner rather than the abstract motion of the turn itself. Marxist critics of the thirties were disconcerted by the Tramp's lack of class awareness, his allegedly Victorian sentimentality, and his gutter opportunism. Today the subject of *City Lights* is more clearly seen as the Tramp himself, precariously balanced between the domains of comedy and tragedy. Charlie is his own Don Quixote and his own Sancho Panza, a knight and a knave, a fool both damned and divine.

City Lights is a film of extremes. If the Tramp has never been more courtly than in the expression of his love for the blind flower girl, one has to go back to his Sennett days to find comparable coarseness in the humor. Audiences are reminded again and again that even while tears flow from the soul, urine still flows from the body. Chaplin's timing is so remarkably precise, however, that the white rose of his romanticism seems to flower in the base soil of his earthiness.

Another paradox in *City Lights* is the virtually equal weight given the themes of courtly love and male camaraderie. Indeed, one of the most interesting characters in the Chaplin canon is the rich man (Harry Myers) who embraces the Tramp during their nocturnal revels, but who invariably forgets their association by the dawn's ugly light after they have sobered up. Chaplin's fear of rejection is thus expressed in both the social and sexual spheres, in terms of both lowly class status and diminutive physique. Harry Myers happened to be a very gifted straight-man comedian in his own right, as demonstrated by his antics with Bea Lillie in the silent 1928 comedy *Enter Smiling*. There is in the Myers persona alongside Chaplin's a stylistic resemblance to Max Linder's early incarnation of the aristocrat as bon vivant. Linder was noted also for his drunk acts, and it is through drink that Charlie's tramp transcends his sorrows in *City Lights* and much, much later in *Limelight*.

Chaplin is the most satisfying of all comedians because he is the most harmonious. He carefully established his character within a dramatic context in each film, and then carefully leads up to that moment when the spectator must identify with the character completely, be he comic, tragic, or merely melancholy. As an example, audiences invariably laugh at the entrance of two *apache* dancers in the night club even before Charlie has seen them. This laughter of anticipation is based on the audience's confidence (and even pride) in the Tramp's chivalry. Indeed, Charlie's chivalry is a mythic mandate of such proportions as to assure the viewer that the Tramp will intervene with beautiful grace and force to right an imagined wrong. No other comedian could so telegraph every pratfall and still make his audience laugh.

Modern Times was hailed or reviled in its time as the first Chaplin film to tackle a theme of social significance with any degree of ideological consistency. Its alleged topicality was always the least of its charms.

Chaplin, like René Clair before him in A *Nous la Liberté* (1931) and Jacques Tati after him in *Mon Oncle* (1958), hated machinery for reasons more aesthetic than ecological, the attitude more Luddite than Leninist. Still, the mechanical feeding sequence in *Modern Times* is probably the funniest episode in all of cinema. It is hardly surprising that the humor is derived not from the historical logic or technological plausibility of the feeder but from Charlie's reaction to his mechanical tormentor. Chaplin's factory may be half René Clair pseudo-modern and half Fritz Lang comic-strip totalitarian, but Chaplin himself is the supreme cinematic performer of all time.

Nonetheless, it is hard to believe today that an astute thirties critic like Meyer Levin could praise Chaplin for aligning the Tramp with the world's working stiffs. The feeling that emerges most clearly from Chaplin's characterization is a studied distaste for his comrades in industry. Nothing personal or anti-socialist, mind you. The Tramp just happens to hate work, and this hatred is consistent with the logic of his classical prototypes. His deepest instincts are more petit bourgeois than proletarian. He may chortle at the dove-like gyrations of a young middle-class married couple, but he ends up yearning for the most grotesque tokens of economic security—a cow to be milked at the front door, grapevines crawling around the cottage like Virginia creeper, and a resourceful street *gamine* as immaculate child bride: Paulette Goddard, here and in *The Great Dictator*, as the urban descendant of Mary Pickford's girl of the rural slums. For the sake of this regressively childlike and sexless ménage, the Tramp announces grandly that he will make the supreme sacrifice and go to work. He is clearly and congenitally one of the poetically unemployed, Mr. Micawber masquerading as Mother Courage.

At times, the Tramp's happiness is uncomfortably opportunistic. Unjustly imprisoned, he thwarts an attempted jail-break and is rewarded with a comfortable cell and other special privileges. The siren call of liberty holds no charm for him, and his fellow convicts, like his fellow workers, sink into the slough of anonymous grayness reserved for abject creatures of necessity. All in all, Chaplin's Tramp gets off quite a few stops before the Finland Station.

Despite the serious overtones in his work, there has always been a tendency on the part of Chaplin's critics to measure his art by the number of laughs per minute he provoked. By this standard, if by not other, *The Great Dictator* and *Monsieur Verdoux* represented Chaplin in decline, and *Limelight* and *A King in New York* were relative disasters. But having survived for so long, Chaplin seemed a study less in decline that in modal metamorphosis, and, if his audiences diminished in size, they gained in appreciation as they contemplated an artist who for more than half a century had used the screen as his personal diary. As he had outgrown Sennett, he had outlasted Hitler, and he had aged with extraordinary grace. He had even got around to recording his awareness (in *Limelight*) that he had lost his mass audience. He remains the supreme exemplification of the axiom that lives and not lenses stand at the center of cinematic creation.

DAVID THOMSON

The Demon Tramp

David Thomson (b. 1941) is best known as the author
The Biographical Encyclopedia of Film, *which has
gone through many revised editions since its first publication in 1975 and is now perhaps the most widely
quoted of cinema reference books. Close to a thousand
pages, it is remarkable both as a one-man production
and as a gathering of the author's prickly, often eccentric opinions — none more so than his view of Chaplin,
reprinted here. Thomson is also a novelist, biographer,
and essayist whose topics range widely over American
popular culture. He is, in effect, the Anti-Sarris, almost
utterly impervious to Chaplin's charms.*

The worldwide appeal of Chaplin, and his persistent handicap, have
lain in the extent to which he always lived in a realm of his own — that
of delirious egotism. Is there a more typical or revealing piece of classic Chaplin than *One A.M.* (or I AM), in which he exists in virtuoso
isolation for fifteen minutes, executing every variation on the drunk-
coming-home theme? It is like a dancer at the bar, confronting himself in a mirror.

The list above includes early films in which Chaplin was only an actor, and which were credited to directors like Mabel Normand and Mack Sennett. But to the world and to Chaplin himself any film in which he appeared has been his own. On *A Countess from Hong Kong* he demonstrated every piece of business for Marlon Brando and Sophia Loren to copy as best they could; and Chaplin the actor has an overbearingly winsome personality that cajoles his films into mawkishness. Chaplin was led to direct because it was a logical extension of the power to be obtained through acting. For there is a paradox between the tramp's woeful simpleton character and the clear-eyed inquisitiveness with which Chaplin the director and owner of the film is prompting our response. Here is a fascinating moment from his *Autobiography* telling how at the age of five he was forced onto the music-hall stage when his mother's failing voice was booed off by a callous audience. The child went on and sang a song:

> Half-way through, a shower of money poured on to the stage. Immediately I stopped and announced that I would pick up the money first and sing afterwards. This caused much laughter. The stage manager came on with a handkerchief and helped me to gather it up. I thought he was going to keep it. This thought was conveyed to the audience and increased their laughter, especially when he walked off with it with me anxiously following him. Not until he handed it to Mother did I return and continue to sing. I was quite at home. I talked to the audience, danced, and did several imitations including one of Mother singing her Irish march song.

A number of inferences can be legitimately based on that passage that throw light on Chaplin's later career:

First, Chaplin's early life was a time of considerable emotional hardship. His father deserted the family when Charlie was an infant and later died of alcoholism. That strain affected the sanity of his mother, whose music-hall career was ruined. When she had to go into an asylum, Charlie was sent to an orphanage—this after being born into a home of enough gentility to keep a maid. He was not born deprived, but saw his family lose almost everything while still a child. "I was quite at home" on the stage is not just the narrative conclusion of the first section of *My Autobiography*, but the emotional escape from such real loss and pain.

Second, there is in Chaplin a strange mixture of coy charm and heartless cold, and it is not too far-fetched to see it as the response to suffering inflicted on a sensitive and lonely child. The pathos in Chaplin's work is always focused on himself. That recollection in tranquility of his first stage appearance is colored by the drama of the child facing the mob, by the romance of championing his mother, and then by the unwitting revelation that he began to imitate her to win more applause.

Chaplin adored his mother, and his films worship women with an ingratiating but crippled awe. The beautiful women in his films are not just dream women that Charlie loves from afar, but emblems of grace that he aspires to. The delicacy of Chaplin's own features, the Italianate daintiness of his gestures, and above all, the mooning after misty emotional contentment are feminine characteristics as conceived by an exquisite man. Indeed, Chaplin's persona is often very close to eighteenth-century sentimentality: a beautifully mannered dreamer who has trained himself into the emotional sensibility that will sometimes shame a woman with its refinement. The history of bisexuality in the movies begins with Chaplin, and the impression of sophistication that he gave in his earliest work is less a quality of the films that his own Cherubino-like refinement amid so much mugging.

But the cruelty in Chaplin is also feminine, impetuous, and instinctive. Chaplin was forever revenging himself on gross, ugly men. His slapstick is often violent and one of the abiding images of Chaplin is of the sharp-toed ballet dancer kicking some thug's ass. As a mime, too, he used impersonation as a weapon. The most famous instance of this is his Hitler caricature in *The Great Dictator*. But just as he was prepared and able at five to imitate his mother, so the tramp relates to the outside world through his ability to master it with mime.

Such egotism expresses Chaplin's hostility to the world, and suggests how his portrait of the little man pandered to the desire for recognition in anonymous audiences. Similarly, Chaplin's wistful admiration of women seems ultimately prettier and more rarefied than any woman is capable of—as witness the last, tremulous close-up of *City Lights*. Was Chaplin's common man so far from Hitler? He spoke to disappointment, brutalized feelings, and failure and saw that through movies he could concoct a daydream world in which the tramp thrives and in which his whole ethos of self-pity is vindicated.

Third, in his line, "This thought was conveyed to the audience," there is the early appreciation of the need to signal emotion and laughter to an audience. The tramp's famous glance into the camera, for all its simpering, is an acute grab for sympathy. Just as in A *Night in the Show*—the film of Chaplin's most successful music-hall act— as the drunken toff in the balcony about to destroy the stage show, he looks at the camera as if to say "Shall we? Let's . . . ," so Chaplin's private world is one that he could only reach out from through personal rhetoric. He does not make an artistic, comic statement on the world but channels it through himself and that demagogic moment when he knows that he has an audience's attention. The instinct for that attention is central to the workings of cinema, and I believe Chaplin understood years before anyone else the way in which audiences might identify with a star. It is no accident that he often employed dream sequences in his early films—for example, *The Bank* and *Shoulder Arms*. Intuitively, he sensed how ready the viewers were to have their fantasies indulged.

But that instinct usually lacked artistic intelligence, real human sympathy, and even humor. Chaplin's isolation barred him from working with anyone else. He needed to fulfill every creative function on a film, whether it is scripting, composing, or directing actors. He is isolated, too, in the sense that his later films seem as cut off from any known period or reality as the earlier ones. That eerie feeling one has in reading the later parts of *My Autobiography*—that Chaplin was still unable to appreciate the world on any other than his own terms— is borne out by the films that supposedly deal with the world's problems but in a social setting that seems increasingly implausible. Only a great egotist could have made films as unspecific as *Limelight*, *A King in New York*, and *A Countess from Hong Kong*. Of course, comedy should be its own world, but Chaplin seems innocent of realities of place, time, character, and situation. And in the end such numbness is disturbing, just as Chaplin's weird old age seemed unreal and deluded. More and more, with that thin, unlocalized voice forever talking the dictionary, and with silver-haired prettiness untouched,

Chaplin looked like a great instinct narrowed by the absence of the other qualities that would mature an artist.

His later films are dreadful, and they are few and far between. The early work seems to me narrow when put beside the films of Keaton and the Marx Brothers. But the early shorts do have a strange sophistication that derives from Chaplin's intuitive skill at easing himself into an audience's mind. Their jokes are usually corny and repetitive, but Chaplin's attempt to charm the viewer is masterly. Those recurring conclusions that iris in on the figure of Chaplin walking away from us are ingenious fosterings of our own sense of loss and hope that he will be back soon. And as an actor/performer who has impinged on the world's huddling round the idea of the oppressed little man, Chaplin may be the most famous image of the twentieth century. It is a marvelous and intriguing story, and one that needs major biographies to make up for the inconsequence of most of his own book.

The facts of Chaplin's career amply bear out the theory of overweening abstraction from the world. He toured America with Fred Karno twice before 1914 when he went to work for Sennett at Keystone. By 1915 he moved on the Essanay, by now the writer and director of all his films. His salary rose prodigiously as in 1916 he went to Mutual. From 1917 he was producing his films independently, to be handled by First National. Then in 1919 he was one of the founding members of United Artists, for whom *A Woman of Paris* was his first film. It was also his first full-length film. After that, in fifty years he made only ten films. Increasingly, around the period 1935–50, his dissatisfaction with the world was voiced in films. Like many more learned men, he feared progress and the agony of choosing between capitalism and socialism. It was only petulance that made him resist sound until 1936, and then horribly misuse it. *The Great Dictator* is an extraordinary mixture of comic mime, halting construction, and an embarrassing sermon at the end.

The crisis in his life came after the war. *Monsieur Verdoux* is by far his most interesting film, the story of a Landru figure and the only undisguised expression of his distaste for women and the world. At this time he was mildly sympathetic to communism and, in 1952, he chose to leave America, hurt by official hostility. His political philosophy was actually threadbare and the move now looks like a final retreat into the cloud cuckoo land of Switzerland. As early as *Easy Street*, Chaplin's withdrawn sensitivity had depicted an intractably town, dominated by bullies, that the cop Charlie made safe for the bourgeois to walk about in. Chaplin's return to Europe was a sorrowful gesture that could only, eventually, prompt a guilty change of heart in America. Eventually, he was reclaimed and must have taken great satisfaction in the way so vast an audience came round. In truth, Chaplin is the looming mad politician of the century, the demon tramp. It is a character based on the belief that there are "little people." Whereas art should insist that people are all the same size.

Charlie Chaplin's Film Heroines

*Stephen M. Weissman, M.D., is a practicing psychia-
trist in Washington, D.C., and professor of psychiatry
at George Washington University. The author of psychological biographies of Frederick Douglass and
Samuel Taylor Coleridge, he has for some years been
working on a similar book about Chaplin. This essay,
though ostensibly about Chaplin's portrayal of women
in his films, is more important for its persuasive speculation about his mother's sudden and mysterious illness, with its disastrous effect on Chaplin's childhood.
So far as I know, no one else has offered so radical (and
tragic) an interpretation of this formative experience in
Chaplin's life.*

". . . in the last few days, Chaplin has been in Vienna . . . but it was
too cold for him here, and he left again quickly. He is undoubtedly a
great artist; certainly he always portrays one and the same figure; only
the weakly poor, helpless, clumsy youngster for whom, however,
things turn out well in the end. Now do you think for this role he has
to forget about his own ego? On the contrary, he always plays only
himself as he was in his dismal youth. He cannot get away from those

From *Film History*, Vol. 8, No. 4, courtesy of Indiana University Press.

impressions and humiliations of the past period of his life. He is, so to speak, an exceptionally simple and transparent case. The idea that the achievements of artists are intimately bound up with their child-hood memories, impressions, repressions and disappointments, has already brought in much enlightenment and has, for that reason, become very precious to us."

—Sigmund Freud to Yvette Guilbert[1]

Generations of filmgoers have laughed with tears in their eyes at Chaplin's scenes in *The Gold Rush* where his boyishly innocent Little Tramp naively attempts to woo and win Georgia, a wistfully soulful dance hall prostitute, away from her hollow life as a good-time girl in a boomtown saloon. But few people realize that the creation of Georgia—like the creation of so many of his other film heroines—borrowed heavily from and reflected dramatically details of the life experiences of his own mother.

Like the high class courtesan in *A Woman of Paris*, the unwed mother in *The Kid*, the suicidally depressed ballet dancer in *Limelight*, and the two other dance hall girls in *A Dog's Life* and *A Countess from Hong Kong*, the figure of Georgia in *The Gold Rush* represents an ambiguous amalgam of a more and less innocent way of viewing a young woman whose problematic sexuality echoes significant issues in Chaplin's own mother's life: before he lost her to a mental illness when he was still a child.

It was that loss and the scars it left that later shaped Chaplin's development of an alter-ego screen character whose core identity (in the feature length films) was the rescue and repair of damaged and fallen women. And of all his rescue films it was *The Gold Rush* which Chaplin later said was the one picture by which he most wanted to be remembered by posterity.

While he was sufficiently dissatisfied with its artistic flaws that he tried to reedit it many years later, he always considered it his favorite film. He probably felt that way because it dealt with first causes. Read

[1] Quoted from Chapter XIV, p. 2–3 of an unpublished biography of Charlie Chaplin in the manuscript collection of the Margaret Herrick Library at the Motion Picture Academy of Arts and Sciences, Los Angeles, California. Title: *Charlie Chaplin: Man and Mime*, Author: Harry Crocker.

from a psychoanalytic perspective, *The Gold Rush* retraced (and symbolically corrected) the original real life circumstances which had ultimately led to his mother's mental illness probably resulting from an incurable case of third stage syphilis.

Like Georgia, Chaplin's mother was in a gold rush (she was in South Africa when gold was first being discovered). And also like Georgia, she may have been a prostitute. Was prostitution the way she first contracted syphilis? And was the third stage syphilis known as general paresis responsible for the insanity that later separated her from her son?

Hannah Chaplin did have syphilis, a disease which was a scourge in the 19th century and until antibiotics were discovered. The diagnosis can be found in her medical records. It was made at the Lambeth infirmary in the fall of 1898. But those records do not state which stage of syphilis she was suffering from at the time young Charlie was languishing in a charity institution. Was it primary, secondary or tertiary syphilis?

It matters because psychosis can accompany an advanced stage of this disease. Primary syphilis is the earliest stage of the sexually transmitted illness. When treated unsuccessfully (as it was in the 1890s) it can lead to secondary and tertiary syphilis. Tertiary syphilis is a complication which can occur from five to 30 (or more) years later. It often shows up as neurosyphilis, a brain infection which can cause psychosis and personality change. And when acutely psychotic patients with neurosyphilis went untreated (as they did in the 1890s) they frequently became chronically psychotic within the span of a few years.[2]

In the fall of 1898, when Hannah Chaplin was diagnosed with syphilis, she had just been transferred from the Lambeth poorhouse to the Lambeth infirmary for emergency evaluation of an acute psychosis characterized by agitation, disorientation, confusion, delusional thinking and an abnormal sensation in her head. After ten days of medical observation, the psychosis persisted and she was transferred to the Cane Hill Lunatic Asylum. She remained there for two months and then was discharged in a state of remission.

---

[2] For a general discussion of the psychiatric manifestations of syphilis see p. 223–236 in Kolb, Lawrence C.: *Modern Clinical Psychiatry*, 8th edition, W. B. Saunders, Philadelphia, 1973.

Syphilis (stage unspecified) was the only specific diagnosis listed in the Lambeth Hospital Register of Lunatics at the time of that first Cane Hill transfer. And none of the surviving transfer records from Hannah's two subsequent Cane Hill admissions in 1903 and 1905 mentions any other diagnosis which could account for her rapidly deteriorating mental condition.

We also know that as her mental illness rapidly progressed from an acute to a chronical phase (ca. 1903–1905), she began having intermittent visual and auditory hallucinations. Each of those signs and symptoms of acute and chronic psychosis are compatible with third-stage syphilis. And her precipitous decline is also compatible with the natural progression of untreated neurosyphilis, as is the age of onset of her first psychosis. The peak incidence of onset for neurosyphilis occurs between the ages of 35 and 45. Hannah Chaplin was 33 years old when she first became psychotic.

Finally, in retrospect, there is one more clue about the evolution and timing of Hannah Chaplin's syphilis. In the 1890s era, before the Wassermann test was developed, syphilis was known as "the great mimic." That well known medical aphorism underscored the fact that syphilis could indistinguishably imitate other conditions, physical and mental. Often a revised diagnosis of masquerading syphilis was made only at the time of autopsy.

In Hannah's case what may have been her masqueraded symptom were headaches of unknown origin. While severe headaches have many causes, important among them in this case are migraine headaches, stress headaches and incipient neurosyphilis. In 1895, three years before her nervous breakdown, Hannah's head began to hurt so badly that she took to her bed for days at a time. Unable to work, she was crippled by splitting headaches, much to the dismay of her young son Charlie. Although his mother's show business career had already begun to hit the skids, he still remained her most faithful fan and admirer.

Having lost her singing voice and solo bookings the previous year (1894), the 30-year-old former vocalist-turned-ballerina was struggling to support herself and her sons by working as a poorly paid ballet girl in the *corps de ballet* of the famous Katti Lanner Troupe at the Empire Theater in Leicester Square. Unable to afford a babysitter, she brought Charlie with her to the theater every night. The stagestruck and worshipful 6-year-old boy was mesmerized by the nightly experience of standing in the wings, watching his graceful and beautiful young mother dance onstage in her glamorous ballet costumes, her pretty features highlighted by her dramatic stage makeup. And he also delighted in being made the backstage center of attention by his mother's showgirl friends and acquaintances. Many years later (1931), one of those women (Nellie Richards) would nostalgically remember Charlie as "a regular little demon," always up to mischief.[3]

During this period of Hannah Chaplin's life, the headaches that crippled her and left her bedridden helped bring down the final curtain on her already declining show business career. And they also marked the start of a series of increasingly traumatic and protracted separations between mother and son. Lambeth Infirmary records reveal that Hannah Chaplin was admitted for headaches on 29 June 1895. She remained in hospital for one month, during which time her child was sent to live with a friend. The boy was told that the mother's headaches were migraine in origin. But it was just as possible that they were caused by an acute inflammation of the blood vessels in her brain lining (a precursor condition of incipient neurosyphilis known as meningo-vascular syphilis). For one thing, medically indigent, otherwise healthy young women with stress or migraine headaches were not kept in hospital for one month in the 1890s (anymore than they would be today in the 1990s). And furthermore, severe headaches are a typical early sign of the initial invasion of the central nervous system by the syphilis microorganism (*treponema pallidum*).

But several important questions remain: Where, when and how did Hannah Chaplin first contract syphilis? Could she have tertiary syphilis without infecting her children? And was Charlie aware of the fact that she suffered from syphilis?

The fact that he never mentioned his mother's venereal disease in *My Autobiography* (1964) doesn't mean he didn't know about it. As a dignified and stodgy 75-year-old paternfamilias, Chaplin could hardly have been expected to air his family in public by frankly revealing his mother's sex life in graphic detail.

[3] *Film Weekly*, 4 April 1931 as quoted in Gifford, Denis: *Chaplin*, Doubleday, New York, p. 12.

But as a fun-loving and lecherous young man in his early thirties—who enjoyed and cultivated his film colony reputation as a debonair ladykiller and womanizer—Charlie Chaplin was of a much different mindset. Defiantly proud of his working class Cockney origins and sexually liberated lifestyle, he told his friend Konrad Bercovici in 1922 that he was toying with the idea of writing and publishing an unexpurgated autobiography. A real eyeopener, Charlie's sensational exposé would reveal in lurid detail "how the children of the poor find out the facts of life by themselves!"[4] He may have begun the book, but he never finished it.

Three years later, he told Bercovici why he abandoned the project: "Oh, Konrad, I shall never be able to tell anybody all the poverty and all the humiliation we—my mother, my brother and I—have endured. I shall never be able to tell, for no one would believe it. I myself at times cannot believe all the things we have gone through."[5]

The extent of his own disbelief was such that, "I don't know, actually, who my father was:" Chaplin privately confided to another friend (Eddie Sutherland). Speaking without bitterness, Chaplin matter-of-factly said that his mother's encounters with men when he was a young boy left him wondering if the man who was his namesake father and psychological parent also was his biological father.[6]

Instead of directly revealing his mother's unconventional love life in a sensational autobiography, Chaplin would seem to have disguised it in a series of films about fallen and damaged women. But it was in a semi-autobiographical novel which he never finished (*Footlights*), that he dealt most directly with the issue of "tragic promiscuity" in a woman whose character suggests a fictionalized version of his mother. In that uncompleted manuscript, the woman's promiscuity is fueled by "an insatiable desire that was pathological."[7]

---

[4] p. 156: Bercovici, Konrad: *It's The Gypsy in Me*, Prentice Hall, New Jersey, 1941.

[5] Bercovici, Konrad: *Charlie Chaplin an Authorized Interview*, Colliers Magazine, 15 August 1925.

[6] p. 298–299: Albert Edward Sutherland, *Columbia University Oral History Archives*, Volume Pop Arts II.

[7] Chaplin Charles, *Footlights Manuscript*, Unpublished, Vevey Archives. N. B. All subsequent quotes from *Footlights* in this article are from the same source. I am grateful to Pan Paumier and the Chaplin Estate for making this manuscript available to me.

As a loyal and worshipful child, Charlie had always sided unconditionally with his mother in her many unhappy relationships with men, including her stormy courtship and volatile marriage to his father. But in *Footlights*, the 60-year-old novelist appears to have revisited their courtship and marriage from his father's point of view. He reexamined his mother's original betrayal of his father in 1884 when she jilted him and ran off to South Africa with a fast-talking Jewish con man of Cockney extraction (Sydney Hawkes) who lured her there under false pretenses by posing as a wealthy aristocrat and promising to marry her.

And afterwards, when 19-year-old Hannah returned back to England from South Africa—unwed and six months pregnant—Charlie's father married her and adopted the unborn child (Sydney) as his own. Nothing if not a two-time loser, Chaplin's father was betrayed six years later when his two timing wife ran off with another man (Leo Dryden) who also impregnated and discarded her (but Dryden kept or stole their baby).

If in *Footlights* (1948), Chaplin disguised and fictionalized his star-crossed parents' courtship and marriage, instead of using one character to tell his mother's story, he has actually used three. In this late *roman a clef*, young Charlie's idealized boyhood image of his mother is portrayed by Terry Ambrose; while Eva Morton (and Eva's mother) are used to convey the mature Chaplin's much more circumspect assessment of his mother as a tragically promiscuous figure who fouled her own nest in spite of herself.

Chaplin the omniscient narrator's only criticism of the otherwise long-suffering and sorely wronged father character in the novel (Calvero) is that "had he known . . . [the full] extent of her [Eva/Hannah's] promiscuity, his attitude might have been different. He possibly might have taken her into his arms as he would a sick child; for that she was; and tended her and cared for her and saw that she had medical treatment. As it was, he felt bitter and resentful."

Four years later (1952) Chaplin used *Footlights* as a screenplay treatment for *Limelight*. In both the film and the book, the male protagonist, Calvero, seems to amalgamate the experiences of Chaplin and his father, Charlie Senior. Acting as one individual (psychologically speaking) this inextricably fused "father/son" pair rehabilitates the "mother's" failed show business career.

The film opens with Calvero dramatically rescuing "a diseased woman on the streets" from suicide. At least that is his initial assumption: why else would a beautiful, comatosed young girl in a sleezy boarding house try to kill herself by taking a lethal overdose of sleeping pills and turning on the gas jets?

But he has misjudged her. When she regains consciousness, Calvero learns that she is not a prostitute. She is a crippled ballerina (Terry Ambrose). Having been stricken by a hysterical paralysis of her legs, this bedridden young woman has lost her job in the *corps de ballet* of the Empire Theatre. While her self-inflicted disability blocks her from becoming a prima ballerina, it also prevents her from becoming a streetwalker. (When Charlie was a child—he confided to Claire Bloom while shooting this film—the prettiest prostitutes in London walked and worked the Promenade of the Empire, soliciting wealthy customers).

By patiently nursing this sick but chaste young woman back to health and restoring her confidence in herself, Calvero rehabilitates her failed show business career. Nothing if not a nostalgic sentimentalist, Chaplin ends his film with Calvero dying in the wings backstage while watching his protégé's triumphant resurrection onstage. As Calvero's life fades in the shadows, hers shines in the limelight as she triumphantly pirouettes her way to fame and fortune as a prima ballerina of the Empire Theater.

Whether Charlie's pretty young mother ever supplemented her meager pay as a ballet girl by moonlighting on the Empire Promenade as her show business days drew to a close is anyone's guess. But less a matter of conjecture is her filmmaker son's obsessive preoccupation with fallen women as film heroines at all levels of society.

Instead of writing that version of his autobiography in the early 1920s, Chaplin sublimated his half-remembered, half-repressed memories and fantasies about his mother in his fallen women trilogy. *The Kid* (1921) portrayed an unwed mother seeking to be reunited with her lost child. *A Woman of Paris* (1923) portrayed a high class courtesan and the man whose heart she broke. And *The Gold Rush* (1925) offered a dance hall prostitute whose "mothering" of an ostensible stowaway earns her the love of a millionaire in disguise.

The last theme—the dance hall prostitute—also occurred in two other Chaplin films: *A Dog's Life* (1918) and *A Countess from Hong*

Kong (1966). It was only after the release of *Countess* in 1967, that the 78-year-old filmmaker finally identified that recurrent figure of the dance hall girl as a prostitute in a *New York Times* interview.[8]

But not content to confine his musings to fallen women, Chaplin also made one film about male prostitution (or its psychological equivalent): *Monsieur Verdoux* (1947). That film was consciously based on the real life story of Henri Landru: a mercenary ladykiller who slept with 283 women and murdered ten over a five year period. At another level, the film also expressed Chaplin the compulsive womanizer's unconscious identification with his mother.

All of this circumstantial evidence suggests that Charlie Chaplin may have believed that his mother Hannah Chaplin had been a part-time prostitute at different times in her life. If so, she was certainly not alone.

As many as one in four women may have shared that same occupational fate in Victorian London. Estimates of the number of prostitutes in late 19th century London range anywhere from sixteen to eighty thousand women (of all types and descriptions) depending on the historical source.[9]

Whatever their number actually was, they came from all walks of life. Some were fulltime professional sex workers whose rates ranged anywhere from a few mean pence to thousands of pounds a night. Other were semi-amateur, part-time prostitutes: working class women who occasionally turned a trick in order to supplement the critical gap between an inadequate honest wage and livable income.

In Hannah's case we know that once her show business days were over, the most she earned was seven shillings sixpence for sweating over a sewing machine fifty hours per week. And we also know that the actual poverty line for a family of four in the 1890s fell somewhere between eighteen and twenty-one shillings per week. How Hannah may have been obliged—from time to time—to supplement her family's precarious finances has never been fully clarified.

---

[8] *New York Times Encyclopedia of Film*, January 7, 1967: "An Irked Chaplin Calls Critics 'Bloody Idiots'."

[9] INTERNET, *Victoria Digest*. Discussions on Prostitution in 19th-Century London, Proceedings of September 10–11 and September 11–12 1996. E-mail Address: Victoria@ IUBVM.UCS.INDIANA.EDU

What has been "clarified" by Chaplin scholars with an ax-to-grind is the notion that Charlie Chaplin did not "really" grow up poor. They pooh pooh Chaplin's claim of having grown up in grinding Dickensian poverty as patently false and exaggeratedly self pitying.

It is true that Charlie, Hannah and Syd never lived in the worst neighborhoods in London; the notoriously filthy and rat-infested slums of the underworld. But it is also true that the psychological reality of childhood poverty which Charlie Chaplin did experience included a daily domestic life of deficit spending in a pawn shop economy, numerous evictions, rare occasions of sleeping on streets, rare occasions of sleeping in homeless shelters, rare occasions of foraging for food in garbage cans, occasions of stealing food, longer periods of living off the charity of church missions and soup kitchens and—finally—two unforgettably humiliating experiences of being officially branded a ward of the state in a London poorhouse. And judging from Chaplin's films and his off-the-record remarks to friends like Sutherland and Bercovici maternal prostitution might well be added to Charlie's long list of unforgettably humiliating and stigmatizing childhood traumas.

Returning to the question of Hannah Chaplin's syphilis: there is no way to determine medically when, where and how she first became infected. The fact that none of her children developed congenital syphilis does not help us pinpoint the time of her original infection. Contrary to popular belief, a case of syphilis (at any stage) in a pregnant woman does not invariably cause congenital syphilis in her child.[10] The fact that none of Hannah's children ever showed signs of congenital syphilis does not mean that she was free of that disease (in one stage or another) at the time of her pregnancy with that child.

Nor of course, is it the case that a woman had to be a whore in order to contract syphilis. Women who are only active with one partner their entire lives can and do contract sexually transmitted diseases. In Hannah's case, it is possible that she first contracted syphilis as an unsuspecting 18-year old when she was conned into eloping to South Africa in 1884. Two years later, stories like hers were commonplace.

---

[10] In a recent study of 262 infants born to mothers with a positive syphilis serology, 26 had congenital syphilis. "Congenital Syphilis and Syphilitic Mothers: Survey of the Past Ten Years," *Spanish Annual of Pediatrics*, 1992 August; 37 (2): 135–9.

In 1886, when the Gold Rush began to reach its peak, the cynical enticement of gullible young Cockney girls to South Africa with false promises of marriage, where they were then raped and forced into lives as white slaves in the boomtown dance halls of the Witwaterstrand by fast-talking Jewish pimps from London's East End was a regular occurrence. Whether this was meant to have been Hannah's fate in 1884—a time when a less sustained and lucrative gold strike had just taken place—is anyone's guess.[11]

Given her filmmaker son's fantasy tale in which his boyishly innocent and comically chivalrous *Little Tramp* tries so valiantly and lovingly to rescue that trapped dance hall girl from her unhappy life in a Gold Rush saloon, there is every good reason to wonder if that might have been the case. But as Charlie told Konrad Bercovici, if he had ever attempted to fully and frankly tell his readers about the many incredible hardships and humiliations his young mother had suffered, no one would have believed it. And so 75-year-old Chaplin summed her up in *My Autobiography* by simply saying: "to judge the morals of our family by commonplace standards would be as erroneous as putting a thermometer in boiling water." With great delicacy and tact, the loving son left the rest of her story to the reader's imagination.

[11] For background see: p. 10 in McNab, Roy: *Gold and Their Touchstone*, Jonathan Bell Publishers, Johannesburg, S.A. 1987 and p. 47–9 and 103–162 in van Onselen, Charles: *Studies in the Social and Economic History of the Witwaterstrand: 1896–1914*, Longmans, S.A. 1982.

ELIE FAURE

The Art of Charlie Chaplin

Elie Faure (1873–1937) was among the first, but certainly not the last, French critics to approach Chaplin—and popular culture in general—in the high Mandarin manner. Nevertheless he has good things to say about why Chaplin must be taken seriously as an artist. Pieces of this kind, written relatively early in his career, projected Chaplin into realms of consequence that other movie stars did not achieve. Faure was an essayist with a wide range—art, philosophy, and literature were all within his purview. His great work was a four-volume history of art that was, in its time, highly regarded in his native country.

I

We still speak of giving sight to the blind; but why, if they prefer not to see? For the blind, from generation to generation, are no more desirous of seeing what is before their eyes than those who have sight are weary of seeing. How, then, can we expect the blind to perceive that which has scarcely yet emerged in barest outline and which so few even of those who have eyes to see can understand? For in the cinema we have a new art, the art of movement, an art based on that which is

---

From *The Art of Cineplastics* (Boston, 1923).

the very principle of everything that exists; an art which is the least conventional of all arts, an immense visual orchestra of which the precursors were the sculptors of the Hindu bas-reliefs and the painters of the drama of lines and of masses in action—Michelangelo, Tintoretto, Rubens, Delacroix; an art which is akin to painting, which moves and renews itself ceaselessly in a visible symphony into which enter the rhythm of the dance and the mysterious changes of a musical poem—enter and sometimes meet and will some day unite. The mechanism of this art is so directed as to bring before man's eyes the whole universe of moving form, reconstituting it for a space in which time precipitates itself, after man has spiritualized and regulated it in his heart. It is a new art which has nothing to do with the theatre. It is a mistake perhaps to associate it with plastic art. It is still inorganic, and will not find its true rhythm till society itself has found its rhythm. How then can we define it? It is still embryonic. A new art must create its own organs. All that we can do is to help to deliver them out of chaos.

So far one man, and only one, has shown that he entirely understands the new art of the cinema. Only one man has shown that he knows how to use this art as if it were a keyboard where all the elements of sense and feeling that determine the attitude and form of things merge and convey in one cineographic expression the complex revelation of their inner life and quality. The master of this new art never speaks, never writes, never explains. He has no need even to mask an ephemeral gesture in the conventional manner of the mimic. In him the human drama possesses an instrument of expression of which people hitherto have had no suspicion, an instrument which, in the future, will be the most powerful of all—namely: a screen upon which falls a shaft of light; our eyes look towards it; and behind the eyes, the heart. Nothing more is needed to draw from the heart a wave of new harmonies, a sudden realization of the inevitability of things, and the everlasting monotomous rhythm of the passions. For there, upon the cinema-screen, are forms that move, faces that reveal, a confused, continuous play of values, lights, and shadows, composing and decomposing unceasingly, uniting the impulses and desires which they express with the feelings and the ideas of the spectator.

Charlie Chaplin is the first man to create a drama that is purely cineplastic, in which the action does not illustrate a sentimental fiction or a moralistic intention but creates a monumental whole; projecting from the inner consciousness a personal vision of the object in a form that is actually visible, in a setting that is actually material and perceptible. There, as it seems to me, we have something very great, an achievement comparable with Titian's concentration of all the sound-elements in time, thus creating from them their very soul and sculpturing it before us. Apparently most people do not perceive this because Chaplin is a clown, and because a poet is, by definition, a solemn person who brings us to knowledge through the door of boredom. Yet to me Chaplin is a poet, even a great poet, a creator of myths, symbols, and ideas, the discoverer of a new and unknown world. I could not even begin to say how much Chaplin has taught me—and always without boring me. Indeed I do not know, for it is too essential to be defined. Every time I see him I have a sense of equilibrium and of certitude which liberates my judgment and sets my ideas swarming. Chaplin reveals to me what is in me, what is truest in me, what is most human. That a man should thus be able to speak to another—is that not strange and unusual?

Somewhere recently I read that Chaplin cannot sleep when he is composing one of his dramas, that he is nervous, irritable, distrait, or seized with sudden enthusiasm; that it takes him as much as six months to find what it is he wants to do, and then his whole soul strains itself in the effort of realization. This does not surprise me. I have read too that Chaplin is thinking of giving up his work for the cinema; but this I do not believe. A man who thinks cannot, if he continues to live, give up thinking; and Chaplin thinks, if I may use such a fearful adverb, cinematographically; therefore he cannot express his thought except by giving it the tangible shape of which chance has given him the symbol. In other words, Chaplin is a conceptualist. It is his profound sense of reality which he imposes on all appearances and movements, upon nature itself, and upon the soul of men and of objects. He organizes the universe into a cineplastic poem and flings forward into the future, in the manner of a god, this organization which is capable of directing certain sensibilities and intelligences, and by means of these, of acting more and more upon the mind of mankind.

But Chaplin is not merely a cinemime. I am speaking of the Chaplin of the last two or three years. Until then he was only a supernumerary in a sort of circus. The later Chaplin does not play a part at all. He conceives the universe in its totality and translates it in terms of the moving picture. He imagines the drama. He gives it its laws. He stages it. He plays the parts of all his associates, as well as his own, and reunites them all in the final drama after having explored it and examined it in all its aspects, like a sculptor shaping and molding a spherical mass according to the conception he has formed of it through his understanding of its projection and its hollows and the contrasts that result from them—all the time ceaselessly selecting, combining, and characterizing; or as a musician controls an orchestra, drawing upon all its tones and rhythms in order to give infinite variety to the expression of his grief, joy, surprise, or disenchantment.

Chaplin's drama is essentially architectural in its construction. Each scene is determined by Chaplin's conception of the whole, just as the smaller cupolas surround the great central cupola in the old Byzantine churches, or as music ordains the song of the spheres and controls the continuous harmony of their motion. This architectural quality exists in the brain of Chaplin and passes with such precision into his gesture, however extravagant that gesture may seem to be, that it always maintains, as in a rhythmic dance, its equilibrium about the central idea, at once sad and comic, from which it derives its motion.

Chaplin is differentiated from the ordinary comedian—who is but an interpreter of ideas, sentiments, and forms which he has not himself combined—but not from the painter, the architect, or the musician, by the camera, the film, and the screen which play the parts of the colors, the brushes, the canvas, the compass, or the instruments of the orchestra. Like the painter, an architect, or a musician, Chaplin enters victoriously into the empire of poets. See him, the sly elf-like figure dancing out of sight in the shadow of a sordid alley or along the border of a wood—it is Watteau, it is Corot, with the great trees framing the garland of the farandole, the green-blue twilight losing itself under the leaves. See the poor boy as he is carried away in his dream, with his worn-out shoes, his charming, grotesque antics, among the nymphs who dance with him across the sunny meadows. Surrounded by the eternal divinities—the sorceress and the siren, Hercules and

the Minotaur, whom with his little walking-stick and his invincible
candor, he drives back into his cave—behold this imp of humanity
bringing into association with his humble joy and his absurd suffering, the grand poetic complicity of the winds, the sunshine, the mur-
muring trees, the reflection of rivers, the plaint of violins.

II

I have said elsewhere that Chaplin makes me think of Shakespeare,
and I repeat it, though doubtless many people will regard my insistence with a scornful smile, for this impression forces itself upon me
every time I see him. Though he is of less imposing complexity—
Chaplin is not yet thirty years old—he has the same bewildering and
yet lucid lyricism that Shakespeare had. In the fertility and creativeness of his heart Chaplin has the same limitless fancy which unites in
a single gesture an ingenuous delight in the magnificence of life and
a smiling, heroic consciousness of its fruitlessness. If Chaplin leans towards the side of laughter, as Shakespeare does towards the side of
lyric ecstasy, it is, again like Shakespeare, to evade vexatious reality.
Chaplin laughs at himself even while he suffers, and even while he
sings. With unsparing clarity of vision he watches the freshest effu-
sions and the most sentimental transports of the heart, at the moment
when they entrust themselves to the welcoming stars.

Poor Charlot! People love him, and pity him, and yet he makes
them sick with laughter. It is because he bears within him, like a burden which he cannot lay aside even for an instant—except when he
calls forth from us a joy which helps him to endure it—the genius
that belongs to the great comic spirits. Like them he has that exquisite
imagination which enables him to discover in every incident and in
every act of daily life, a reason for suffering a little or much, for laughing at himself a little or much, and for seeing the vanity that lies beneath the charm and splendor of appearances. Before Chaplin came
we knew that beneath all drama there is farce, and beneath all farce
there is drama, but what do we not know now? This man appears, and
by his revelation he has taught us to recognize all that we dimly knew
before. His are the simple methods that belong to greatness: in the
midst of danger an immense distraction seizes him; has he some great

sorrow?—he allows some grotesque pleasure to make him forget it; does a lofty sentiment fill his heart?—man or nature intervenes to make it ridiculous; and if love itself condemns him to some pathetic gesture he is overtaken by hiccoughs.

The irony of human passions and of life itself has so made Chaplin that he sees all things, as it were, through this irony. Yet the fearful thing is that he, too, experiences the passions and desires of life. Who can divine his remorse, his suffering, his exquisite feeling, when, as a poor man, he silently strips himself for the sake of one who is poorer than he? Who can realize his hunger for goodness? He loves, and no one sees that he loves. He is hungry, and no one knows that he is hungry. But this does not anger him; it does not even astonish him; for he sees himself and cannot take himself seriously; and in order to perceive these contrasts, in revealing which all his gestures bear the stamp of his comic power, he has no need to observe the world about him. These contrasts are within himself; and his gestures are the discerning expression of the cruel spectacle which his own thought offers him.

To make these gestures supreme Chaplin has merely to carry them into the domain of morals (which determines the progress of his time and endlessly compares his loftiest illusions with the sordid reality) and into the infinitely vaster domain of social and psychological life where beneath each face, each gesture, each object, the unseen god watches slyly to plunge a poisoned dart into the heart of innocence or to humble it with a smile of triumph, stupidity, or brutality. . . . Thus, perhaps, Chaplin is fighting; but when a policeman appears he dances; or while he is being dragged away by his feet, drunk, he plucks a flower on the way; or just as he is settling down to sleep in an open field, he fills up a hold in a fence in order to stop a draught; or in a flooded trench, he rolls himself up in his blanket, yawns, stretches his limbs, and disappears peacefully beneath the water; or walking along with his eyes gazing into the eyes of the beloved, he falls down a well—but I could go on forever telling these things!

Chaplin's wretchedness—for he is always wretched, this bohemian, this wanderer, this dreamer, this lazy dawdler, so lazy that in order to live he must be ceaselessly imaginative and ingenious, and so simple that in order to realize that a fist is threatening him he must actually feel it on his nose—this wretchedness of his is the canvas on which he paints the golden colors of his wonderful and abounding fancy. We see him carefully deposit his ragged clothes in the great safe of a bank, pull at his imaginary cuffs and regard himself complacently in the non-existent polish of his cracked and broken boots, dust his can carefully and convey a sense of exquisite elegance by his handling of it, and by his tipping of his shabby old hat down over his eyes. His whole bearing, his manners, bows, and smiles, are those of a complete man of the world, and serve to heighten the contrast with his appearance—shirtless, his rags held together by pins—the amazing silhouette of a tattered dandy. It is a figure which possesses the comic fascination which the Anglo-Saxon genius has reveled in from Shakespeare down to the latest popular clown, as well as a tremendous quality of originality.

What that originality consists of I cannot easily say. It is something joyous and yet somber; a grave imperturbability in the midst of farce, the constant presence, in every gesture, of man's organizing will and the catastrophes of chance. It is the confusion of the visionary before life's drama and his surprise when he is caught up in it, and the pitying return to himself when he finds that he cannot escape from it. Chaplin maintains himself on one of the steep summits attained by the genius of man by the unfailing quality of style and distinction which he imprints upon his art. It is an impressive style, which, in the economy of its essentials, is allied with that of the ancient theatre, even while it gives to the personality of the artist a quality of inevitability as irresistible as the march of the days and the seasons, as death and destiny—and yet at the same time it is quite impersonal.

I have spoken of Chaplin's cane and hat, of his boots and his tatters, as unchangeable as the mask and cothurnus of the Greek drama; but what is one to say of his walk, which possesses such a musical rhythm, of his protruding feet, of his leaps of jubilation and light-heartedness, of his despairing staggerings on one heel, of his sudden turns at right angles, of his fantastic steps in moments of danger or when his is fighting, of the silhouette of this droll mechanical clown before which all humanity shakes with laughter?

To sum up, the man who seeks to explain himself to us, does so only when his is telling us of the adventures he has met with in life, and then only if he knows how to relate them—his spiritual adventures, I mean, of course, for only those are of any moment. Chaplin expresses his unfitness for life, which the philosopher knows is every man's unfitness as well; an unfitness for which the artist consoles himself by giving an appearance to his illusions and, with these lost illusions, playing out a heroic farce which he watches as in a mirror. Always beaten, always conquered, Chaplin avenges himself, but always with good temper. He avenges himself by means of jokes or, what is even funnier, by means of blunders which oblige others to bear a part, sometimes the greater part, in his humiliations. When from behind the board-fence he unties the shoe-strings of the policeman who is seeking him, one knows, of course, that he is doing it on purpose, but one is less sure of his intention when he steps on the gouty foot of the man who is persecuting his sweetheart. His innocence and his malice go hand in hand, and by means of his malice he reveals his innocence. When he arrives late at his master's house and submits his poor body to the kick that does not come; when, from his bed, he rattles his wash-basin and drags his shoes about the floor to make his master think that he is getting up, a divine joy fills us, for he is avenging us all, those who have passed and those who are yet to come. Through his resignation and through his vitality he is the conqueror of fate and of despotism. What does death matter, or trouble? He brings laughter through his suffering. The gods flee in all directions.

The gods flee because Chaplin judges impersonally the passion which devastates him; and even if he accepts their domination, he refuses to yield them his respect. Thus he wins the right to judge our passions and to make us face without shame our own infirmity, our own wretchedness, and our own despair. He does not laugh at this one or at that one, he laughs at himself and therefore he laughs at us all. A man who can laugh at himself delivers all men from the burden of their vanity, and, as he thus conquers the gods he himself becomes a god to other men. Think of it, Chaplin can make us laugh at hunger itself. His meal at the coffee-stall, his tricks to hide his pilferings and to appear absent-minded and indifferent, even at the moment when his hunger is sharpest, when he is meek and pale with it, and the policeman is approaching; these things draw their comic force from sufferings that seem least suitable for laughter. Why, then, do we laugh, when we ourselves have been hungry, when our children have been hungry? Mainly, I think, especially where the contrast is all the more terrible, because of the victory of the spirit over our own torment. Than this there is nothing which so stamps a man as a man, whether he be a clown or a poet.

This pessimism, constantly conquering itself, makes of this little buffoon a spirit in the great line. The man who never fails to oppose reality to illusion and who is willing to play with the contrast between them is allied, as I have said, to Shakespeare, and can claim kinship with Montaigne. It is unnecessary to ask whether Chaplin has read these authors—I have heard that Chaplin is never without his Shakespeare, but whether it is true or not he has had no need of him. For without knowing it one may wear the features of a most remote ancestor. In any case, it is the modern spirit, like Shakespeare's, like Montaigne's, that has guided Chaplin and has illumined him with the light of dawn: this man, drunk with intelligence, dancing on the summits of despair. There is, however, a difference; with Chaplin the manner of expression is no longer that of convention; the word is suppressed, and the written symbol of the word, and even the sound of it. It is with his feet that he dances, though they are shod with such incredible wrecks of leather.

As he hops from one of these feet to the other—these feet so sad and yet so absurd—he represents the two extremes of the mind; one is named knowledge and the other desire. Leaping from one to the other he seeks the centre of gravity of the soul which he finds only to lose it again immediately. In this search lies the whole of Chaplin's art, as does the art of all great thinkers, of all great artists, and of all those who, without expressing themselves, wish to live deeply and understandingly. If dancing is so close to God, it is, I imagine, because it symbolizes with the most direct gesture and the most invincible instinct, the vertigo of thought which can find its equilibrium only on the hard condition of turning unceasingly about the unstable point which it occupies, of seeking for rest in the drama of movement.

ANDRÉ BAZIN

Charlie Chaplin

A vivid and passionate stylist, André Bazin (1918–1958) was co-editor of Cahiers du Cinema, *perhaps the most influential film journal ever published, and revered mentor to that postwar generation of French filmmakers who collectively entered film history as the "Nouvelle Vague" ("New Wave"). His essay on Chaplin is typical of his best work—patient, kindly, extraordinarily alert to nuance. His intelligence is as high as the highest of French Mandarins, but his style, unlike theirs, is approachable, reluctant to inflate either his own ideas or the achievements of the artists he wrote about so persuasively.*

CHARLIE IS A MYTHICAL CHARACTER

Charlie is a mythical figure who rises above every adventure in which he becomes involved. For the general public, Charlie exists as a person before and after *Easy Street* and *The Pilgrims*. For hundreds of millions of people on this planet he is a hero like Ulysses or Roland in other civilizations—but with the difference that we know the heroes of old through literary works that are complete and have defined

From *What Is Cinema?* by André Bazin (1967), by permission of the University of California Press.

once and for all, their adventures and their various manifestations. Charlie, on the other hand, is always free to appear in another film. The living Charlie remains the creator and guarantor of Charlie the character.

BUT WHAT MAKES CHARLIE RUN?

But the continuity and coherence of Charlie's aesthetic existence can only be experienced by way of the films that he inhabits. The public recognizes him from his face and especially from his little trapezoidal moustache and his duck-like waddle rather than from his dress which, here again, does not make the monk. In *The Pilgrim* we see him dressed only as a convict and as a clergyman and in a lot of films he wears a tuxedo or the elegant cutaway coat of a millionaire. These physical "markings" would be of less than no importance if one did not perceive, more importantly, the interior constants that are the true constituents of the character. These are however less easy to define or describe. One way would be to examine his reaction to a particular event, for example his complete absence of obstinacy when the world offers too strong an opposition. In such cases he tries to get round the problem rather than solve it. A temporary way out is enough for him, just as if for him there was no such thing as the future. For example in *The Pilgrim* he props a rolling-pin on a shelf with a bottle of milk that he is going to need in a minute or two. Of course the rolling-pin falls onto his head. While a provisional solution always seems to satisfy him he shows a fabulous ingenuity in the immediate circumstance. He is never at a loss in any situation. There is a solution for everything even though the world (and especially things in it rather than the people) is not made for him.

CHARLIE AND THINGS

The utilitarian function of things relates to a human order of things itself utilitarian and which in turn has an eye to the future. In our world, things are tools, some more some less efficient, but all directed towards a specific purpose. However, they do not serve Charlie as they serve us. Just as human society never accepts him even provisionally except as a result of a misunderstanding, every time that Charlie wants to use something for the purpose for which it was made, that is to say, within the framework of our society, either he goes about it in an extremely awkward fashion (especially at table) or the things themselves refuse to be used, almost it would seem deliberately. In *A Day's Pleasure* the engine of the old Ford stops every time he opens the door. In *One A.M.* his bed moves around unpredictably so that he cannot lie down. In *The Pawnshop* the works of the alarm clock that he had just taken to pieces start moving around on their own like worms. But, conversely, things which refuse to serve him the way they serve us are in fact used by him to much better purpose because he puts them to multifarious uses according to his need at the moment.

The street lamp in *Easy Street* serves the function of an anaesthetist's mask to asphyxiate the terror of the neighborhood. A little later a cast-iron stove is used to knock the man flat, whereas the "functional" truncheon only gives him a slight singing in the ears. In *The Adventurer* a blind transforms him into a lampstand, invisible to the police. In *Sunnyside* a shirt serves as a tablecloth, as sleeves, as a towel, and so on. It looks as if things are only willing to be of use to him in ways that are purely marginal to the use assigned by society. The most beautiful example of these strange uses is the famous dance of the rolls which contribute to a sudden outburst of highly unusual choreography.

Let us look at another characteristic gag. In *The Adventurer* Charlie thinks he has disposed of the warders pursuing him, by pelting them with stones from the top of a cliff. The warders are actually lying on the ground more or less unconscious. Instead of seizing the opportunity to put daylight between himself and them, he amuses himself by throwing more stones, pebbles this time, by way of refining on the operation. While he is doing this he fails to notice that another warder has arrived behind him and is watching him. As he reaches for another stone his hand touches the warden's shoe. His reaction is something to marvel at. Instead of trying to run away, which would in any case be useless, or having sized up his desperate plight, handing himself over to the officer, Charlie covers the ill-met shoe with a handful of dust. You laugh and your neighbor laughs too. At first it is all the same laughter. But I have "listened in" to this gag twenty times in different theaters. When the audience, or at least part of it, was made up of intellectuals, students for example, there was a second wave of laughter of a different kind. At that moment the hall was no longer filled with the original laughter but with a series of echoes, a second wave of laughter, reflected of the minds of the spectators as if from the invisible walls of an abyss. These echoed effects are not always audible; first of all they depend on the audience but most of all because Charlie's gags are often of such short duration that they allow just enough time for you to "get it," nor are they followed by a time lag that gives you a chance to think about them. It is the opposite of the technique called for in the theater by the laughter from the house. Although he was brought up in the school of the music hall, Charlie has refined down its comedy, refusing in any way to pander to the public. This need for simplicity and effectiveness requires of the gag the greatest elliptical clarity, and once he has achieved this he refused to elaborate on it.

The technique of Charlie's gags naturally calls for a study to itself, which we cannot undertake here. Sufficient perhaps that we have made it clear that they have attained a kind of final perfection, the highest degree of style. It is stupid to treat Charlie as a Clown of genius. If there had never been a cinema he would undoubtedly have been a clown of genius, but the cinema has allowed him to raise the comedy of circus and music hall to the highest aesthetic level. Chaplin needed the medium of the cinema to free comedy completely from the limits of space and time imposed by the stage or the circus arena.

Thanks to the camera, the evolution of the comic effect which is being presented, all the while with the greatest clarity, not only does not need boosting so that the whole audience can enjoy it, on the contrary it can now be refined down to the utmost degree; thus the machinery is kept to a minimum, so that it becomes a high-precision mechanism capable of responding instantly to the most delicate of springs.

It is significant, furthermore, that the best Chaplin films can be seen over and over again with no loss of pleasure—indeed the very opposite is the case. It is doubtless a fact that the satisfaction derived from certain gags is inexhaustible, so deep does it lie, but it is furthermore supremely true that comic form and aesthetic value owe nothing to surprise. The latter is exhausted the first time around and is replaced by a much more subtle pleasure, namely the delight of anticipating and recognizing perfection.

CHARLIE AND TIME

Whatever the facts, one can clearly see that the gag referred to above opens up under the initial comic shock a spiritual abyss which induces in the spectator, without giving him a chance to analyze it, that delicious vertigo that quickly modifies the tone of the laughter it provokes. The reason is that Charlie carries to absurd lengths his basic principle of never going beyond the actual moment. Having got rid of his two wardens, thanks to his capacity to exploit the terrain and whatever objects are to hand, once the danger is past he immediately stops thinking about building up a reserve store of supplementary prudence. The consequence is not long delayed. But this time it is so serious that Charlie is not able to find an immediate solution—rest assured that he soon will—he cannot go beyond a reflex action and the pretence at improvisation. One second, just time enough for the gesture of dismissal and the threat, in illusion, will have been effaced by the derisory stroke of an eraser. Let no one, however, stupidly confuse Charlie's gesture with that of an ostrich burying its head in the sand. The whole bearing of Charlie refutes this; it is sheer improvisation, unlimited imagination in the face of danger. The swiftness of the threat, however, and above all its brutal nature in contrast to the euphorious condition of the mind in which it takes conscious shape, does not allow him, this time, to escape immediately. Besides who can tell—because of the surprise it gives to the warden who was expecting a gesture of fear—if his action will not in the end allow him that fraction of a second that he needs to make his escape? Instead of solving the problem Charlie has no recourse other than to pretend things are not what they seem.

As a matter of fact this gesture of brushing aside danger is one of a number of gags peculiar to Charlie. Among these should be included the celebrated occasion when he camouflages himself as a tree in *Shoulder Arms*. "Camouflage" is not really the right term. It is more properly a form of mimicry. One might go so far as to say that the defense reflexes of Charlie end in a reabsorption of time by space. Driven into a corner by a terrible and unavoidable danger, Charlie hides behind appearances like a crab burying itself in the sand. And this is no mere metaphor. At the opening of *The Adventurer* we see the convict emerging from the sand in which he was hiding, and burying himself again when danger returns.

The painted canvas tree in which Charlie is hiding blends in with the trees of the forest in a way that is quite "hallucinating." One is reminded of those little stick-like insects that are indiscernible in a clump of twigs or those little Indian insects that can take on the appearance of leaves, even leaves that caterpillars have nibbled. The sudden vegetable-like immobility of Charlie-the-tree is like an insect playing dead, as is his other gag in *The Adventurer* when he pretends to have been killed by a shot from a warden's gun. But what distinguishes Charlie from the insect is the speed with which he returns from his condition of spatial dissolution into the cosmos, to a state of instant readiness for action. Thus, motionless inside his tree he flattens out, one after the other, with swift precise movements of his "branches," a file of German soldiers as they come with range.

THE SWIFT KICK CHARACTERIZES THE MAN

It is with a simple and yet sublime gesture the Charlie expresses his supreme detachment from that biographical and social world in which we are plunged and which, for us, is a cause for regret and uneasiness, namely that remarkable backward kick which he employs to dispose alike of a banana peel, the head of Goliath and, more ideally still, of every bothersome thought. It is significant that Charlie never kicks straight ahead. Even when he kicks his partners in the pants he manages to do it while looking the other way. A cobbler would explain that this was because of the points of his outsize shoes. However, perhaps I may be allowed to ignore this piece of superficial realism and to see in the style and frequent and very personal use of this backward kick the reflection of a very vital approach to things. On the other hand, Charlie never liked, if I may dare to say so, to approach a problem head on. He prefers to take it by surprise with his back turned. On the other hand, especially when it seems to have no precise purpose, a simple gesture of revenge for example, this back-kick is a perfect expression of his constant determination not to be attached to the past, not to drag anything along behind him. This admirable gesture is furthermore capable of a thousand nuances ranging all the way from peevish revenge to a gay "I'm free at least," except, that is to say, when he is not shaking off an invisible thread attached to his leg.

THE SIN OF REPETITION

His use of the mechanical is the price he is forced to pay for his nonadherence to the normal sequence of events and to the function of things. Since for him things have no future in the sense of being planned to serve an end, when Charlie is involved with an object for some time he quickly contracts a sort of mechanical cramp, a surface condition in which the original reason for what he is doing is forgotten. This unfortunate inclination always serves him well. It is the basis for the famous gag in *Modern Times* when Charlie, working on the assembly line, continues spasmodically to tighten imaginary bolts; in *Easy Street*, we observe it in a more subtle form. When the big tough is chasing him round the room Charlie shoves the bed between them. There then follows a series of feints in the course of which each moves up and down his side of the bed. After a while, in spite of the continued danger, Charlie becomes used to this temporary defense tactic, and instead of continuing to direct his movements by the movements of his adversary, ends by running up and down on his own side as if the gesture were sufficient of itself to ward off all danger forever. Naturally, no matter how stupid the other man might be, all he has to do is to switch rhythm, to have Charlie run right into his arms. I am confident that in all Charlie's pictures there is not one where this mechanical movement does not end badly for him. In other words, mechanization of movement is in a sense Charlie's original sin, the ceaseless temptation. His independence of things and events can only be projected in time in the shape of something mechanical, like a force of inertia which continues under its initial impetus. The activity of a social being, such as you or I, is planned with foresight and as it develops, its direction is checked by constant reference to the reality that it is concerned to shape. It adheres throughout to the evolution of the event of which it is becoming part. Charlie's activity on the contrary is composed of a succession of separate instants sufficient to each of which is the evil thereof. Then laziness supervenes and Charlie continues thereafter to offer the solution proper to a previous and specific moment. The capital sin of Charlie, and he does not hesitate to make us laugh about it at his own expense, is to project into time a mode of being that is suited to one instant, and that is what is meant by "repetition."

I think we should also include in this sin of repetition the category of well-known gags in which we see a joyous Charlie brought to order by reality, for example the famous gag in *Modern Times* when he wants to bathe and dives into a river that is little more than a foot deep or again, at the beginning of *Easy Street* when, converted by love, he walks out of a room and falls on his face on the stairway. Subject to a more precise check, I would be willing to suggest that every time Charlie makes us laugh at his own expense and not at that of other people, it is when he has been imprudent enough, one way or another, to presume that the future will resemble the past or to join naively in the game as played by society and to have faith in its elaborate machinery for building the future . . . its moral, religious, social and political machinery.

A MAN BEYOND THE REALM OF THE SACRED

One of the most characteristic aspects of Charlie's freedom in respect to the demands of society is his total indifference to the category of things held sacred. Naturally by sacred I here mean, first of all, the various social aspects of the religious life. Charlie's old films add up to the most formidable anticlerical indictment imaginable of provincial puritan society in the United States. One has only to recall *The Pilgrim* and the incredible faces of those deacons, sacristans, and sharp-featured, toothy, bigoted females, the solemn and angular Quakers. The world of Dubout is a world of child's play alongside this social caricature worthy of Daumier. But the principal strength of this portrait derives from the fact that the acid which has etched this engraving is in no sense anticlericalism. It is rather what ought to be called a radical a-clericism, and this keeps the film within the bounds of what is acceptable. There is no sacrilegious intent. No clergyman could take offense at Charlie's outfit. But there is something worse here, namely a sort of nullifying of whatever justification there is for such people, their beliefs and their behavior. Charlie has absolutely nothing against them. He can even pretend to go through the Sunday ritual, to pantomime the sermon for their pleasure or to remove the suspicions of the police. It is almost as if he had introduced a Negro dance into the ritual. In one blow, ritual and faithful are relegated to a world of the absurd, reduced to the condition of ridiculous, even of obscene objects, by being deprived of all meaning. By way of a derisory paradox the only actions throughout the ceremony that make any sense are in fact Charlie's gestures when he tests the weight of the collection-bag, rewarding the generous with a smile and the mean with a frown. Another example is the way he returns several times after his sermon to bow to his audience like a contented vaudeville actor. Nor is it a matter of chance that the one spectator who enters into the game and applauds is a snotty-nosed urchin who has spent the entire service, in spite of his mother's remonstrances, fly-watching.

However, there are other rituals besides the religious. Society approves a thousand forms of acceptable behavior which are a sort of permanent liturgy that it performs in its own honor. This is particularly true of table manners. Charlie never really manages to master the use of his knife and fork. He regularly gets his elbow among the plates, spills his soup on his pants and so on. The high spot surely is when he is himself a waiter, as in *The Rink*. Religious or not, the sacred is everywhere present in the life of society and not only in the magistrate, the policeman, the priest but in the ritual associated with eating, with professional relations, and public transportation. It is the way that society retains its cohesion as if within a magnetic field. Unknowingly, every minute of our time we adjust to this framework. But Charlie is of another metal. Not only does he elude its grasp, but the very category of the sacred does not exist for him. Such a thing is, to him, as inconceivable as the color of a pink geranium is to someone born blind.

To put it more precisely, a good part of Charlie's comedy is born of the efforts he makes (to fit the needs of a temporary situation) to imitate us, as for example when he forces himself to eat politely, even with delicacy, or when he adds a touch of derisive coquetry to his dress.

I I

In the Beginning

The Art of Charles Chaplin

Minnie Maddern Fiske (1865–1932) was one of Amer-
ica's great actresses—a naturalist in a theatrical age
when the prevailing acting manner was more presenta-
tional than psychological. Equally at home in Ibsen,
Shakespeare, and contemporary comedies and melo-
dramas, she was a redoubtable enemy of the theatrical
trust, which for a long period kept a deadening hand
on theatrical enterprise in the United States. As a rebel
against all forms of traditionalism, it was perhaps to be
expected that she would write so welcomingly about
Chaplin—a new artist in a new medium in whose work
she obviously discerned something of her own spirit.

It will surprise numbers of well-meaning Americans to learn that a
constantly increasing body of cultured, artistic people are beginning
to regard the young English buffoon, Charles Chaplin, as an extraordinary artist, as well as a comic genius. To these Americans one may
dare only to whisper that it is dangerous to condemn a great national
figure thoughtlessly. First, let us realize that at the age of twenty-six
Charles Chaplin (a boy with a serious, wistful face) has made the
whole world laugh. This proves that his work possesses a quality more

From *Harper's Weekly*, May 6, 1916.

vital than mere clowning. Doubtless, before he came upon the scene there were many "comedians" who expressed themselves in grotesque antics and grimaces, but where among them was there one who at twenty-six made his name a part of the common language of almost every country, and whose little, baggy-trousered figure became universally familiar? To the writer Charles Chaplin appears as a great comic artist, possessing inspirational powers and a technique as unfaltering as Rejane's. If it be treason to Art to say this, then let those exalted persons who allow culture to be defined only upon their own terms make the most of it.

Apart from the qualified critics, many thoughtful persons are beginning to analyze the Chaplin performances with a serious desire to discover his secret for making irresistible entertainment out of more or less worthless material. They seek the elusive quality that leavens the lump of the usually pointless burlesques in which he takes part. The critic knows his secret. It is the old, familiar secret of inexhaustible imagination, governed by the unfailing precision of a perfect technique.

Chaplin is vulgar. At the present stage of his career he is frankly a buffoon, and buffoonery is and always has been tinctured with the vulgar. Broad comedy all the way through history has never been able to keep entirely free from vulgarity. There is vulgarity in the comedies of Aristophanes, and in those of Plautus and Terence and the Elizabethans, not excluding Shakespeare. Rabelais is vulgar, Fielding and Smollett and Swift are vulgar. Among the great comics there is vulgarity without end. Vulgarity and distinguished art can exist together. When a great buffoon like Chaplin is engaged in making people laugh at the broad and obvious facts of life, he is continually so near the line that separates good taste from bad taste that it is too much to expect him never to stray from a moment on the wrong side of the line. If, in the name of so-called refinement, we are going to obliterate Chaplin and set him down as not work considering, we must wipe all buffoonery off the slate and lay down the absolute rule that it is not a legitimate part of public entertainment.

Further, we must remember that the medium of Charles Chaplin's expression is entirely new. He has had only two years to develop his particular phase of the moving picture art. We all know it to be still in its infancy. The serious side of this newest medium of expression has received more attention than the comic side. Why is it not probable that the comic side may develop to a point where Chaplin's art will have opportunity to express itself in really brilliant and significant burlesque?

Anyone who has seen the primitive and meaningless comic scenes in which Chaplin began his career will see the difficulties under which his art was at first forced to express itself. Undoubtedly he will fare better in the future. It is said that his newest travesty, now current, shows that with a really intelligent scenario to aid him he can be supremely comic and at the same time free from vulgarity. Those of us who believe that Charles Chaplin is essentially a great comic artist look forward to fine achievements. We think that we know, perhaps better than he knows himself, what he is capable of accomplishing, and we are confident that he will attain the artistic stature to which it seems he is entitled.

It was a very humble entrance—the entrance of Charles Chaplin into the realm of comic art. Anyone could see him for a few pennies. It is said he came from a life of sadness. And at twenty-six he has made the world laugh. Quite a beautiful thing to do!

GILBERT ADAIR

The Tramp

Gilbert Adair (b. 1944) is an English novelist, biographer, and translator with an occasional taste for odd subjects (one of his books is a biography of the young boy who served as the model for the seductive child in Thomas Mann's Death in Venice*). He has written or co-written several books about the movies, the most entertaining of which is* Flickers, *from which this essay is taken. In it he chooses what he regards as the most interesting film of each year from the beginnings of film through 1995. His novel,* The Dreamers, *was the source for Bernard Bertolucci's film of the same name.*

To every great clown of the cinema, silent or sound, is attributable what might be called a recurrent fetish image, an image, that is, in which the quintessence of his poetics, his personal mythology, is to be located: Lloyd dangling haplessly from a vast clock face, Laurel scratching his scalp with a grin of beatific idiocy, Keaton sheltering under a bedraggled, broken-backed brolly, Groucho lurching into the frame of the screen with a leer, an obscenely curvatured spine and a phallic cigar, right up to Woody Allen expostulating with his leading lady on a crowded Manhattan street. The forerunner of all such fetish images was, of course, Charlie Chaplin's climactic stroll into the sunset (giving his right leg a shake from time to time like an infant who has wet his pants), of which the example illustrated opposite, from *The Tramp*, is only one of many in his oeuvre. If this book had had to encapsulate a century of film history by virtue not of a hundred images but of a single one, this, unquestionably, would have been it.

The unique beauty of Chaplin's art resides in the tension that it sustains between the conventionalized figure of the clown (whose codified costume of baggy trousers, flapping shoes and bulbous red nose always represented, in any case, a stylized sublimation of a tramp's tatterdemalion dignity) and a realism founded on personal experience and observation: watching Chaplin's tramp, one is made simultaneously aware of the interrelated traditions of the circus and the ghetto, a tinsel and sawdust, which is why Fellini is his direct descendant. Keaton, by contrast, is a white clown, an Auguste. Like those of Jacques Tati, his gags are brilliantly contrived but often simply too lovely, too clever, to be laughed at. They lack that fundamental component of humour, one all but ubiquitous in Chaplin's work, *vulgarity*. If Chaplin's art is vulgar, though, his is the vulgarity not of the lowest common denominator but of the *deepest* common denominator. The pathos (inevitable word) of his films is rooted in the sweatshops of the East End of London and the Lower East Side of New York. And his earliest audiences, those audiences for whom he was not a petrified icon of cinema history, as he has since become, but an adorably disreputable Everyman of the slums, were moved by him even as they laughed at him because they could identify his condition so intimately with their own.

In this real, literal sense Chaplin was incomparable. No one else — not Keaton, whoe responses to his environment were those of a character out of Kafka (Buster K?); not Harry Langdon, who brought to his impersonation of a long-trousered baby something of the eerie craft of the show business transvestite; not Laurel and Hardy, sublime as they were — none of these could claim quite the universality that would be his. The basic difference between Chaplin and Keaton, for example, is encapsulated in the celebrated scene of *Steamboat Bill, Jr* in which the poker-faced Keaton tries on a series of different hats, including the boater that was destined to become his trademark: he admires it on himself for an instant or two before, to our amusement and amazement, rejecting it out of hand. It's an extraordinary moment, but one in which Keaton stands outside his own public persona in order to pass ironic comment upon it: one can almost see him winking at his public. The gesture, however, is ultimately divisive. It splits the audience into two, into those who know and those who don't, something that Chaplin would never have done (not, at least, until a late professional embitterment was made manifest in films like *Limelight* and *A King in New York*).

It's arguably the case that, if Chaplin is to be judged by the standards of pure *mise-en-scène*, by the strict consideration of the visual and plastic qualities of the films for which he was responsible, as actor, director, writer and even composer, then Keaton is the more stylish, more polished and more felicitous artist. Certainly, Keaton was a very fine filmmaker, many of whose films were masterpieces, and he had, throughout a long and turbulent career, his cortège of devoted champions. But Chaplin was *greater than the cinema*. Every one of his films was a masterpiece. And his public was the world.

GILBERT SELDES

"I Am Here To-day"

The invaluable Gilbert Seldes (1893–1970) was the first American critic to write seriously about all the popular arts — movies, of course, but also jazz, comic strips, Broadway revues, and so on. His The Seven Lively Arts, *published in 1924, was the first trickle of what would eventually become a flood of writing, by hundreds of critics, that implicity argued for the vitality and significance of supposedly "low" cultural forms which had previously been ignored by the literati. Seldes's shrewd but unpretentious manner (he also wrote mystery novels under a pen name) was very much in the best spirit of the works he championed.*

For most of us the grotesque effigy dangling from the electric sign or propped against the side of the ticket-booth must remain our first memory of Charlie Chaplin. The splay feet, the moustache, the derby hat, the rattan walking-stick, composed at once the image which was ten years later to become the universal symbol of laughter. *"I am here to-day"* was his legend, and like everything else associated with his name it is faintly ironic and exactly right. The man who, of all the men of our time, seems most assured of immortality, chose that particularly transient announcement of his presence, "I am here to-day," with its emotional overtone of "gone to-morrow," and there is always something in Charlie that slips away. "He does things," said John S. Sargent once, "and you're lucky if you see them." Incredibly lucky to live when we have the chance to see them.

It is a miracle that there should arise in our time a figure wholly in the tradition of the great clowns—a tradition requiring creative energy, freshness, inventiveness, change—for neither the time nor the country in which Charlie works is exceptionally favourable to such a phenomenon. Stranger still is the course he has run. It is simple to take *The Kid* as the dividing line, but it is more to the point to consider the phases of Charlie's popularity, for each phase corresponds to one of the attacks now being made upon his integrity. He is on the top of the world, an exposed position, and we are all sniping at him; even his adherents are inclined to say that "after all" he is "still" this or the other thing. One goes to his pictures as one went to hear Caruso, with a ghoulish speculation as to the quantity of alloy in the "golden voice." It is because Charlie has had all there ever was of acclaim that he is now surrounded by deserters.

That he exists at all is due to the camera and to the selective genius of Mack Sennett. It is impossible to dissociate him entirely from the Keystone comedy where he began and worked wonders and learned much. The injustice of forgetting Sennett and the Keystone when thinking of Chaplin has undermined most of the intellectual appreciation of his work, for although he was the greatest of the Keystone comedians and passed far beyond them, the first *and decisive* phase of his popularity came while he was with them, and the Keystone touch remains in all his later work, often as its most precious element. It was the time of Charlie's actual contact with the American people, the movie-going populace before the days of the great moving pictures. He was the second man to be known widely by name—John Bunny was the first—and he achieved a fame which passed entirely by word of mouth into the category of the common myths and legends of America, as the name of Buffalo Bill has passed before. By the time the newspapers recognized the movie as a source of circulation, Charlie was already a known quantity in the composition of the American mind and, what is equally significant, he had created the

first *Charlot*. The French name which is and is not Charlie will serve
for that figure on the screen, the created image which is, and at the
same time is more than, Charlie Chaplin, and is less. Like every great
artist in whatever medium, Charlie has created the mask of himself—
many masks, in fact—and the first of these, the wanderer, came in the
Keystone comedies. It was there that he first detached himself from
life and began to live in another world, with a specific rhythm of his
own, as if the pulse-beat in him changed and was twice or half as fast
as that of those who surrounded him. He created then that trajectory
across the screen which is absolutely his own line of movement. No
matter what the actual facts are, the curve he plots is always the same.
It is of one who seems to enter from a corner of the screen, becomes
entangled or involved in a force greater than himself as he advances
upward and to the centre; there he spins like a marionette in a
whirlpool, is flung from side to side, always in a parabola which seems
centripetal until the madness of the action hurls him to refuge or
compels him to flight at the opposite end of the screen. He wanders
in, a stranger, an impostor, an anarchist; and passes again, buffeted,
but unchanged.

For a book about popular American entertainment, the number of
French words used is perhaps excessive. The one I am most inclined
to defend is *Charlot* for the character Chaplin created on the screen
before he began to make feature-length pictures. It is used to distin-
guish "the little tramp" on the screen from the citizen, taxpayer,
house-owner, individual; it is an attempt to say in a single word, that
Charlie Chaplin was a creative artist, that unlike many excellent and
many second-rate people who played in the movies he was *not playing himself.* "Charlie" was after all, the name we called Chaplin—
whereas the figure on the screen had no name until the French invented one for him. I could have used "the little tramp" or put the
name "Charlie" in quotes but both seemed awkward. I did not, as a
critic implied, attach an "arcane significance" to the French name,
but when the same critic said that *Charlot* meant nothing more than
Charlie Chaplin he was simply wrong. *Charlot* was a figure existing
only on the screen and the great critical error was in confusing him
with the man whose imagination brought him to life there.

The description of the typical line of movement Chaplin created for that figure seems to me accurate, but I wish I hadn't described it so exclusively in geometrical terms. Or that the terms excited the visual imagination more immediately. The high degree of Chaplin's control of his material (including himself) is proved by the fact that a diagram of his movement can be made—but it remains a diagram.

The Keystone was the time of his wildest grotesquerie (after *Tillie's Punctured Romance*, to be sure), as if he needed, for a beginning, sharply to contrast his rhythm, his gait, his gesture, *mode*, with the actual world outside. His successes in this period were confined to those films in which the world intruded with all its natural crassness upon his detached existence. There was a film in which Charlie dreamed himself back into the Stone Age and played on God of the Waters—wholly without success because he contrasted his fantasy with another fantasy in the same tempo, and could neither sink into nor stand apart from it. But in *His Night Out* the effect is perfect, and is intensified by the alternating coincidence and syncopation of rhythm in which Ben Turpin worked with him. Charlie's drunken line of march down a stairway was first followed in parallel and then in not-quite-parallel by Turpin; the degree of drunkenness was the same, then varied, then returned to identity; and the two, together, were always entirely apart from the actuality of bars and hotels and fountains and policemen which were properties in their existence. In this early day Charlie has already mastered his principles. He knew that the broad lines are funny and that the fragments—which are delicious—must "point" the main line of laughter. I recall, for example, an exquisite moment at the end of this film. Turpin is staggering down the street, dragging Charlie by the collar. Essentially the funny thing is that one drunkard should so gravely, so soberly, so obstinately take care of another and should convert himself into a policeman to do it; it is funny that they should be going nowhere, and go so doggedly. The lurching-forward body of Turpin, the singular angle formed with it by Charlie's body almost flat on the ground, added to the spectacle. And once as they went along Charlie's right hand fell to one side, and as idly as a girl plucks a water-lily from over the side of a canoe he plucked a daisy from the grass border of the path, and smelled it. The function of that gesture was to make everything that went before, and everything that came after, seem funnier; and it succeeded by creating another, incongruous image out of the picture before our eyes. The entire world, a moment earlier, had been aslant and distorted and wholly male; it righted itself suddenly and created a soft idyll of tenderness. Nearly everything of Charlie is in that moment, and I know no better way to express its elusive quality than to say that as I sat watching the film a second time, about two hours later, the repetition of the gesture came with all the effect of surprise, although I has been wondering whether he could do it so perfectly again.

This was the Charlie whom little children came to know before any other and whose name they added to their prayers. He was then popular with the people; he was soon to become universally known and admired — the Charlie of *The Bank* and of *Shoulder Arms*; and finally he became "the great artist" in *The Kid*. The second period is pure development; the third is change; and the adherents of each join with the earlier enthusiasts to instruct and alarm their idol. No doubt the middle phase is the one which is richest in memory. It includes the masterpieces *A Dog's Life, The Pawnshop, The Vagabond, Easy Street*, as well as the two I have just mentioned, and if I am not mistaken, the *genre* pictures like *The Floorwalker, The Fireman, The Immigrant*, and the fantastic *Cure*. To name these pictures is to call to mind their special scenes, the atmosphere in which they were played: the mock heroic of *The Bank* and its parody of passion; the unbelievable scene behind the curtain in *A Dog's Life*; Charlie as policeman in *Easy Street*, which had some of the beginnings of *The Kid*; Charlie left marking time along after the squad had marched away in the film which made camp life supportable. Compare them with the very earliest films, *The Pile Driver* and the wheel-chairman film and so on: the later ones are richer in inventiveness, the texture is more solid, the emotions grow more complex, and the interweaving of tenderness and gravity with the fun becomes infinitely more deft. In essence it is the same figure — he is still a vagrant, an outsider; only now when he becomes entangled in the lives of other people he is a bit of a crusader, too. The accidental does not occur so frequently; the progress of each film is plotted in advance; there is a definite rise and fall as in *A Dog's Life*, where the climax is in the curtain scene toward which tends the first episode of the dog and from which the flight and the rustic idyll flow gently downward. The pace in the earlier pictures was more instinctive. In *The Count* the tempo is jerky; it moves from extreme to extreme. Yet one gets the sense of the impending flight beautifully when, at the close, Charlot as the bogus count has been shown up and is fleeing pell-mell through every room in the house; the whole movement grows tense; the rate of acceleration perceptibly heightens as Charlot slides in front of a vast birthday cake, pivots on his heel, and begins to play alternate pool and golf with the frosting, making every shot count like a machine gunner barricaded in a pillbox or a bandit in a deserted cabin.

It was foreordained that the improvised kind of comedy should given way to something more calculated, and in Charlie's case it is particularly futile to cry over spilled milk because for a long time he continued to give the *effect* of impromptu; his sudden movements and his finds in the way of unsuspected sources of fun are exceptional to this day.

In *The Pawnshop* Charlie begins to sweep and catches in his broom the end of a long rope, which, instead of being swept away, keeps getting longer, actively fighting the broom. I have no way to prove it, but I am sure from the context that this is all he had originally had in mind to do with the scene. Suddenly the tape on the floor creates something in his mind, and Charlie transforms the back room of the pawnshop into a circus, with himself walking the tight rope—a graceful, nimble balancing along the thin line of tape on the floor, the quick turn and coming forward, the conventional bow, arms flung out, smiling, to receive applause at the end. Again, as ever, he has created an imaginary scene out of the materials of the actual.

"The egregious merit of Chaplin," says T. S. Eliot, "is that he has escaped in his own way from the realism of the cinema and invented a *rhythm*. Of course the unexplored opportunities of the cinema for eluding realism must be very great."

It amused me once, after seeing *The Pawnshop*, to write down exactly what had happened. Later I checked up the list, and I print it here. I believe that Chaplin is so great on the screen, his effect so complete, that few people are aware, afterward, of how much he has done. Nor can they be aware of how much of Chaplin's work is "in his own way"—even when he does something which another could have done he adds to it a touch of his own. I do not pretend that the following analysis is funny; it may be useful:

Charlot enters the pawnshop; it is evident that he is late. He compares his watch with the calendar pad hanging on the wall, and hastily begins to make up for lost time by entering the back room and going busily to work. He takes a duster out of a valise and meticulously dusts his walking-stick. Then proceeding to other objects, he fills the room with clouds of dust, and when he begins to dust the electric fan, looking at something else, the feathers are blown all over the room. He turns and sees the plucked butt of the duster—and carefully puts it away for to-morrow.

With the other assistant he takes a ladder and a bucket of water and goes out to polish the three balls and the shop sign. After some horseplay he rises to the top of the ladder and reaches over to polish the sign; the ladder sways, teeters, with Charlot on top of it. A policeman down the street looks aghast, and sways sympathetically with the ladder. Yet struggling to keep his balance, Charlot is intent on his work, and every time the ladder brings him near the sign he dabs frantically at it until he falls.

A quarrel with his fellow-worker follows. The man is caught between the rungs of the ladder, his arms imprisoned. Charlot calls a boy over to hold the other end of the ladder and begins a boxing match. Although his adversary is incapable of moving his arms, Charlot sidesteps, feints, and guards, leaping nimbly away from imaginary blows. The policeman interferes and both assistants run into the shop. By a toss of a coin Charlot is compelled to go back to fetch the bucket. He tiptoes behind the policeman, snatches the bucket, and with a wide swing and a swirling motion evades the policeman and returns. He is then caught by the boss in another fight and is discharged.

He makes a tragic appeal to be reinstated. He says he has eleven children, so high, and so high, and so high—until the fourth one is about a foot taller than himself. The boss relents only as Charlot's stricken figure is at the door. As he is pardoned, Charlot leaps upon the old boss, twining his legs around his abdomen; he is thrown off and surreptitiously kisses the old man's hand. He goes into the kitchen to help the daughter and passes dishes through the clothes wringer to dry them—passes a cup twice, as it seems not to be dry the first time. Then his hands. The jealous assistant provokes a fight; Charlot has a handful of dough and is about the throw it when the boss appears. With the same motion Charlot flings the dough into the wringer, passes it through as a pie crust, seizes a pie plate, trims the crust over it, and goes out to work.

At the pawnshop counter pass a variety of human beings. Charlot is taken in by a sob story about a wedding ring; he tries to test the genuineness of goldfish by dropping acid on them. Sent to the back room, he takes his lunch out of the safe, gets into another fight, in which he is almost beating his rival to death when the girl enters. Charlot falls whimpering to the floor and is made much of. He returns to the counter and the episode of the clock begins.

A sinister figure enters, offering a clock in pawn. Charlot looks at it; then takes an auscultator and listens to its heartbeat; then taps it over crossed fingers for its pulmonary action; then taps it with a little hammer to see the quality, as with porcelain; then snaps his thumb on the bell. He takes an augur and bores a hold in it; then a can-opener, and when he has pried the lid off he smells the contents and with a disparaging gesture makes the owner smell them, too. He then does dentistry on it, with forceps; then plumbing. Finally he screws a jeweler's magnifying glass into his eye and hammers what is left in the clock, shakes out the contents, measures the mainspring from the tip of his nose to arm's length, like cloth, squirts oil on the debris to keep it quiet, and, lifting the man's hat from his head, sweeps the whole mess into it and returns it with a sad shake of the head.

A pearl-buyer has meanwhile come in and Charlot retraces his steps to the back room (carefully stepping over the buyer's hat) and begins to sweep. His broom becomes entangled with a piece of tape, which fights back and gets longer and longer. Suddenly Charlot begins to tight-rope upon it, balancing with the broom, and making a quick turn, coming forward for applause. A final quarrel with the other assistant ensues. As they are swarming round the legs of the kitchen table, the boss comes in and Charlot flees, leaps into a trunk, and is hidden. As the others enter the room, the pearl-buyer, who has stolen all the valuables, holds them up with a revolver. Charlot leaps from the trunk, fells the robber, and embraces the lovely maiden for a fade-out.

All of this takes about thirty minutes. I have put down nearly everything, for Chaplin is on the scene virtually all of the time. I am fairly certain that ninety per cent of this film could not have been made, even badly, by anyone else. Analysis of A *Dog's Life* would give the same result: the arrival at the climax being a little more certain and the drama of the climax (the curtain scene — compared with the clock scene above) being more involved in the course of action.

In his book on Chaplin, Theodore Huff has done a sequence-by-sequence analysis of the same picture. Comparing the two, I find that in spite of all my care I had omitted a few bits. Proof of my point, that it is impossible to see everything Chaplin does, was double: Huff hadn't seen a few of the bits I recorded!

The plotting of these comedies did not destroy Charlie's inventiveness and made it possible for him to develop certain other of his characteristics. The moment the vagrant came to rest, the natural man appeared, the paradoxical creature who has the wisdom of simple souls and the incalculable strength of the weak. Charlie all through the middle period is at least half Tyl Eulenspiegl. It is another way for him to live apart from the world by assuming that the world actually means what it says, by taking every one of its conventional formulas, its polite phrases and idioms, with dreadful seriousness. He has created in Charlot a radical with an extraordinarily logical mind. Witness Charlot arriving late at the theatre and stepping on the toes of a whole row of people to his seat at the far end; the gravity of his expressions of regret is only matched by his humiliation when he discovers that he is, after all, in the wrong row and makes his way back again and all through the next row to his proper place. It is a careful exaggeration of the social fiction that when you apologise you can do anything to anyone. The same feeling underlies the characteristic moment when Charlot is fighting and suddenly stops, takes off his hat and coat, gives them to his opponent to hold, and then promptly knocks his obliging adversary down. Revisiting once an old Charlie, I saw him do this, and a few minutes later saw the same thing in a new Harold Lloyd; all there is to know of the difference between the two men was to be learned there; for Lloyd, who is a clever fellow, made it seem a smart trick so to catch his enemy off guard, while Chaplin made the moment equal to the conventional crossing of swords or the handshake before a prize fight. Similarly, the salutation with the hat takes seriously a social convention and carries it as far as it can go. In *Pay Day* Charlot arrives late to work and attempts to mollify the furious construction-gang boss by handing him an Easter lily.

The Kid was undoubtedly a beginning in "literature" for Charlie. I realize that in admitting this I am giving the whole case away, for in the opinion of certain critics the beginning of literature is the end of creative art. This attitude is not so familiar in America, but in France you hear the Charlot of *The Kid* spoken of as "theatre," as one who has ceased to be of the film entirely. I doubt if this is just. Like the one other great artist in America (George Herriman, with whom he is eminently in sympathy), Charlie has always had the Dickens touch, a thing which in its purity we do not otherwise discover in our art. Dickens himself is mixed; only a part of him is literature, and that not the best, nor is that part essentially the one which Charlie has imported to the screen. *The Kid* had some bad things in it: the story, the halo round the head of the unmarried mother, the quarrel with the authorities; it is an unnecessary amount of realism and its tempo was uncertain, for it was neither serious film nor Keystone. Yet it possessed moments of unbelievable intensity and touches of high imagination. The scenes in and outside the doss-house were excellent and were old Charlie; the glazier's assistant was inventive and the training of Coogan to look like his foster-father was beautiful. Far above them stood the beginning of the film: Charlot, in his usual polite rags, strolling down to his club after his breakfast (it would have been a grilled bone) and, avoiding slops as Villon did, twirling his can, taking off his fingerless gloves to reach for his cigarette case (a sardine box), and selecting from the butts one of quality, *tamping it* to shake down the excess tobacco at the tip—all of this, as Mr Herriman pointed out to me, was the creation of the society gentleman, the courageous refusal to be undermined by slums and poverty and rags. At the end of the film there was the vision of heaven: apotheosis of the long suffering of Charlot at the hands of the police, not only in *The Kid*—in a hundred films where he stood always against the authorities, always for his small independent freedom. The world in which even policemen have wings shatters, too; but something remains. The invincible Charlot, dazed by his dream, looking for wings on the actual policeman who is apparently taking him to jail, will not down. For as they start, a post comes between them, and Charlot, without the slightest effort to break away, too submissive to fight, still dodges back to walk round the post and so avoid bad luck. A moment later comes one of the highest points in Charlie's career. He is ushered into a limousine instead of a patrol wagon—it is the beginning of the happy ending. And as the motor starts he flashes at the spectators of his felicity a look of indescribable poignancy. It is frightened, it is hopeful, bewildered; it lasts a fraction of a second and is blurred by the plate glass of the car. I cannot hope to set down the quality of it, how it becomes a moment of unbearable intensity, and how one is breathless with suspense—and with adoration.

For, make no mistake, it is adoration, not less, that he deserves and has from us. He corresponds to our secret desires because he alone has passed beyond our categories, at one bound placing himself outside space and time. His escape from the world is complete and extraordinarily rapid, and what makes him more than a figure of romance is his immediate creation of another world. He has the vital energy, the composing and the functioning brain. This is what makes him aesthetically interesting, what will make him for ever a school not only of acting, but the whole creative process. The flow of his line always corresponds to the character and tempo; there is a definite relation between the melody and the orchestration he gives it. Beyond his technique—the style of his pieces—he has composition, because he creates anything but chaos in his separate world. "You might," wrote Mr Stark Young, wise in everything but the choice of the person addressed, "you might really create in terms of the moving picture as you have already created in terms of character." As I have said, the surest way to be wrong about Charlie is to forget the Keystone.

This is precisely what Mr Stark Young would like him to do—and what Charlie may do it the intellectual nonsense about him is capable of corrupting his natural wisdom and his creative gift. Mr Young has addressed an open letter to "Dear Mr Chaplin"* in which he suggest that Charlie play *Liliom* and *He Who Gets Slapped* and *Peer Gynt*. (Offended as I am by these ideas, I must be fair. Mr Young does say that better than all of these, "you could do new things written by or for you, things in which you would use your full endowment, comic and otherwise . . . develop things calculated strictly for it [the screen] and for no other art, made up out of its essential quality, which is visual motion and not mere stage drama photographed. . . .") This is, of course, corruption. It means that Mr Young has either not seen the Charlie of before *The Kid* (as I suspect from the phrase about creating in terms of character) or not liked him (which I am sure about); he has failed to recognize in *The Pawnbroker* "his full endowment, comic and otherwise." It implies to me that Mr Young would prefer a "serious film" and that suggests the complete absence of a critical sense, of taste and gusto, of wisdom and gaiety, of piety and wit. "The larger field" . . . "serious efforts" . . . "a more cultured audience" . . . "the judicious"—O Lord! These are the phrases which are offered as bribes to the one man who has destroyed the world and created it in his own image!

There is a future for him as for others, and it is quite possible that the future may not be as rich and as dear as the past. I write this without having seen *The Pilgrim*, which ought to be a test case, for the two films which followed *The Kid* (*Pay Day* and *The Idle Class*) determined nothing. If the literary side conquers we shall have a great character actor and not a creator; we shall certainly not have again the image of riot and fun, the created personage, the annihilation of actuality; we may go so far as to accomplish Mr Stark Young's ideal and have a serious work of art. I hope this will not happen, because I do not believe that it is the necessary curve of Charlie's genius—it is the direction of worldly success, not in money, but in fame; it is not the curve of life at all. For the slowing-up of Charlie's physical energies and the deepening of his understanding may well restore to him his appreciation of those early monuments to laughter which are his greatest achievement. He stood ten shod in absurdity, but with his feet

---

*It appeared in *The New Republic* and will probably be found in *The Flower in Drama* (Scribners).

on the earth. And his danced on the earth, an eternal figure of lightness and of the wisdom which knows that the earth was made to dance on. It was a green earth, excited with its own abundance and fruitfulness, and he possessed it entirely. For me he remains established in possession. As in spins under his feet he dances silently and with infinite grace upon it. It is as if in his whole life he had spoken only one word: "I am here *to-day*"—the beginning before time and the end without end of his wisdom and of his loveliness.

What am I, as a critic, to make of this? It is excited writing toward the end and I am brought up sharp by the word "adoration" which I wouldn't use now, the word having, even more than it used to, the foolish overtone of "adorable" (as for babies). But I still think that Chaplin was entitled to something vastly more complex than admiration, that a portion of gratitude and even something of the profound respect we call awe is his due.

I have shifted to the present tense. I cannot write as I once did, but I can express my deep feeling that Chaplin has been badly treated and that the critics of his art were stupidly affected by the enemies of his politics. When *M. Verdoux* appeared—the masterpiece of his later style, a picture before which the critics should have bowed in silent respect—some of them had the effrontery to suggest that Chaplin go back to the baggy pants and the rattan walking stick—but it was not Chaplin's youth they were trying to recapture, it was their own. He had followed a natural line of growth—a rare phenomenon in the distracting world of the movies—and they were asking him to have died twenty years ago.

Fortunately for the world, Chaplin was wiser than his critics, he outgrew his youth, he was not afraid of maturity, he escaped from his own formula, not into something unsuited to his talents, but into the full flowering of those talents which the formula was beginning to strait-jacket. One of the things for which we can without reservation thank the sound track is that it compelled Chaplin to develop all his capacities. He was resentful under this compulsion, he had never needed words (and as Élie Faure pointed out many years ago, he was the only one who never "talked," never made the motions of talking, in the silent pictures). But he had implied sound. Looking at one of his old pictures in a projection room, without piano or orchestra, you "heard" the glissando of a harp as he slid across a dance floor and the thump of the drums, the plucking of violin strings, the spiral of wood-winds and a hundred other sounds—his movements were music.

His words were not. His decision to be his own writer was probably the right one; it eliminated the dreadful dialogue of the kind of script-writer who is not in essence a writer at all; it brought a kind of plain talk to the screen. It was flawed by the same kind of sentimental clichés one finds in his situations and gestures, by a flatness corre-sponding to the primitive settings and the uninspired camera-work of all his pictures. He made movies year after year as if the rest of Holly-wood didn't exist, as if the cinematographer was still cranking the cam-era by hand in the glare of the sun, as if lighting hadn't become a spe-cial skill and the set-designer was still a carpenter. In part this can be traced to Chaplin's unique situation as the only star financing his pro-ductions with his own, not bank, money. But beyond this imposed economy, a kind of austerity operated to keep the pictures simple, to concentrate attention, not to disperse it. The language of the dialogue-movie would have been inappropriate and Chaplin seemed always to be trying to arrive at the concision and plainness of the silent-movie ti-tle, sometimes falling into its stereotyped phrases, but usually avoiding its flowery "mood" language.

As a writer and as composer of music for his films, Chaplin re-mains an amateur. He gains because his movies (and his alone) are the product of a single individual, as a novel is or a poem. But the the-atrical arts are not novels or poems, and a powerful man can use the skill of others, as Wagner did, to carry out his intent, without doing everything himself. There was evidence in A *Woman of Paris* that Chaplin could be a great director, but all we can be sure of is that he was the best director for his own films. They would have been better, they would have contributed more to the art of the movies, if he hadn't insisted on himself as the solitary source of all the inspirations a movie requires.

Yet he created masterpieces.

One of the consequences of writing this book was that I came to know some of the people I admired and Chaplin was one of them. Our connection was professional, our meetings always had to me some of the atmosphere of an interview arranged by a press-agent, which they were not. In perhaps a dozen meetings, I can recall only one during which anything that was personal transpired. I had come West to work on a radio program and saw Chaplin at Dave Chasen's restaurant on Christmas or New Year's eve, I've forgotten which, and he asked me to dinner the next night. When I arrived he inquired about my health and (it was wartime and accommodations in hotels were difficult to get) whether I was comfortable. I reassured him on all points, but said that I didn't sleep well in Hollywood, at which he said, "Gilbert, no one sleeps well any more." I note this as the only general comment on the human condition I ever heard him make; everything else was either about his work or about his ideas which, at that time, obsessed him. For most of the evening he was protesting against the stupidity of the networks (I was working for CBS at the time) in refusing him a regular quarter-hour a week to talk to the armed forces. When I suggested that he had a better way to express what he wanted to say, he brushed me aside, as if I had asked him to do a *Shoulder Arms* again.

Professionally he was pleased that I had written about him, as he was pleased with any critical praise. He knew that I was not the first to appreciate his genius—Waldo Frank and Vachel Lindsay had long preceded me and a writer in an English weekly, whom I read in 1916, had done a remarkable study of *A Night at the Show*. I had referred with pleasure to Chaplin and with displeasure to his imitators as early as 1916, but priority in these matters is of small account. Some time after the release of *M. Verdoux*, and English actor asked Chaplin if he was pleased with what I had written about him. Chaplin replied that no one had ever written anything significant about him except the French. (Those who believe that Chaplin was "spoiled" by the critics may take note of this.)

I am sorry my work hadn't given him greater satisfaction and I wish I knew precisely what he found in the admirable French criticism of his work that made it significant to him because that would give us a clue to what he thinks the essence of his genius is. I suspect that he cannot express that essence in words, that it must be conveyed in his work—and there are many interesting attempts in every major language to make the discovery for him. I am deterred from adding to them. But not from recording my pleasure.

The greatest performance I ever saw him give occurred on the same night as his bad-tempered attack on the networks. I had finally shifted his thoughts to the picture he was then doing, which was *Verdoux* . . . It surprised me that in view of the publicity about his private life he had chosen to do a movie about a man who murders one wife after another, but the moment he began to tell me about the picture I fell completely under his spell. It was Chaplin's habit to act out his pictures—I think it was part of his creative process—and I had seen him do it once before, when he played all the great moments of *Modern Times* after dinner at Sam Goldwyn's house. He did *Verdoux* for me at the restaurant and came to the scene of the streetwalker whom Verdoux takes to dinner, dropping poison into her wineglass. The whore tells her story, stopping now and again to reach for her glass, to lift it, to set it down again, unsipped. At the end, exhausted, she puts her hand out again for the glass. "Then I reach over," said Chaplin, "and I say 'I think there's a bit of cork in your wine' and I flick it out . . ." At this point he made a gesture, almost imperceptible, so accurate, so controlled and delicate, that I was dazzled—and it didn't seem to me that the moment came off nearly as well in the film. I had seen the creative event itself.

But, of course, we all have seen it, over and over again. The feeling I had, watching the gesture in *His Night Out*, wondering whether he could do it as well the next time, marks precisely the difference between Chaplin and all the others, of whom we know with certainty that it will be the same and will remind us that this is a repetition, whereas with him it always seems created, fresh and new and dazzling, on the spot.

His defects do not rise out of his virtues, they rise from that part of his total personality which is at war with his genius. Whenever a picture runs into a bad patch it is because Chaplin is doing something under some intellectual compulsion, which may be only the compulsion to make a picture successful at the box-office and is often the compulsion to prove a point, some intellectual concept he has defended, to prove himself right. It would give me the greatest pleasure if he proved me wrong with the picture he has made abroad. The publicity suggests that it is a criticism of those unfortunate American attitudes which exiled him. In the dispute between him and the State Department (and with that portion of the American people the State Department attitude represents) I am totally on his side. But I do not think he is his best defender. He is the best defender of others, of those deprived of defence who have to turn to him to represent them in the high courts of justice. He has pleaded their cause against the brutality of the world and I wish he were content to let others plead his.

ALISTAIR COOKE

Fame

Alistair Cooke (1908–2004) was famous in his native
England for his weekly Letter from America *radio*
broadcasts on the BBC, which began in 1946 and con-
tinued until almost the moment he died in 2004. He
was famous in his adopted country for the impeccable
urbanity with which he hosted Masterpiece Theatre
on PBS for some two decades. One of his great interests
was the movies, which he reviewed for a time in the
1930s. When he first arrived in the United States he be-
came friends with Chaplin, and this piece is an unruf-
fled but acute consideration of fame's impact on him.
It is excerpted from Six Men, *which collected his por-*
traits of famous acquaintances in politics and the arts.

The fans, they sift around the entrance to the Dorchester or huddle
against a knifing wind on the sidewalk outside the Broadway stage
doors: miniature traffic cops with their little books out, poised for the
kill. They palpitate up against the improvised stage on any field large
enough to enclose the pandemonium of a rock festival. Like Olympic
relay runners, they stretch their arms to the limit over the barricades
at Wembley or Yankee Stadium waiting for the touch of the afternoon

hero. They used to mob department stores where Sean Connery was rumored to be shopping. I have seen them as a congregation of dolls, bobbing behind the customs barrier at Tokyo, waiting for the Rolling Stones to wing in from Seattle or Hawaii. They are the distorting mirrors in which the stars see their images blown up beyond any human scale.

What this ceaseless adoration does to the psyche of the victims is something that the victims rarely seem to examine, though they reveal it in various touching or unlovely ways. They learn to practice self-deprecation by way of fake surprise. Or they bear with it as the inevitable codicil to a million-dollar contract. Or, more often than is pleasant to see, they wallow in the ocean of their narcissism and accept it as no more than the due of their uncanny beauty or talent.

But the fans today are not to be confused with the public. They are specialists, devotees of a particular cult that may be worldwide but is exclusive nonetheless. The disciples of Elton John have never heard of Giscard D'Estaing. Girls and matrons dizzy with desire for Robert Redford would not know Saul Bellow or Bjorn Borg, or maybe even Nelson Rockefeller, if they fell over him. Perhaps only Presidents of the United States and the Queen of England—Muhammad Ali dissenting—can bring out a general crowd, and then only during an election campaign or a coronation. Somewhere along the falling graph of our allegiance to authority, the general public seems to have exhausted its naïve impulse to appear en masse for the arrival of the famous one—except in those "people's republics" where a million people can be commanded to appear on the double in the great square, or else.

But most of all, in our century, more people have come out everywhere to catch a glimpse of Charles Chaplin than did so far any other human in history. This sentence seems a contradiction: no celebrity could be seen by more people in more countries, though in the bacterial stew of the early cinemas, than Charlie Chaplin was. But he was the first world entertainer whose film persona seemed too real to be true: to see Charles Chaplin was to come face to face with the living Aladdin whose lamp had conjured up the genie we all loved and laughed at.

To say that anyone is the most famous, or the best, the greatest, the most beautiful, is—like all rhetoric—a method of bullying the reader into sharing a prejudice. The journalists who garnish a magazine profile with such superlatives, like the authors of screenplays about some chosen eminence (Pasteur, Beethoven, Sister Kenny), are writing from the focal center of their idol's local fame and assume that the din of it reverberates out from center to the farthest corners of the earth. This convention can produce scenes of hilarious innocence in the movies, where, say, an enterprising producer offers us a Parisian soirée at which our heroine George Sand is an invited guest. To foster a little desperate verisimilitude, the camera pans over the assembled company, and you get a glimpse of an Orson Welles bulk addressed as "M. Balzac," a passing remark addressed to a dandy with whiskers ("Tell me, Mr. Dickens"), a French lieutenant deferring to a fellow called Bismarck (no matter whether the Iron Chancellor had ever been in Paris or not). They are all hushed into reverence by the arrival of Merle Oberon in a tuxedo, for although the casual spectator may have thought of this as the Age of Revolution or the Reform Acts, he is meant to realize that the whole world swooned at the appearance anywhere of George Sand. In dull fact, George Sand and Charles Dickens, even with Bismarck in tow, could probably have roamed through Paris or London arm in arm and gone unrecognized by all but a chance acquaintance or an aficionado of daguerreotypes. Johnny Carson cannot go into a delicatessen anywhere between the Florida Keys and Fairbanks, Alaska, without a chorus of oohing and ahing and a rush of autograph hounds.

A year or two ago a New York magazine concocted a list of the 100 "most famous men and women in the world." By the most generous count, not more than a dozen of them could have been heard of outside the regular readers of the American editions of *Time* and *Vogue*, the nighttime audience for American television talk shows, dentists' patients, and the addicts of *The New York Times*'s proliferating gossip columns. The composers of the list had plainly ignored the fact that our world includes the inhabitants of Europe, Communist China, and Upper Volta, not to mention all of South America and Australasia.

Yet Will Rogers was saying nothing but the literal truth when he wrote, in 1931, that "the Zulus know Chaplin better than Arkansas know Garbo." Throughout the 1920s and into the early 1930s, Chaplin was the most famous man on earth. It is impossible to pick another person of any nationality to whom such a legion of other international celebrities was eager to be introduced. At one time or another, they included the Crown Prince of Japan, Woodrow Wilson, Prince George of Greece, Nijinsky, Lord Louis Mountbatten, Franklin Roosevelt, Georges Carpentier, Diego Rivera, Albert Einstein, Pandit Nehru, Pablo Calals, Nikita Khrushchev, Jean Cocteau, and Chou En-lai.

As early as 1917, when Chaplin had been making two-reelers for only three years, his studio was the court to which trooped the most eminent of touring artists: Paderewski, Godowsky, Heifetz, Harry Lauder, Dame Nellie Melba. In 1921, on his first return to Britain since he had left it as an obscure vaudevillian, the crowds at Waterloo lifted him on their shoulders from the boat train, and the streets along the three-mile route to the Ritz were lined as for a coronation. Ten years later, over 100 police were required to guard him between the Tokyo docks and the Imperial Hotel. On a two-month visit to Europe in 1931, which included a short detour into Africa, he had to abandon shopping expeditions in Algiers and Marrakech. In Berlin, he was the guest of the Reichstag. In Paris, the Briand Cabinet attended his investiture into the Legion of Honor. In London, he was toasted at a public banquet by Winston Churchill, and among the great

Ones who sought him out were H. G. Wells, J. M. Barrie, Emil Ludwig, Lloyd George, Lady Astor, the King and Queen, the Prince of Wales, the Duke of Connaught, and Bernard Shaw. Shaw broke a lifetime's vow by wearing evening dress to appear with him at the opening of *City Lights*. Mahatma Gandhi was the only innocent in this majestic procession of fans. Told that it was important for him to meet the great man, he replied, "Who is Mr. Chaplin?" He saw him nevertheless.

This celebrity list is not compiled to elicit gasps of astonishment. It is meant merely to sharpen the point that whereas the Beatles, for example, may have enjoyed an idolatry as widespread, it was only among their fanatical followers. Chaplin was mobbed by ordinary people of all types, of all ages, was known to every country, and was the sought-after guest of kings, statesmen, authors, artists, celebrities of every sort.

It has to be borne in mind as a burden on the ego quite beyond the imagining of the rest of us. There is one story that Chaplin loved to tell which shows that in the beginning no one was more overwhelmed by the extent of his fame than Chaplin himself. This may at first sound suspicious as fact and coy as a confessional, because we think of fame as something that burgeons and can hardly amaze its object, unless it mushrooms overnight, as with Lindbergh.

It happened to Chaplin when he was already earning $1250 a week, a salary which would have been handsome enough for an opera star. (Within a year, he signed for $10,000 a week.) He was, at the time, the most financially precious property in the movies. But it is hard for us now to appreciate how inbred was the American motion-picture business in its infancy, how much of a colony in exile its practitioners had created.

In 1915, there were studios on Long Island, in Chicago, and in the hills across the bay from San Francisco. But Hollywood, only four years away from the status of a sheeptown without a post office, was already the world's motion-picture factory. It was all so new and so self-absorbed in its productiveness that its workers formed as parochial a community as the scientists laboring in their hideout in Los Alamos to make the atom bomb. An Englishman I knew for many years who had gone out to Utah in 1908 to look over his father's investment in a copper mine, and who subsequently drifted to San Francisco and tapped a little silver in the Tonopah strike, used to exercise his horse by signing up as an extra for the primitive Westerns being made at Niles Canyon by "Bronco Billy" Anderson, a partner in the S & A (for Spoor and Anderson) company, which, as Essanay, signed Chaplin to a contract that quadrupled his former salary. This worldly Englishman told me how he had struck up a friendship with Mabel Normand, an early and beguiling film comedienne, and how he went down one time to Santa Monica to watch the shooting of a Chaplin film in which she appeared. For two or three days—which was as long as it took in those days to do the whole filming—he hung around with the cast and dined with them in the evenings. He must have been as flattered as any other European visitor to be socializing with the legendary "Charlie." But he told me what a shock it was to notice the crudity of Chaplin's table manners, his brusqueness with waiters, his cocky assumption that he was the smartest moviemaker in town. Which indeed he was, even though his conceit was a kind of bluster covering up the rueful knowledge that he was no more than a big fish in a tiny and socially rather murky pond of Southern California.

On lonely evenings—and Chaplin always prized the good artist's retreat into the loneliness that breeds ideas—he liked to go over to a favorite café in Santa Monica owned and run by one Nat Goodwin, a light comedian who had long ago established himself in London as what Max Beerbohm, among others, thought of as the supreme "American mime." Goodwin had retired to California and there looked back with anecdotal amusement over the ease of his theatrical fame and the strain of eight marriages, one of them to Maxine Elliott, a mountainous beauty whom he recalled as "the Roman Senator." Chaplin knew all about Goodwin's fame and looked on him, no doubt, as the first among equals. He went to Nat Goodwin's café as to a court and listened to the King recall his triumphs. But Goodwin was far more aware of Chaplin's fame than Chaplin was.

There came a time in the beginning of 1916 when Chaplin was exhausted by the frantic routine of making thirteen films in fourteen months. He had just finished cutting *Carmen*, his parody of the opera, and he decided to accept the invitation of his brother, Syd, to rest and play in New York. It would be the first time he had seen the big city since he had left it as a member of Fred Karno's vaudeville company. Goodwin told Chaplin that he would be lionized and gave him a little avuncular advice: "You'll be invited everywhere, but don't accept. Pick out one or two friends and be satisfied to imagine the rest. . . . John Drew was a great favorite with society and went to all their houses, but they would not go to his theater. They had had him in their drawing rooms."

Well primed by this cautionary tale, Chaplin boarded the train for the journey east and relaxed into the five days of anonymity that would precede the social whirl he had been warned to expect from the actors and actresses and social-theatrical hangers-on in New York. On the evening of the second day, he was standing in his underwear, shaving in the washroom, as the train pulled into Amarillo, Texas. He was aware of a vague baying sound as the train slid into the station. He peered out and saw a dense crowd on the platform and a line of trestle tables piled with refreshments. Like any other traveler, he assumed that Amarillo was out to welcome some local hero—a football star, the Governor perhaps—and he went back to his lathering. The baying sound came into focus as the chant: "Charlie! Charlie! Charlie! Where's Charlie Chaplin?" There was a rush of footsteps along the corridor and a deputation caught him. He was allowed to wipe his face and pull on a shirt and tie and descend to a roar of cheers, as the Mayor stepped up to invite him to "have a drink and a light refreshment" with, apparently, the entire population of Amarillo. At any rate, the crowd was too boisterous for safety, and the Mayor, slammed against the train with a rumpled Chaplin, as the cops strode and shouted, performed a Groucho switch of mood and snapped, "All right, Charlie, let's get it over with."

In the retelling of it, Chaplin recalled this line as the one delightful memory of what had been a trauma. When it was all over, and the train moved off, he sat in his compartment, huddled against the pointings and gigglings of the people who had lately seen a fellow passenger and now recognized a marvel. He was, he would admit, at first wildly flattered, then frightened, and, long before New York, facing for the first time the fact of universal fame and the psychological problem, peculiar I image to ventriloquists, of being worshiped as the creator of a being outside himself.

It was the same in Kansas City and Chicago. Along the route, where the train ran through suburban stations, people stood in clusters or long lines beside the track waving at the Man who must be in there somewhere. It was no longer the Southern Pacific transcontinental daily out of Glendale. It was the Chaplin Train, as one would say the Lincoln Train.

From then on, he had to learn to acquire the protective affability, and the stoicism, that recognizable celebrities must live with. It was not easy for him. He discovered with some alarm that he cherished his privacy, which was now invaded night and day. He was also highly opinionated, and while he responded extravagantly to anyone who sincerely sought advice about some private turmoil or future of capitalism, he was insulted by general questions that might be put to any other celebrity, and he was rattled to the point of outrage by gossip-column queries about his taste in women, in food, whether he would every play Hamlet or become an American citizen. He refused to perform for a shipboard concert. At Cherbourg, a ship's reporter wondered whether he considered Lenin or Lloyd George the greater man. He snapped, "One works and the other plays," thus planting an ominous hint of other innumerable offhand sallies that would get him into a thicket of public squabbles in the years ahead.

When he had acquired some self-possession, which he once admitted to me deserted him most often when most he needed it—namely, in the presence of newspapermen out to bait him—he was most concerned to dispose briskly of the interview, the war bond speech, the balcony appearance, and lock himself into his privacy. This impatience to have done with the adulation—which he once significantly remarked "is given, after all, to the little fellow, not me"—brought him unfairly the reputation of a misanthrope. Simply, but hopelessly, he discovered, after the first return to New York, that he could enjoy no such luxury of choice as Nat Goodwin had recommended: "Pick out one or two friends and be satisfied to imagine the rest."

For, it is fair to say, the next twenty years or so, the shoals of mail (in London 73,000 letters in two days) never ceased, nor the flood of invitations, nor even the celebrity-seeking raids of other celebrities. It forced his private life to be surreptitious, and few public figures had for so long such a continuously turbulent private life. From his earliest slapstick days, when director, cast, actors, and crew were vagabonds, there was always some mischief brewing with one or other of the Mack Sennett bathing beauties. Chaplin, it should be remembered, was not only a dapper and amusing man, an enchanting mimic from childhood on. He was also remarkably handsome, extremely attractive to women and instantly susceptible to them. To two types more than most: the *femme fatale* and the child-woman. The gamut is represented at its polar opposites by Pola Negri (for all that she was born Appolonia Chalupek) and his first wife, Mildred Harris. Time and again he found himself involved with earthy, lusty women. But the ones he sought were nubile adolescents. He married three of them: Mildred Harris at sixteen, when he was twenty-nine; Lita Grey at seventeen, when he was thirty-five; Oona O'Neill at eighteen, when he was fifty-five. I state this as an interesting but probably inexplicable emotional pattern.

Most of this, all the accumulated detail of his fame as the one and only Charlie Chaplin, was known to me—and much of it was flooding through my mind—on a still and brilliant midsummer morning in 1933 when I sat on the deck of a yacht anchored twenty-odd miles southwest of Los Angeles Harbor, looking across the shimmering water to the small mountainous island called Catalina. The yacht was, by Riviera or even Hollywood standards, modest, a fifty-footer Chaplin had named the *Panacea*. There were five of us aboard. Chaplin, then forty-four. Paulette Goddard, an enchanting twenty-two-year-old brunette, as trim and shiny as a trout, whom Chaplin had known for little more than a year. Andy, the skipper, a gnarled, good-natured man of few words (and a former Keystone Kop). And Freddy, a Japanese cook. And there was I, a lean, black-haired twenty-four-year-old Englishman on a two-year fellowship at Yale. In another place, or applying for a job on paper, I would have explained that I was a young man of mixed but lively aspirations to be either a theatrical director of the stature of Reinhardt, Piscator, or Meyerhold *or* a playwright of deafening fame (I was undecided just then whether to be the acknowledged successor to Noel Coward or Eugene O'Neill). But sitting there for the first time on anybody's yacht, waiting for my host to wake up and emerge from the bacon odors misting up from the galley, I was a fortunate nobody immersed in a glow of vanity, wondering, as the reader must be, how I had got there.

This is a thought which brings up, as dazzling accidents do in everyone's life, a sequence of unanswerable "ifs." If, on my arrival in New Haven, Connecticut, toward the end of 1932 I had not written out of the blue to J. L. Garvin, the venerable editor of the London *Observer*, hinting that I was well qualified to write occasional reviews of the New York theater; if he had not agreed; and if, when I brashly proposed a six-part series of articles on Hollywood, to appear in the summer, his celebrated film critic, Miss C. A. Lejeune, had not arranged to take a six-week holiday, thus providing a hiatus which I could neatly bridge, I should never have met the great man. But I no sooner had Garvin's consent than I sketched out the series under five heads (director, cameraman, shooting on location, English star, and Chaplin—just Chaplin), and wrote off letters of request to Ernst Lubitsch, Lee Garmes, George Cukor, C. Aubrey Smith, and Chaplin. (The choice of Smith as the English star may now sound odd, but I was writing for an English paper, and at the time he was symbolizing the British Empire to a gaping world a good deal more heroically than Stanley Baldwin. I got a charming handwritten note from him, provoked perhaps by my having mentioned that my father remembered him warmly as "Round-the-Corner-Smith," a sporting tag he had acquired, long before his acting days, as a famous amateur England cricketer. He was a bowler with a peculiar run-up to the wicket that has not, so far as I know, been imitated since: starting at eight o'clock, he ran down and around a fishhook curve up to one o'clock and then delivered the ball. Since, from the batsman's point of view, he started way right of the umpire and then suddenly appeared close to his left side, Smith offered the menacing illusion of being two bowlers instead of one.)

The last reply to come in was a curiously cordial letter from one Alfred Reeves, manager, telling me that Mr. Chaplin would be pleased to see me if I would appear at the studio office at ten o'clock on a certain morning in July.

Chaplin's reputation as the Caesar of independent producers, a multimillionaire, and a ferocious disciplinarian hatched in my fancy a vision of his studio as easily the most imposing of the Hollywood lots, patrolled between pictures by a private army of guards and subservient underlings. I was frankly nervous when I drove along Sunset Boulevard in my $60 secondhand Ford and watched for the turnoff into North La Brea. I drove past the studio several times before checking with a nearby lunch counter, whose owner assured me that the address I had scribbled down was indeed that of the one and only Chaplin studio.

It was a row of linked brick-and-stucco cottages, one with a turret, another with a Victorian bow window, two chimney stacks, four gables with imitation beams of brown-painted wood. My dented Model A seemed exactly right. Righter still was the little man who greeted me, Alfred Reeves, a wiry, courteous Cockney sparrow, impossible to place in any fantasy of the Hollywood hierarchy as anything but a gaffer, a carpenter maybe, one of those strange, self-contained Englishmen one meets in the unlikeliest places in America, who must have been fired at some point by the rumor of the American dream and who settle for a lifetime in a humble job without any apparent sense of disillusion.

Alfred Reeves had come over on the ship with Chaplin and the London vaudeville troupe, and until he died he was Chaplin's only manager. He offered in person a first proof of something very appealing about his boss. Chaplin could sustain outrageous feuds with business partners, drop old friends on a whim and walk in on them again with a grin, issue imperial edicts banning this titan or that from his studio, and summarily jilt houris both obscure and famous. But he was unflaggingly loyal to his old-time staff, in the manner of a sergeant who has been through years of trench warfare with a motley pack of privates and ever afterward uses them as a protective base of sanity against the fits and starts of the higher-ups. At least a half dozen of the vaudevillians who appeared in the earliest Chaplin primitives could be spotted in character parts a quarter century later. As the most creditable example, there was Rollie Totheroh, who was Chaplin's cameraman at Essanay in 1915. As Chaplin became Shaw's "one artist of the cinema" and moved out of two-reelers into the grandeur of full-length feature films, with a correspondingly grander investment to protect, it would have been entirely sensible for him to cast around for new and spectacular talents. But Totheroh, a diffident and thoroughly competent craftsman, was still there shooting *Monsieur Verdoux* thirty-two years later. He was there, in fact, on the day of my arrival, filing some old prints and pottering around in a leisurely fashion, on full pay, though there would be no more filming for another two years.

Reeves took me off into Chaplin's office, another shock but one softened by the inoculation of the first: the row of workers' mock-Tudor cottages which constituted the façade of the studio itself. The office was the central room of the small bungalow. It had worn oilcloth on the floor, and if it was ever wallpapered, the paper had rotted in the fungi of mildew. There was one small window, three straight-back wooden chairs, an old table, about half a dozen books with peeling spines, and an ancient upright piano hideously out of tune. It was probably about as luxurious as any of the rooms Chaplin rented in the boardinghouses of prewar England, and as I was to learn, in working there the following year, it reflected Chaplin's deep distrust of elegant surroundings whenever there was serious work on hand. It was also, it now strikes me, the reassuring home base that some men whose childhoods have been grindingly poor require in the years of their affluence. Chaplin himself had noticed the same trait in Bronco Billy Anderson and may have caught from him the courage to indulge it ("It was dark when we entered his bungalow . . . the place was empty and drab. In his room was an old iron bed with a light bulb hanging over the head of it. A rickety old table and one chair were the other furnishings. Near the bed was a wooden box upon which was a brass ashtray filled with cigarette butts. . . . This was the home of G. M. Anderson, the multi-millionaire cowboy").

Reeves was saying something about Chaplin's frequent burnings at the hands of the press but how, for some unstated reason, "this is different and he'll be happy to see you," when the man himself stepped smartly through the door and came into the room. The first impression was of being suddenly with two optimistic midgets in the office of a failing vaudeville agent. Neither Reeves nor Chaplin could have been much over five feet. We exchanged the usual nervous grins and "Well, well!" handshakes, and Reeves, assuring himself that Chaplin was in an affable mood (the precaution of a swimming teacher who is satisfied that the children are playing safely at the shallow end), bowed out and left us along.

You expect a small man to have a small hand, but it was not until you doubted for a moment whether it was flesh you were holding or some ivory knickknack that you looked up at its chuckling owner and said to yourself, He certainly is a tiny man. His feet were in scale, peeking out like mice from under high-held trousers. Above the trousers were a white angora sweater, and above that a tanned face, small ears set flat behind the cheekbones, gray eyes of a dancing mobility, and above them a monumental forehead and hair piled like a melting snowball. I like to think I would have been arrested anywhere by the face: features evenly sculptured into a sensuous whole, strong and handsome beyond any guess you might have made by mentally stropping away the black half-moon eyebrows and the comic mustache. This startling disparity between Chaplin and "Charlie" might be thought to have protected his identity from the fans, and I remember once, coming out of a movie theater with him, how a young man nudged his girl and hissed, "There's Charlie Chaplin!" She made the obvious comment that it didn't look like him, to which the young man irritably snapped, "You can't expect anybody to *look* like Charlie Chaplin." In the early days, he could wander incognito through the cities of California. But by the time of that first railroad journey east, the news of his presence anywhere was so trumpeted in the papers or by word of mouth that people had to see him in order to believe that the creator of the immortal tramp was the same person in another guise. So seeing Chaplin for the first time was a more curious pleasure than having the screen image of any other star confirmed in the flesh.

Reeves's notion that this press interview would somehow be "different" was explained by the sort of lucky coincidence that can transform a wary first meeting into a starting friendship. Reeves had warned me that Chaplin, after a spate of more or less scurrilous articles about him (the papers had made a messy thing out of his second divorce), had cut himself off from all access to the press, thereby compounding his normal isolation from Hollywood and all its denizens. In the two summers I spent with him, the only movie people—the only people, for that matter—who ever appeared at the house were King Vidor, Frank Reicher, and old German character actor, and Dr. Cecil Reynolds, his stagestruck doctor.

On his recent visit to England, Chaplin had been warmly entertained by the Astors, who owned the paper I was writing for. He had also struck up a congenial relationship with another Alistair, the son of Prime Minister Ramsay MacDonald. It was a simple as that. At any rate, the "interview" dissolved into lively conversation, and from there we went to lunch and then up to his house, where I was introduced to "my friend, Miss Goddard." A routine mannerly hint from me that I ought to be on my way was brushed aside, and through the long afternoon we sat round the empty swimming pool (there was a polio epidemic that summer), and I left at sundown on a promise to be back next day to dinner. After that, I was up at the house almost every day, and then he invited me for a weekend aboard the *Panacea*.

It was the beginning of a friendship that was as close as could be through that summer and the next. But I come back to the first cruise on the *Panacea*, because during its four or five days Chaplin opened himself up in the most natural and revealing way, and very little that happened afterward was much of a surprise to me. The impression I picked up then, confirmed later by other close friends—Frank Reicher, John Steinbeck, and more than any other Dr. Reynolds—was that when Chaplin took to anyone, he was wide open from the start, spontaneous, generous, gabby, confidential, as if taking up again where he had left off with a favorite, long-lost brother. I could see then how, if it were a woman who attracted him, he would soon be as deep in intimacy as Macbeth was in blood and find "returning as tedious as go o'er." This instinct to plunge into a relationship with all the defenses down can be darkly ascribed to a helpless reflex of egocentricity. And Chaplin undoubtedly needed to dazzle a new friend with the whole panoply of his charm, humor, talent, knowingness, and—which was a little less impressive to anyone used to thinking—his intellect. But, instant psychoanalysis apart, it ought to be said that whatever the spring of its motive, it was a warming thing to receive. There was nothing of the poltroon about Chaplin. Neither in love nor in friendship did he ever tread water. He regularly took a header into deep water, and the splash usually shocked his envious neighbors. Much of the public uproar about his matrimonial troubles came from highly moral women's groups, who, no doubt correctly, felt their own marriages threatened by the possible contagion of Chaplin's gallantry. In his autobiography, and looking back from the cool sanctuary of old age, he put it very succinctly: "Procreation is nature's principal occupation, and every man, whether he be young or old, when meeting any woman, measures the potentiality of sex between them. Thus it has always been with me."

Looking across to the little boats bobbing gently by the quayside at Avalon, I was startled by a deferential cough and turned to see Chaplin standing over me. He had come up from below as lightly as a grasshopper and was standing there in the attitude of a butler awaiting orders, head cocked expectantly, a napkin over the left forearm, his right hand poised in a kindly-step-this-way freeze. It was the silent movie call to breakfast, and we went below. I have seen only one other man dispatch a meal with such speed. But whereas Adlai Stevenson, belying his general reputation for delicacy, shoveled the stuff in with hands as pudgy as baseball mitts, Chaplin disposed of eggs and bacon

and a wad of pancakes almost as a display of sleight of hand. One of
the permanent pleasures of being with him was to watch the grace
and deftness with which he performed all physical movements, from
pouring syrup to swerving like a matador just out of the line of an on-
coming truck.

"My friend, Miss Goddard" was not yet up, so we took the dinghy
and rowed over to the shore and went for a walk. I suppose we were
gone for no more than a couple of hours, but in them he managed to
elaborate on most of his life, as if he were doing the first rough dicta-
tion of a biography or giving a deposition by free association. "I am
the renowned Charlie Chaplin," he seemed to say, "and you are a
new friend who might well turn into my Boswell. Very well, let me begin to tell you some things you ought to know."

He told it in no sort of sequence but began touching base with me
on his recent memories of England, and from there went into flash-
backs of his childhood and youth. He started by making it plain that
in spite of his hobnobbing with royalty, with the Tory leaders in London, and international socialites on the Riviera, he was neither a roy-
alist nor a Tory and, what's more, took the standard radical view that
in forming a national government, Ramsay MacDonald had betrayed
the Labor Party and was not much more than a lackey of what today
we call the Establishment. All this was a little puzzling to me, for I
was at the time about as apolitical as it is possible to be, and I have
been amazed, in going back through the political history of Britain
during the years I was at Cambridge, to see how casually unaware I
was of budget deficits, the American debt problem, the departure
from the gold standard, and other weighty matters which Chaplin
went hotly on about as he sat squeezing the sand between his toes in
the hills above Avalon.

This was not quite what I expected of the world's ranking clown,
and he must have guessed that my ahs and ums and other grunting responses proceeded from no very deep conviction or even from a passing acquaintance with the facts and dogmas he trotted out. But I often noticed at other times that he was anxious to tell strangers what he
was *not taken in by* rather than to say where he stood politically. (All
his life his much-abused "radical philosophy" was no more than an
automatic theme song in favor of peace, humanity, "the little man,"

and other desirable abstractions — as hum-drum politicians come out for mother love and lower taxes.)

But I had been in Germany two summers before and seen all around me the blue faces and bloated bellies of starving people. I had enough political instinct, however uninstructed, to sense the depths of despair from which the mass of people could look up to Hitler as to the only possible savior. And I had just driven halfway round America and told him how roused I had been by the contrast of a listless nation suddenly galvanized into energy and confidence by Franklin Roosevelt. Roosevelt! I had made the connection: the dense pupil suddenly says a bright thing. He was all for Roosevelt, believed he had saved the country from revolution, and saw the New Deal as a promising halfway house on the road to "true Socialism," which, I gathered, was not Ramsay MacDonald's spurious brand but something on which Joseph Stalin had the only legitimate patent. (In his autobiography, Chaplin is frank enough to leave in the recollection of a conversation with H. G. Wells, whose fears of dictatorship and the suppression of civil liberties in Russia are dismissed by Chaplin as growing pains or tactical "mistakes" not to be compared in grossness with "the repudiation of foreign loans.") There is an interesting psychological point here. Chaplin always talked about capitalism as a more or less failing system and showed no anxiety about its doom. But I was told by people who knew him as a businessman that he was as alert as a radar specialist to the rise and fall of the stock market. He told me, that summer, in a moment of offhand pride, that he had felt in his bones the coming of the 1929 crash and astutely transferred his holdings to Canada and South Africa and other places where the collapse was less painful. He had, he once boasted, lost little or nothing in the Depression.

I was beginning to think that actors, like writers and opera stars, were never the same at home. Certainly, the world's funniest man would have turned into the world's most hectoring bore if he had gone on and on even as long as these recollections. But I have, unfairly, lumped his political sermons into a running credo. He was always reciting them in snatches, at the unlikeliest times, and in the end they led to his banishment from the United States, an outcome that no one could possibly have predicted on that August morning as Chaplin preached to the Catalina hills and to me. But a funny memory of the

First World War incidentally revealed on that occasion a wound long forgotten in England and, I should guess, hardly known about in the United States. As soon as Chaplin had established his no-nonsense political credentials, he fell into reminiscences of the old music-hall songs, and, cued by my mention of some of the great gone names, he went off into a bout of marvelous total recall, ballooning before my eyes into the bosomy swagger of Marie Lloyd and bawling out "A Little of What You Fancy Does Y'Good," then shrinking into the exquisite shape of Vesta Tilley, the pocket Astaire, and singing "I'm Colonel Coldfeet of the Coldstream Guards" and "Into a cookshop he goes dashin',/Who should bring his plate of hash in,/But the girl he had been mashin',/By the sad sea waves." I told him that my father had kept for me, and I still had, a wartime record of "Oh, the Moon Shines Bright on Charlie Chaplin."

"That," he said, in sudden alarm, "scared the hell out of me."

What I'd forgotten in mentioning that song, though it was neither hard nor pleasant to recall, was the insensate jingoism of wartime Britain, the hounding of German shopkeepers, the cretinous women patriots handing a white feather to young men in civilian clothes, and the holy indignation of comfortable editorial writers against any famous Englishman abroad who had not dashed home to join Our Boys Out There on Flanders Fields. Chaplin was a glaring target, and there was much doltish sarcasm at his expense, until it was discovered that few imports from England bucked up Our Boys Out There like the Chaplin films shown behind the lines. For a nasty spell he was Chaplin the Slacker in the London press and "Good Old Charlie" in the trenches, after which the hunt was abandoned. At this height, somebody sent Chaplin the new song. In its American original it was about an Indian maiden called "Little Red Wing," but the lyrics were changed in the British version, whose chorus went:

Oh, the moon shines bright on Charlie Chaplin,
His books are crackin'
For want of blackin',
And his little baggy trousers they need mendin'
Before we send him
To the Dardanelles.

"I went home," said Chaplin, "and read about the Dardanelles after that, and for a time I was certain they were out to get me." He laughed now, but he had remembered it as a threat long enough to begin hustling around addressing war bond rallies with bouncing enthusiasm once the United States was in the war.

The songs led naturally to the old vaudeville days in England and the seedy rooms, in dark provincial towns, that he had shared with Stan Laurel. I don't think he saw much of Laurel in Hollywood, certainly not in my time, but he spoke affectionately of him and told me why. There was a time during a provincial tour when Chaplin was often absent from his lodging, till one Saturday night he came back petrified with fright that his girl in the show was pregnant. Laurel evidently confronted this life crisis as mildly as he contemplated the crasser ordeals of Oliver Hardy. He went off to his trunk and fumbled round in it for a while and came back with a handful of pound notes. They were such savings as he could have scratched up from a fifteen-shilling-a-week salary. Chaplin never said whether the offer had to be taken up, but the memory of it made him more indulgent to the antics of Laurel and Hardy than to any other of the Hollywood comedians, of whom he was uniformly contemptuous. The Marx Brothers were just then getting into their swing, and Chaplin was almost defensively scornful of them. "Nothing but anarchists," he'd say, which—considering the implicit anarchy of his own film character—suggested that Chaplin thought the best way to mock society was not to fight it but to join it by way of parody.

He talked in a touching and rambling way about his childhood, but neither then nor ever later did he moon over his poverty or sentimentalize the groveling times (he left the tearful touch, regrettably, for the heroines in his movies). As he went on, acting out with great spirit and delicacy his early attempts at shabby gentility when he got into vaudeville, and then went further back to miming a wealth of characters fixed forever in his boyhood—in the workhouse, the pickle factory, chemist's shops—I had the odd feeling that I had heard and seen all this before. Charles Chaplin was Charles Dickens reborn. As documentary support for a thesis merely, there is eerie similarity between *Oliver Twist* and the first sixty pages or so of Chaplin's *Autobiography*. But as a reincarnation of everything spry and inquisitive and

Cockney-shrewd and invincibly alive and cunning, Chaplin was the young Dickens in the flesh. I had started to read Dickens when I was not more than nine, and by the time I was twelve I had gone through all the novels and whatever I could lay my hands on by way of memories and biographies, from Forster and Dolby to Mamie Dickens' *My Father as I Recall Him*. I was so absorbed in his fictional world that the streets I lived in were more alive with Dickens characters than the actual humans who peopled them. If I ever mentioned this to Chaplin, I can't now recall it. He would have been only mildly interested. I doubt he ever read any fiction; he was too busy manufacturing it.

For the rest of that cruise he was in manic good spirits. We fished for swordfish with mackerel, and catching nothing, and being fresh out of mackerel, we then fished for mackerel. I had just bought an 8 millimeter movie camera, and with his extended thumbs touching and his palms at the parallel he would fix the frame for me and retreat to mime a range of characters he picked up from the headlines of the only newspaper we had brought aboard. Jean Harlow had just eloped, and I still have Chaplin's outrageous cameo of the happy, if bewildered, bride. A famous female impersonator had been given a "friendly push" and drowned, a disaster which, however harrowing in life, was reenacted by Chaplin as a neat and ribald playlet. The Prince of Wales was seen to be making a speech: Chaplin tugged at nonexistent cuffs, acknowledged the thunder of the mob, licked a nervous lip, and bobbed his head in nervous modesty from side to side: almost a prevision of the melancholy future King.

Chaplin had a mild but steady obsession with royalty, some secret need to deflate it in mimicry, as if he would thereby expose the hypocrisy of hereditary thrones as compared with the one he had constructed with so much sweat and talent. He had dined with the royal family, and one time he was going on about the anachronism of monarchies in the twentieth century. As always, the sermon was prolix and dull, but the dramatization of it in mime was wonderful. He remembered having once seen a newsreel of Edward VII coming out of the house at Sandringham before a shooting party. Chaplin walked ahead of the invisible retainers, froze his stance, and very slowly raised his elbows in a position to receive his cape. He never looked behind him but gazed confidently out to the horizon, slumped his shoulders as the cape descended, gave a heavy grunt, and—for all Chaplin's tiny gymnastic form—was the huge patrician buffalo to the life. After that, there was no need for moralizing tags about the arrogance of empire, the absolute assumption of hereditary superiority to the human clay that cooks the meals, beats the bushes, mines the coal.

Chaplin was so relaxed on that cruise, so naturally restless and inventive, that in retrospect I can see he was revealing himself as if by describing an endless series of Rorschachs. One thing led on impulse to another, and after some talk about the future King George VI and his stammer, Chaplin suddenly asked me to take some photographs, both still and in motion, of himself as Napoleon. (The frontispiece to this chapter is one of them.) He pulled his hair down into a ropy forelock, slipped one hand into his breast pocket, and slumped into a wistful emperor. He started to talk to himself, tossing in names strange to me—Bertrand, Montholon—and then took umbrage, flung an accusing finger at me, and, having transformed his dreamy eyes into icicles, delivered a tirade against the British treatment of him on "the little island." His face was now a hewn rock of defiance. I have it still on film, and it is still a chilling thing to see.

It will occur to the reader, and it has been said time and again with tedious clairvoyance by people who disliked him, that the trouble with Chaplin was a Napoleon complex. We are on touchy ground here. Tall men make a habit of explaining a lively sex life in small men as a crippling Napoleonic fantasy, though in my experience the small men seem to hop from bed to bed with singular and enjoyable agility. The truth in this instance was that Chaplin had been thinking for some time of doing a film about Napoleon on St. Helena. And he was serious enough about it to write to me the following winter and say that if I was free to come out to Hollywood the next summer, he would like me to do the research and help him with the script. Needless to say, I jumped at it, and drove out from Cambridge, Massachusetts, to Hollywood, set myself up in a room at the Mark Twain Hotel, and again presented myself, this time as an important employee, to Alfred Reeves. Now it was possible to get close to another Chaplin, to the professional, to one as far removed in action from the social Chaplin as a jolly general from the same man preparing the invasion of France.

He came scurrying into the bungalow every morning on the dot of ten in cap, tieless shirt, white slacks, and the angora sweater; sat down at the creaky little table; and said, "Shall we go?" For a week or two, I fed him stuff from books I'd picked up at the public library, with Las Cases' *Memorial of Saint Helena* as the principal source book. Then we started the script, and the first thing he taught me was that you don't begin at the beginning. "We look," he said, laying down the law with a firm index finger tapping the table, "for some little incident, some vignette that fixes the other characters. The audience must never be in any doubt about them. We have to fix them on sight. Nobody cares about *their* troubles. They stay the same. You know them every time they appear. This is no different from the characters who surround 'the little fellow.' *He's* the one we develop." (This, by the way, sounds like another Dickens prescription.)

Sometimes we had along Carter De Haven, whom Chaplin had hired to be assistant director on *Modern Times*, which was then beginning to brew in Chaplin's mind. Almost always, except during the knottier historical stretches, there was his massive old friend, spiritual uncle and adviser Henry Bergman, who had played in some of the early two-reelers as every sort of foil from a fat lady and a bum to a pawnshop owner. Bergman was a huge, gentle old German to whom Chaplin always referred some promising scene or gag. He said very little, but if Chaplin had doubts, in the moment of improvising, he would look over to Bergman, say, "No?" and Bergman would shake his head, and we'd forget it.

In the ramshackle bungalow, whenever we were stuck, Chaplin would pace around, mimic all the parts, mutter variations on a line I'd written, inflect it this way and that, sigh, smoke, stroke the piano keyboard, and say, "Let's try again after lunch." We went off always to the same place, Musso Frank's, and Chaplin made a point of banning all talk of the script. At the end of the meal, he would make a silent sign to Bergman, who produced the money and paid the bill. I never remember Chaplin carrying money, and once I asked him about this. He put it down to the childhood days when he was being shuttled between the workhouse and various board schools, and to the memory of his father, who, if ever he appeared with money, would exhibit it as proof of solvency at last but would then blow it in a drunken evening.

Chaplin told me how when he was first offered $60 a week to go to Hollywood, he thought the money was a bribe and would never last. Years later, when he barely knew he was world-famous, he lived in a room at the Hollywood Athletic Club, until one day his brother, Syd, took matters into his own hands. "Look," he said, "it's crazy for you to go walking down the road always looking for a cab, you're a rich man. Buy yourself a car." They finally went downtown to a showroom, where the first thing Chaplin saw was a large, high sedan. Chaplin, telling this, went at once into his act of the high-hat millionaire commanding empires. "Tell me, my good man, is that a good car? I want nothing but the best." It *is*, said the main, *the* best. Chaplin waved an imperious wrist: "I'll take it." But it took his brother another year to get him to move out of the Athletic Club into a house, which he had steadily refused to do. "Syd, I remember, put on his coat and had one last try. He begged me to go and consult my bank balance." They went off together, and Chaplin was appalled to discover he had upwards of $900,000 in a checking account. "You see," roared Sydney. "You can *buy* yourself a *home!*" Chaplin went out and bought himself the one and only home he ever lived in in Beverly Hills. "But," he said, riding back to the studio in a Rolls, "I don't trust it, I still feel it'll never last," and chuckled.

Script sessions are as never-racking a bit of committee work as any board of directors ever has to face. One bad day, when I was being more than usually obtuse about how some tricky scene could be resolved into sight as well as sound, Chaplin gently suggested, like a doctor to a dithering hypochondriac, another, possibly more soothing, form of treatment. We would go for a stroll through the relics of the sets for *City Lights*. We gazed down into the arid cement basin which had been his suicide's intended grave. We walked along the embankment. He sat down on the stony bosom of the unveiled statue, which was now lying on a broken plaster elbow. And he started to go over well-remembered scripting crises in *City Lights*. A famous one will suffice to show what agonies of sweat and tension could go into the distillation of a scene which in the playing seemed as effortless as quicksilver.

"I began," he said, "with a hazy idea of a blind flower girl sitting on the sidewalk. She is going to be the heroine. And this is the first time the little fellow meets her. She must sell him a flower, and she must mistake him for a rich man. That's what I started with." He gave this simple rundown to his assistant, who drafted some sequences that conveyed the general idea. They were filmed, argued about, and destroyed. Chaplin sat down in the bungalow and tried again and again. "I was a terror to be with," he said, and I could believe it. He paced around the bungalow, flew into quick rages, refused food and rest, dragged his assistant by night to the house, and tried again. He shuffled every conceivable formula employing girl, flowers, sidewalk, rich man, poor man, five-dollar bill, expensive automobile, police whistles, crowds. He shot these fumbling scenes and found them as clumsy as the others. "Then, one day I wondered how the girl—a blind girl—could possibly be aware of the automobile." It took three weeks for the sparking detail to occur that would animate the whole idea. "I came down one morning, very glum, a bear, and I looked at the automobile and it hit me: *a slamming door!*"

All that happened in the end was that the tramp approached the girl, and as he did so, an automobile braked against the sidewalk. Its occupant walked rapidly to the park railings beside the girl. The tramp bought a flower and tendered his last dollar bill. While he was waiting for his change, and she was feeling for it, the smart steps retreated to the car, she heard the door slam and the purr of a luxurious engine. She hesitated, said, "Thank you, sir," and the tramp, distraught about his vanished change but not wanting to shatter this pretty vision, backed away on tiptoe. In the finished movie, the incident flowed like water over pebbles, smooth and simple for all to see with no hint of the groaning pressure that had gone into it.

But these agonies exacted a high price from his friends, his staff, and all his business relationships on the outside. When any such script crisis was unresolved, he would retreat to the house, alone or with one assistant, and give his Japanese servants the sternest orders that he was home to nobody and would not answer the phone. He would call up the faithful Alf Reeves to say he was out to anybody who might call, write, or cable. Reeves would then make a list of every outstanding social or business commitment and send the word out, to cronies and board meetings alike: "He can't see you and he won't talk to you. And if it's any consolation, I'm on the blacklist, too."

When Chaplin started to brood over the script of *The Great Dictator*, the Los Angeles police department was using all its regulation ingenuities to get in touch with him. They had a little matter of a subpoena to discuss. One Michael Kustoff was claiming that Chaplin had plagiarized the story of *Modern Times*. The process servers started by knocking on the front door and subsequently tried getting in as laundrymen, doctors, and Western union messengers. Months later, the courts finally gave up and the judge signed an order to allow the subpoena to be served by publication.

If anything, the moment of release from filmmaking was worse, for Chaplin's friends, than the throes of creation. He felt that the easing of the strain relieved him also of the social obligations he had ignored or postponed. One afternoon, after a tense but rewarding session with the Napoleon script, he asked me back to the house to relax and "and mooch around the piano." We got to arguing about Shakespeare. Chaplin never overcame the prejudice that Shakespeare is an unactable poet and that on the stage his language is as embarrassing as the theatrical conventions of opera. The previous winter, I had directed a theater group at Harvard in *Cymbeline* and done it in modern dress as a scandal in the diplomatic corps in Rome. By this device, it had come to life again as a rich and malicious Noel Coward comedy. It satisfied me anyway, although it shocked the critic of the Boston *Evening Transcript* into a fatal coronary. Chaplin was fascinated by this idea, called for some tea, and asked me to read the play aloud to him. I read on into the twilight, by which time I knew he was supposed to be on his way to a party that Sam Goldwyn was throwing in his honor. I looked at the clock and reminded him. He erupted into a fury and stalked around the room like the outraged Little Corporal himself: "A party! Good God, what is a cocktail party, and a bunch of Hollywood ninnies, compared to this? You'd think they owned me! The one thing that money gives you is the right to change your mind and do what you want, *when* you want to do it. Keep going!" (It was a trait I noticed later in other very poor boys who had grown very rich: a willful desire to flout the idea that there is any such thing as a duty or a social obligation.)

About an act later, he bared his teeth and gave the slit-eyed grin that made him look like a jolly Oriental. "I think," he said, "I'd better call poor old Sam." The moment he was connected, he startled me by begging to be excused in a voice croaking with advanced laryngitis. It was a pathetic sound. He was deeply sorry, in more misery than he could tell, he'd been hoping against hope the thing would clear up, he would surely call the first day he felt he was going to survive. He hung up the phone, make a large mock-heroic gesture, and cried in a resounding baritone: "On with Iachimo, let's get to the adultery!" We read on until midnight, when he thought it would be amusing to have supper at a geisha house he knew in Los Angeles' Little Tokyo. The proprietor's voice at the other end was fawning with delight. So Chaplin routed out his chauffeur, Kono, from a deep sleep, and we were out until three in the morning. (Eight years later, I ran into Kono sitting at the door of a wooden shack with a handkerchief over his mouth against the swirling dust storms of the Owens Valley. He was one of the Japanese-Americans who had been carted off to the concentration camp, discreetly called a "relocation center," in Manzanar, on the eastern, the safe, side of the Techachapi Mountains.)

By the end of the summer, we were coming along well with the Napoleon script, and one evening I was up at the house playing piano duets with him of *Titine*, which he was to use in *Modern Times*. After a break, he came back into the living room, took out a toothpick, sucked his teeth, and said, "By the way, the Napoleon thing. It's a beautiful idea—for somebody else." He said no more, and we never wrote another word or referred to the project again. It was the same with two other ideas he had during the summer. One was to be "a film revue," containing three or four short films. He got very excited, for several nights, with the notion of a nightclub scene in which the floor show was to be a dead-solemn miming of the Crucifixion. Another was the old French legend of "Our Lady and the Tumbler," the slight and tragic sketch of a starving tumbler taken in by a nunnery. In gratitude for his care, he goes into the chapel but is ashamed to offer up his ignorant prayers, so he gives his all, by way of his tumbling talent, and breaks his back. As he lies dying, the Virgin comes down and blesses him.

Chaplin simplified the whole legend in his head and one night mimed it for me—the stumbling prayers, the shamed interval, the half-comic realization that his acrobatics could be enough of a trib-ute: for positively one evening only, he was every shape and name of humility. But he didn't bring it up again, and when, days later, I dared to, he said almost snappishly, "They don't pay their shillings and quar-ters to see Charles Chaplin doing artistic experiments. They come to see *him*."

At the end of August, 1934, I was to be married. My father-in-law to be was the President of the American Public Health Association, which was holding its annual meeting in Pasadena, and so that was the ob-vious place for the ceremony. I asked Chaplin if he would be my best man. His alacrity in consenting was touching, and he made much comic play, as the day approached, with the imagined disasters of a marriage service that misfired.

When we got to the Pasadena registry office, my father-in-law was already there talking to the magistrate. Quite simply, Chaplin never showed up. Luckily, a Harvard friend of mine, who lived in Pasadena, was along, and after an hour's fretful wait, he stood in for me.

Days went by before I dared to call the house. Kono told me that "Mr. Chaplin has gone with Miss Goddard to Arrowhead." There was no other word. But the following evening, I called again and Chaplin came on as blithe as a robin. When was he going to see the bridal cou-ple? Where and when should we hold the wedding party? We must come up to the house at once.

Without ever referring to his nonappearance at the marriage cer-emony, he walked up and down in bubbling spirits, setting the date we'd dine and dance at the Coconut Grove, and nothing would do but white tie and tails. So it was, and we had a marvelous evening, with Chaplin the soul of friendship, courtesy, tenderness, and drollery. This was apparently the first time in many months, if ever, that he had taken Paulette to a nightclub, and she came alive and shining at the prospect of breaking with some regularity out of the Chaplin cloister-on-the-hill into the high life. If that was what was on her mind, she was soon dismally disillusioned.

The midnight show at the Coconut Grove was coming to its end in the usual melancholy atmosphere of reeking smoke, flat cham-pagne, and lovers staring at the table and having second thoughts.

The star performer was one Gene Austin, a sugary crooner who had an alarming, but highly admired, habit of modulating his final notes a whole octave higher and so giving out the sound of a boy soprano or castrato. "Revolting," muttered Chaplin, who had declined into a brooding silence. Riding home, Paulette kept up the heartbreaking pretense that from now on her evenings would be agog with music and dancing. Chaplin gave her a black parental look. He started in about the cacophony of jazz, which he hated, and went on about the decadence of night life, the excruciating "eunuch" sounds to which we had been subjected, and the fate, similar to that of Sodom, which would shortly overtake the Republic. Paulette saw her vision collapse like the Ghost of Christmas Present. A tear ran down her enchanting face and her eyes fairly popped in frustration as she said, "What are we going to do evenings—stay home and *write theses?!*" Well, Chaplin replied, "One night a year is enough of that rubbish."

At the house, his spirits revived, but there was no champagne to help them along. He never, through the two years I knew him best, drank or offered any alcohol. To make things worse, he enforced this abstinence on his guests not from forgetfulness but from evangelism. He ordered his man to fetch a huge pitcher of water and the required number of tumblers. Our wedding party ended on a scene that would have warmed the heart of a Southern Baptist. We sat there yawning slightly, throwing in monosyllabic responses to Chaplin's elegy on the modern world, and took long meditative drafts of pure cold water. It did not help to recall an old and feverish Sunday school song: "My drink is water bright, water bright, water bright!"

However, before we left to go east, and from there on to England and my first job—as the BBC's film critic—Chaplin came down alone to our hotel, took dinner with us in our small suite, and was his gentle, brimming self. At one point, he motioned me out onto the terrace overlooking the hills and asked me quite directly if I would like to stay and be his assistant director on *Modern Times*. Though shocked into a daze of vanity, I replied just as directly that the Commonwealth Fund, whose fellowship I had been holding for the past two years, required that all fellows return to some part of the British Empire for at least two years. (I later discovered that the fund would have waived this requirement at the mere mention of a job with

Chaplin.) He thought it was a pity, and then said an astounding thing. Apparently, it was not a training in film direction that he had in mind. "If you stay with me," he said, "I'll make you the best light comedian since Seymour Hicks." Hicks was then as adroit a light comedian as any on the English stage. But a comedian still. As I have mentioned, I was thinking just then of becoming Eugene O'Neill. We thanked the maestro warmly for all his kindness, and I went to bed still marveling that an artist of Chaplin's sensitivity and lightning perceptions could offer to cast O'Neill as a light comedian.

After those two memorable years, I saw him only intermittently, the last time in a London restaurant, where I was dining with his publisher and mine. He was off at a table with his wife and several children, but he came over and sat down, and though he was now in his late seventies, he shed the years as he reminisced and chuckled, and—as I recalled the first passage on the *Panacea*—he threw his head back and crooned with a faked bronchitis: "Oh, the moon shines bright on Charlie Chaplin. . . ." He was the old incomparable charmer again.

I saw him not at all during the bad years of the late forties and early fifties, and this is a memoir, not a life. But I ought to say something about them, if only for people too young to have picked up much more than the rumor of Chaplin's pesky "radicalism." I told earlier how the implied threat of the old song about the Dardanelles had genuinely scared him, and how—whether reacting to that threat or not—he had been a busy seller of war bonds once the United States was in the First War. In the Second War, he sold no bonds. And he conspicuously turned down all invitations to perform at USO concerts and the like. Closeted in Beverly Hills, he became a fairly unpopular figure in the movie colony, especially among the male stars who had not joined up and were all the more anxious to prove their machismo and their patriotism by "morale" tours of army camps. In 1942, Chaplin came out of his isolation and, in a single act of misjudgment, laid up years of grief for himself.

He yielded to an invitation to replace the ailing former American Ambassador to the Soviet Union and address a rally in San Francisco for Russian War Relief. After that, heady with the pride of having turned in one night from mere funny fellow into political spellbinder, he made a long-distance telephone speech to a Madison Square Garden mass meeting that was sponsored by the Congress of Industrial Organizations. It had the support of such simon-pure Americans as Wendell Willkie, the 1940 Republican presidential candidate, and Mayor Fiorello La Guardia, who was an early speaker. It was admittedly a rally to urge the opening by the United States and Britain of "a second front" to relieve the Russian armies sagging on the eastern front. With these two speeches, which blazed with unqualified praise for the gallant Russians ("On the battlefields of Russia democracy will live or die!"), Chaplin probably sealed his dubious reputation among old America Firsters and other professional patriots who were, within a decade, to rise again and bedevil prominent liberals, as well as crypto-Communists, who could be shown to have been "premature" (i.e., pre-Pearl Harbor) "antifascists." At any rate, when the country recoiled, for good reason, from the old American-Soviet alliance in the early years of the Cold War, Chaplin's number was up, both as an off-the-cuff public speaker and as an adored public entertainer. His first postwar film, *Monsieur Verdoux*, was at first banned by the Motion Picture Association's censor. In its final form it was picketed vigorously by Legionnaires, had a rocky short run in New York, and provoked a spate of abuse of Chaplin as a renegade, a "fellow traveler," if not actually a secret Communist, and a "paying guest" of the United States who, in spite of paying out millions of dollars in American taxes, was an ungrateful alien who ought to be thrown out of the country.

He was harassed and investigated for several years. Nothing could ever be dredged up to show that he was other than the "non-conformist of no political party" he had always claimed to be. No indictments were ever handed down. After releasing *Limelight*, he packed for a holiday in Europe, and he and his wife boarded the *Queen Elizabeth* on the seventeenth of September, 1952. Once the ship was well out at sea, the United States Attorney General rescinded Chaplin's reentry permit on the vaguely rhetorical ground that he was "an unsavory character" about whom the Department of Justice had "plenty of information available." If so, it was never authenticated or even made public. Chaplin was left in the now familiar limbo of rumor and untested assertion, until he had had enough and chose his own exile by turning in his reentry permit to the American vice-consul in Geneva. I had it from the Solicitor General of the United States two years later that Chaplin's politics had nothing to do with the excluding order, and that there were no constitutional grounds on which he could have been deported. Some people, unidentified, in the government "felt" that he had come close to deportation in a paternity suit he had lost. Others "felt," on no evidence I could adduce, that he had been chronically cavalier with such things as subpoenas and so had shown contempt for the courts and laws of the United States.

In short, he was a vague nuisance, and a tiresome talking point among the noisy patriots who never felt that the government's "loyalty" procedures proceeded far enough. Chaplin was all the more offensive in that he could never, after endless investigating, be pinned down as a criminal. He was simply turned in—by, we should remember, the Truman administration—as a useful sacrifice to the witches who were then supposed to be riding high exclusively on the broomstick of Senator Joseph McCarthy. The Chaplin expulsion was a squalid episode in a shabby period. The most accurate and honorable account of it I ever read appeared in—of all improbable places—a Madrid daily during the heyday of the fascist Franco.

The film industry, which in the scary decade after the Second War had hastened to keep him at a distance, the better to take a dim view of him, made it up to him in a stagy, sycophantic way when he was in his eighty-sixth year and had practically to be carried across the ocean back to the country he had loved and come to deplore. They gave him a special Oscar and a dinner in his "honor" in New York. As the crowds surged around him in Lincoln Center, and the televised Hollywoodites rose and pounded their hands, he shuffled carefully to a microphone and forlornly wished them well and said in not much more than an amplified whisper that he loved them all. The tears drenched the audiences 3000 miles apart. He was very old and trembly and groping through the thickening fog of memory for a few simple sentences. A senile, harmless doll, he was now—as the song says— "easy to love," absolutely safe to adore.

III

The Early Features

FRANCIS HACKETT

The Kid

Francis Hackett (1883–1962) was an Irish-American historical novelist and playwright who frequently reviewed movies for The New Republic *in the teens and twenties of the last century. His work in this field was marked by uncommon common sense. One of his pieces, about the racism of D. W. Griffith's* The Birth of a Nation, *remains, after all these years, unsurpassed as a dissection of that historically important, morally irredeemable film.*

The best motion pictures, I hear, are written with the scissors. The scissors, at any rate, have a great deal to do with the triumph of Charles Chaplin in (and with) *The Kid.* It is a movie stripped to its emotional essentials. The result is form, in which practically all American movies are just as much lacking as are our industrial architecture, display advertising, public cooking, and private conversation. In certain American institutions one does find form. Women's public meetings usually have it. The better sort of women's hats have it. So do certain kinds of house interiors and New England domestic architecture and those expositions of chamber music, baseball, and tennis which have never failed of appreciation here. But the movies are usually like

---

From the *New Republic*, March 30, 1921.

the Sunday newspapers, Golden Oak furniture, Yonkers carpets, the snub-nosed and stub-toed Ford car. The moviemakers have simply wallowed in the license extended by American incompetence and indulgence, knowing that a people which puts its hotels in the noise-area and its hotel kitchens in the dust-area will be content to have its movies as loud and as insanitary as its life. It has remained for Charlie Chaplin to scout this indulgence, to adopt a standard absolutely and relatively high, and to be rewarded by the gratitude of millions. For millions of harassed and dissatisfied movie patrons are finding joy in the integrity of *The Kid*.

This integrity is to be enjoyed least of all in the anecdote itself. It is a silly enough story of a woman who is reunited with the child she deserted after a separation of some time and considerable space. A woman might conceivably abandon her baby in this fashion. There must be a score of abandoned babies for every few hundred abandoned women. But to fail to trace the baby at the time and yet to run into the growing child some years later—years gilded with success and yet yearning with heartache—is almost Shakespearean in its absurdity. Still, an excellent bean may be grown on the humblest of bean poles, and that is the case with *The Kid*. Chaplin knows that the story of his adopted waif is a joke between the experienced movie patron and himself. The merchantable maternal instinct and the surefire lost child and the beautiful Lady Bountiful and the glad reunion—he glides over them with a touch like a light beam. What he has to play with is his own gorgeous predicament as the victim of a maternal problem. He has himself to present in the role of a Madonna. It is this preposterousness, with its possibilities of pathos and vulgarity, which he brings successfully through.

He does it as only a superb interpreter could. He realizes that when he, the authentic splay-footed, cane-twirling comedian, inherits the baby, he must steer his course clean away from farce in the direction of sentiment, but must keep enough comedy to correct the least hint of sentimentality. It gives him just the chance that his fine creativeness demands. With a boldness that no other comedian could attempt, he exhibits himself feeding and providing for the baby. This boldness, which he pushes far enough to earn laughter and not so far as to exploit it, he immediately banks up against his first exhibition of real feeling. And his exhibition of feeling is preserved from excess or unreality by a resourcefulness in byplay which is beautifully right. He makes a contrast between The Kid's deportment, so sternly inculcated, and his own dilapidation, which never fails to give amusement; and he carries that dilapidation to extraordinary lengths. But just as he seems to have violated taste by projecting the dirty sole of his bare foot out of bed, his head is slipped through a hole in his bedspread—converting it into so comical a dressing gown that the very invasion of good taste is turned to grotesque account. This is only one of twenty tricks that he wins in his sly game with (or against) his audience. He plays on his audience with an audacity that conquers prig and groundling in the same instant, and gives both of them a chance to be amused and moved.

Chaplin's relations to his audience may once have been deferential. Now he is an artist who uses his medium as he wills. When he opens the sewer trap and debates whether to slip the baby into it, he gains the credence which is only won by complete expressiveness. And his audience accepts his sincerity in this role of foster father with precisely the shade of amusement that he artfully conveys. To dominate photography with a personality is in itself marvelous. It is all the more marvelous when one remembers that Chaplin is not a projection of the average but a variation, a sport. This violates in every detail the Philistinism which seems to be the motion-picture religion.

Without the Coogan boy it couldn't be done. It is dreadful to think of such a perfection as this child pushing out of his treble exquisiteness into something perhaps theatrical and overstimulated and unstable. But in his present manifestation, under the hand of Chaplin, he is as expressively and imaginatively nature as if he himself had Chaplin's genius. His eyes speak, and they say not only direct and eloquent things but things indirect, troubled, complicated. And not only do his eyes speak, but so do the turn of his head, his entrances and exits, his place on a lonely doorstep, or on a curb. No child that I have ever seen on the stage created so full a part before. No child that I have ever seen on the stage created so full a part before. Most of the children one sees are limited to one or two postures. They appear but do not represent. This "Kid" represents, and with a lovely mobile countenance, a countenance that is at once quite childlike and deep as an Italian masterpiece.

The dream of Heaven I thought highly amusing. What amused me was its limitedness, its meagerness. It was like a simple man's version of the Big Change, made up from the few properties with which a simple man would be likely to be acquainted. The lack of inventiveness seemed to me to be its best point. Others tell me that it was a failure of inventiveness. Mayhap. But after suffering the success of movie inventiveness so many times, with the whole apparatus of the factory employed to turn out some sort of slick statement or other, I rejoice over this bit of thin and faltering fantasy. And I venture to believe that it represents exactly what Chaplin intended. It was the simplified Heaven of that antic sprite whom Chaplin has created and whose inner whimsicality is here so amusingly indulged.

Chaplin's lightness of touch is shown not merely in the pictures, with the sporting elimination of unnecessary detail and the occasional note of mocking sophistication. It is shown technically in the admirable insistence that the pantomime must tell the story without any particular help from the desiccated medium of words. To read titles is to impede the flow of feeling rather than to aid it. It is to distract the pictorial mind. By cutting out as many titles as possible Charles Chaplin and his company keep close to the visual, and the visual in their case is frequently the beautiful, because of the effort that has been made to represent by hieroglyphic, to eliminate and simplify. Nothing could be better than the way *The Kid* is launched: the mother's plain clothing, her Salvation Army bonnet, her listless walk, and her short brooding in that open-air cathedral of broken humanity, the city park. The quickening of pace when she sees the wealthy motor, just before it is stolen (with her baby in it), tells everything that a world of newspaper-readers needs to know. And the discovery of the baby, its awkward removal, its abandonment in the meanest of lanes until it falls into the surprised hands of the little hobo—this is also sufficiently pointed by the expert action of the company Chaplin has wisely chosen. His wisdom, his sincerity, his integrity, all exhibited in this film, should go some way to revolutionize motion-picture production in this country. From an industry *The Kid* raises production to an art. An art it should be, in spite of the long-suffering public.

ROBERT E. SHERWOOD

The Pilgrim

*Robert E. Sherwood (1896–1955) is now a half-forgotten
figure. But he holds the record for most Pulitzer Prizes
ever won by an individual—three for plays (*Idiot's Delight, Abe Lincoln in Illinois, There Shall Be No
Night), *one for his joint biography of Harry Hopkins
and Franklin D. Roosevelt, whom he served as a speech-
writer during World War II. He also won an Academy
Award for his screenplay for* The Best Years of Our
Lives. *In his early years he was a witty but never condescending movie reviewer for* Life, *in its pre-Luce incarnation as a sophisticated humor magazine.*

*Written and directed by Charles Chaplin.—Distributed by First
National.—Released March, 1923.*

CAST OF CHARACTERS
The Pilgrim . . . . Charles Chaplin
The Girl . . . . Edna Purviance
Her Mother . . . . Kitty Bradbury
The Deacon . . . . Mack Swain
The Elder . . . . Loyal Underwood
The Boy . . . . Dinky Dean

From *The Best Moving Pictures of 1922–23* by Robert E. Sherwood (Boston, 1923).

His Mother . . . . Mai Wells
Her Husband . . . . Sydney Chaplin
The Crook . . . . "Chuck" Riesner
The Sheriff . . . . Tom Murray

Charlie Chaplin has made comedies that may be rated above "The Pilgrim" in point of hilarity—and if you must have instances, I offer "Shoulder Arms," "A Dog's Life" and "The Kid"—but there has been none in all his long list of comic triumphs that was so typically a Chaplin picture.

"The Pilgrim" was almost a dramatization of Chaplin himself—an exposition of his point of view, a recitation of his creed.

The fundamental trait in Chaplin's character is his sublime irreverence. He is the supreme gamin, strutting about in the mantle of genius and thumbing his nose at all institutions that suggest dignity, importance and fat-headed pomposity. Nothing is sacred to him—except humanity; nothing is immune from the thrust of his satire or from the slam of his explosive slap-stick.

Chaplin is a persistent kidder. The person who, on meeting him, dares to take him seriously, instantly becomes an attractive target for his sly raillery. In this time, Chaplin has kidded the most profound intellectual into believing that he is a deep thinker; he has kidded clergymen into believing that he is as spiritual as a nun; he has kidded radicals into believing that his life is devoted to the accomplishment of a world revolution; he has kidded members of the aristocracy into believing that he is one of them. And all the time, he has retained the identity of Charlie Chaplin; he has remained an agnostic, in the most inclusive sense of the word.

Thus, when Chaplin impersonated a convict who disguised himself in clerical garb, he approximated autobiography. He arrived in a small Western town, and was accepted by the local congregation as the shepherd of its flock. He delivered a spectacular sermon on David and Goliath, concluding with a flood of oratory so dramatic that it moved a small boy to unseemly applause—in response to which Charlie took a number of breathless curtain calls.

During the collection, Charlie reached nervously for a cigarette, tapped it reflectively on his thumbnail, and was about to guide it to his lips when the horrified countenances of the choir reminded him that clergymen don't smoke in church.

This was all Chaplinesque in the extreme. It emphasized strongly his utter disregard for the conventional, his unquenchable drollery and his ability to bamboozle the strait-laced, kiddable gentry who believe that virtue is its own protection against ridicule.

In "The Kid," Chaplin realized the beauty of childhood, and of the love which childhood inspires. His scenes with Jackie Coogan were rich with legitimate sentiment. There was nothing of heart interest or sob-squeezing hokum about it; it was genuine, honest, real. But in "The Pilgrim," Chaplin sought to make atonement for his glorification of childhood as it was embodied in Jackie Coogan. Characteristically enough, he represented childhood in its most obnoxious form.

After the spectacular church service, the minister was invited to tea at the home of a parishioner. His fellow guests at this mild affair were a garrulous lady, her subdued husband, and their child—the most offensive infant in the history of the world.

The child's father, played in remarkably adroit fashion by Syd Chaplin, engaged in embarrassed conversation with the rector, while the dear little kiddie frolicked about over their laps, hitting them vigorously, poking at their eyes, plastering them with fly paper and deluging them with gold-fish. Charlie Chaplin feebly resisted these advances, humbly suggesting to the mischievous little fellow that he "go play with momma." But it was all useless. The child continued to maul the helpless visitor—just as thousands of children have mauled thousands of innocent bystanders since the day when the first infant learned to pipe the words, "Do it again."

Chaplin terminated this incident in the most unexpected and yet the most logical manner. When the guests marched into the dining room to partake of the afternoon collation, the terrible child trotted obediently at the minister's heels, endeavoring to ham-string him. Chaplin turned on the brat and, obeying an impulse that had been surging within him throughout the ordeal, administered a painless but authoritative kick against the child's abdomen, and sent him hurtling across the room.

There are many, no doubt, who will decry this seemingly brutal behavior; but there are others who will murmur, devoutly, "God! How I've wanted to do that."

At the conclusion of "The Pilgrim," Charlie reverted to the beatific mood of "The Kid," by way of proving that there is something sacred, after all. The little minister had been exposed, and turned over to a sheriff for delivery at the jail whence he had come.

The sheriff was a kindly soul, with a sense of charitable leniency that is sadly misplaced in an official. He led Chaplin along until they came to the Mexican border.

"Do you see those flowers?" the sheriff inquired, pointing into neutral territory. "Go pick me some."

Charlie Chaplin dashed obediently across the border and the sheriff, smiling, rode off. But Charlie, a stern slave to duty, sprinted after him, waving the bunch of flowers. The sheriff promptly kicked him back across the border.

Here was an episode that was as eloquent, as impressive, as profound as Wordsworth's "Ode to Duty." It was also considerably more amusing.

I have dwelt heavily upon the significant aspects of "The Pilgrim" (it is always a temptation to soar into symbolism when considering a Chaplin picture), but the real meat of the piece was furnished when the terrible child slipped a derby hat over a plum pudding, and when the villain applied a lighted candle to that portion of Charlie Chaplin's anatomy which George Jean Nathan politely terms his "sit-spot."

Charlie Chaplin is a great artist, an inspired tragedian — and everything else that the intellectuals say he is — but there never can be any doubt of the fact that he is fundamentally a clown; and it is when he is being most broadly, vulgarly, crudely funny that he approaches true genius.

Perhaps the most hilariously humorous aspect of "The Pilgrim" was provided by the Pennsylvania censors, who barred the picture from that sacrosanct State because, said they, it made the ministry look ridiculous.

A number of interested observers have been waiting, since then, to hear that the Pennsylvania censors have suppressed several thousand clergymen on the same charge.

"Dear Mr. Chaplin"

*Except for a year when he was the drama critic for the
New York Times, Stark Young (1881–1963) reviewed
plays for* The New Republic *from 1921 to 1949, always
in a highly intellectual and quite influential manner.
He occasionally wrote about film in a similarly high-
toned way. He was also a novelist, whose most famous
title was* So Red the Rose. *As with Robert Sherwood,
his work has not worn particularly well, but in his day
he was a figure to be reckoned with.*

Dear Mr. Chaplin: You get hundreds of letters every week no doubt,
but I have seen your last picture—which they say completes your contract and leaves you free to do what you like—and I must write to say
that I hope this will indeed be the last of its kind and that now you
will go on to a larger field. How many people have said this to you I
have no way of knowing. But your friends, I am sure, insofar as they
are able to see, must have said it often.

This is how it stands. You have created one of the great clowns of
all time. This Charlie of yours needs no portrait anywhere: he is foolish, pathetic, irrepressible, flickering, comical, lovable beyond all
words; he is light as air; he is a blunderer with a heart not solid but

---

From *The New Republic*, August 23, 1922.

worn like a flower on a child's sleeve; a sexless gallantry; he is a tire-less curiosity drawn to things as a monkey to a peephole or a moth to a flame; a gentle blithe dreamer and acrobat; a mask; he is a little, grotesque music; a dear laughter carried lightly in everybody's breast; a gay, shy classic; a world figment.

But you have finished your creation. It was perfect long ago. Already it begins to slow down. It shows a falling off in invention and zest; it shows a kind of boredom in you despite the great art with which you sustain the flow of it, the lightness, the airy intensity. Better still it is than all the clowns in the world put together could do, or comic artists anywhere; but it is yet not quite its own best; it is a little weak judged by itself. You have the achievement of it, however, to rest on, whatever happens, whatever you turn to. And you have your own genius and accomplishments to go forward on. The greatest actor in English you are very easily. You have a technique completely finished for your needs so far; an absolute accuracy of the body and the idea, a perfect identification of gesture and intention. You have the musical quality without which no acting is consummate; it appears in your incomparable fluidity of action and in your beautiful, unbroken continuity of style. You have precision and extraordinary economy. You have invention. And—what is the last test—you have been able to give to all this craft and abundance of technical resource that final genius of vitality that makes it really universal, of the people, who long before the critics ever knew of you recognized your credit though your craft was hid from them.

But with all this you have done only one thing. Why not go on? There are so many things that you could do. There is *Liliom* for example. What could you not do with that part where Mr. Schildkraut made it a role that was expert only, always crowded in motif and business and nearly always touched with vulgarity and insistence? You could do *He Who Gets Slapped*. Or with study you could do *Peer Gynt*, and many other parts. But better than all of these, you could do new things written by you or for you, things in which you would use your full endowment, comic and otherwise. And finally you might do the one most important of all things so far as moving pictures go, and that is to develop things calculated strictly for it and for no other art, made up out of its essential quality, which is visual motion and not mere stage drama photographed. In sum, you might really create in terms of the moving picture as you have already created in terms of character.

But all this will have to be a real change, Mr. Chaplin, or at least a real and definite openness to change and to new embarkations. It cannot be done by writing Charles instead of Charlie on the bill-boards, or altering the makeup of your eyes and mustache or shortening your riotous shoes. Such ventures in change amount to nothing and get nowhere. Go in at your full tilt. Go in for what you yourself like, for what satisfies you completely. And say that if the taste of the public does not like your work the taste of the public will have to change.

I think we can all understand some of the difficulties you have to struggle with when you think of taking such a step. There is first of all the natural desire to hold on to what you have won for yourself, to your enormous following. And always, of course, there are people around you who at the very mention of it will tell you that you will lose your place in the sun; who will try to hold you back, out of ignorance or kind solicitude or avarice or jealousy or general timidity. And there is the dread that you might feel of having your serious efforts laughed at, though you can master that if you choose, and can even use it to great ends, use superbly this tension and confusion of laughter and tears together. And not least in your way there is the peculiar money standard in our theatre, not the love of money exactly but its acceptance as a gauge of success, a measure of an actor's height; and you, naturally, may be human enough to compete with the others on their own grounds, however little they can compete with you on what is really yours. But all this is obvious: you know your own dream.

The truth is, you—like many an artist and many men not artists in America just now—are at the crossroads. You have got to choose. It grows clearer and clearer to us all that we are like children getting what we want, but what we want only in competition with each other, not profoundly, not out of ourselves. As time goes on and our relative values get more and more defined, we observe that much of the kind of success we see means only more gasoline, more food, more Victrola records made by other people, more motion. It is forced on us that if we want more life we must look ahead to get it, and must choose what after all we will go after if we are not to be lost. We can see at any artists' club, the crowd of such as have taken for their art the watchword of business success, poor wise arrivals who knew how to play the game, knew what the public wanted and put it over as soap and collars and varnishes are put over with us, and who are now empty-faced, gregarious, unsubtle, unoriginal, bored, vivacious and stale. The necessity for a choice has grown very clear. These last few years especially for many an artist and many another man have been a comment on that experience that Francis Thompson wrote of, that divine pursuit, that flight down the nights and days and arches of the years, and the labyrinthine ways of one's own mind, and in the midst of tears, and under running laughter, from those strong feet that followed, followed after. The folly of that flight is one of those spiritual practicalities we cannot dodge, the common sense of the soul.

And whatever you may think, the cold facts remain, the truth in plainsong. Your public has had an instinct. It has liked the right thing, the best to be had. But the large public is like the natural world: it uses up for its own ends what it finds and then throws it aside. For a while, then, your great public will like, as it has liked, your best art as it comes along. Then later you will have the humiliation and the disillusionment of seeing them applaud equally or even more loudly—partly as the fruit of long habit—your less good things, applaud the bad more than the good was applauded. And this is the bitter last scene of all for a great artist, who can only sustain it easily by increased vanity and egotism. The public's way—which is nature's—of using and throwing aside is right almost, however cruel; for otherwise we should have in the end a survival of what is worse than dead. And yet there is a degree of devotion and survival that is a good thing. There is a degree of permanence of interest and of ideal relationship to art, among cultured men, that is good for art and its complete unfolding; just as there is a degree—though strictly limited and easily carried to unhealthy excess—of sublimation of the natural body into something of more ideality and a more permanent essence. And this you would find among a more cultured audience, of the judicious, as Hamlet would say, however few they might be at first compared to your old millions. And then, too, there is the hard biological fact not to be blinked, of your going off, the sheer physical decline from perfection. And, whether that descent has already begun or not, it is certain at least that this particular thing that you have done is possible physically only a few years more. The spring will go out of it.

And, in conclusion, dear Mr. Chaplin, the main thing is that you be happy as an artist in your own living. And that one can see from your pictures you are not. You have your dreams, we can see that, a passionate and delicate insurgence within you, a poetry and a music and a poignancy that eats into you. One feels that this man we see there on the screen knows very well that most of the people around him know little about him; knows that he has accepted too much cheap praise already and inferior court. He knows that he, like any creative artist, must always be alone and strange, as the mystery of creation is always alone in the material world; he must always be alone exactly as that little figure of his Charlie always stands out from any scene around him by its wistful luster and pathetic vividness. And this pathos, but half expressed, is what gives you now a good part of your appeal—for even little boys want to take you in their arms as they do their teddybears. It is like the pathos of life itself, which arises from our sense in life of the half expressed, the passionate and tender and violent pushing against the dumb obstacles of fact and matter. If in your work this pathos goes no further than it does now, it will in time be lessened and gradually become a gap, a lack, or a mere pitifulness and half-defeat. But if you carry what is yourself further toward its full expression in a more complete art you will express more life, something more beautiful, comic, tragic, and profoundly characteristic of you. That of course is what you want, one sees it behind that mask of yours. And it seems only fair to tell you that there are those among your admirers who want you to have it, and believe that you need not fail except as every artist must fail, by comparison, as Leopardi said, with your own dream.

On "A Woman of Paris"

Penelope Gilliatt (1932–1993) was in her day a highly regarded short-story writer and an occasional novelist and screenwriter, most notably of Sunday Bloody Sunday. *She was also a film critic, first for* The Observer *in London, then for* The New Yorker, *where for some years she wrote reviews for six months of the year, standing aside for Pauline Kael the rest of the time. She was particularly interested in comedy;* To Wit, *from which this piece is drawn, is an excellent and warmhearted survey of the field.*

Just as the hosts in a visited country will so regularly greet a foreign traveler with the question "When are you going back?", meaning no harm in the world but succeeding in making the guest feel thoroughly unwelcome to stay a day more, people are quick to turn on anyone who has made them laugh and has then committed the sin of doing something else. They want to know when he is going back, this spoiler of the fun. *A Woman of Paris*—Chaplin's legendary "serious" comedy, written and directed by him in 1922 and 1923—provoked just that response. The public expected horselaughs and was furious about being robbed, furious about being given instead a sophisticated comedy

From *To Wit* by Penelope Gilliatt (New York, 1990), courtesy of the author's estate.

(which was greatly to influence Lubitsch, for one). Audiences wanted back Chaplin's baggy trousers and clownish trudge. They paid hardly any attention to a film that forgot the little tramp. In the late twenties, Chaplin withdrew the picture from circulation. The self-imposed ban lasted nearly fifty years. Then, in 1976, he wrote a musical score for it and consented to its theatrical redistribution. The film, which was long thought lost, has been transferred from nitrate to glittering 35mm safety stock. In content, it amounts to a king's ransom dredged up from the ocean bed of sunken movies. It has all of Chaplin's wit and none of his whimsy. Strange, lively, reviving, to see evidence of the innovative mind of the figure too familiar to us in the guise of the little man.

This is a film with a sense of comedy which is debonair and elegant and bitterly close to the bone. The woman of Paris is acted by Edna Purviance, fulfilling a promise of Chaplin's that in their long career together he would one day write a dramatic part for her. As the subtitles announce, the Marie St. Clair she plays is the key figure in "a drama of fate." We are in a small village "somewhere in France." Parted by disapproving parents from her love, who is a glaze-eyed, very silent-film figure called Jean Millet (Carl Miller), she goes to Paris alone on the train on which she was to have eloped with him. she gets involved with a handsome dandy called Pierre Revel, played with a benign wink at craftiness by Adolphe Menjou. The characterization of the figure makes it seem as though Chaplin toyed with — perhaps feared — the idea that he himself was this dandy.

In the cutting of one of the picture's many restaurant scenes, there is a mettlesome juxtaposition of gossip. Revel is called the richest bachelor in Paris by a woman at a far table. Revel, smoking rapidly, remarks out of her hearing that she is one of the richest old maids in Paris. We see him making a study of eating as he makes a study of everything, this scholar and taster of "the good things of life." He goes into the expensive restaurant to inspect the cooking. The scene is a Chaplin mêlée of tired and overworked servants observed by an alert and underworked bigwig. His office is his plumply pillowed bedroom, and for doing a rich man's office chores he wears embroidered pajamas. He gets engaged to an heiress but laughs gaily at the idea that this should in any way perturb his set-up with Marie. *A Woman of Paris* is a film of ironic social acuity, full of women trailing long skirts that they kick aside in pretended irritation with expense, and of *luxe et volupté* that lack any kindness or exhilaration except for what is imparted by the character of the movie itself. Marie's friends have pinchbeck souls, and Chaplin shows the fact. These are people who thrive in margins. They chat indestructibly through everything. They allow the passing of time to make strangers of intimates, and they allow politesse to black out sensibility. Marie is caught up by the charade. Marie is trapped by Revel's fury about her when she says, with all too much credibility, that she's so depressed she doesn't want to go out. Marie is trapped by the Latin Quarter parties at which girls are hoisted like hooked fish to float among balloons. Marie is trapped by the party sight of a striptease done by a girl bandaged like a mummy, who slowly lets go the bandage—which is rewound about the stomach of a fat man in evening clothes—and who goes out of the scene, to poke her head around at us with nothing of her nakedness showing but a gleaming bare arm and a merry head with a finger held to the lips. Marie is trapped by the rich society that, by the duplicity of its kind, encourages her to lead a double moral life so well that she doesn't even notice that her maid has spilled out of her tallboy a man's telltale stiff collar in front of her badly-off Millet. He has followed her to Paris and become a painter, anxiously trying to mend things at least to the extent of painting her portrait. At a fine moment when she is standing for the portrait, she yawns in a pause when he is busy painting her, out of sight behind the canvas; and, by some flight of ESP, infects him with the yawn. More of silent comedy's visual puns.

It is a scene of emotion made strict, of yearning not allowed: Millet has made her promise not to look at the canvas because it presents the girl she once was, and not the counterfeit she has come to be.

There is no lack of wit or fault of sentiment in this film. Marie, in a tantrum with Revel, tears off her pearl necklace and throws it into the street, and then breaks a shoe heel when she has had second thoughts about the necklace and gone after it. Revel laughs at her greed. He consoles himself with a so-called friend of Marie's. Then follows the massage scene, so often described by film-lovers: the heroine is invisibly massaged by an inattentive, angry woman. Only the masseuse's irate hands show in the frame with occasional flashes of

Marie's hand. They are intercut with shots of another friend, who is bringing Marie cruel gossip and flicking cigarette ash into a saxophone idly left in a chair. In a last and marvelous celebrated sequence, after Marie has found her self-willed fate, two vehicles meet and pass: Revel's splendid car, and Marie on a farm wagon with a child. Neither principal has seen the other. This is a beautifully put comic moral tale about matters of innocence and ignorance.

The New Chaplin Comedy

Edmund Wilson (1895–1972) was America's great man of letters for something over forty years, a writer of limpid clarity with vast knowledge of the world's literature and languages, a great reviewer for both The New Republic *and* The New Yorker, *and the author of such seminal works as* Axel's Castle *(a pioneering study of literary modernism),* To the Finland Station *(a monumental study of how history is written and acted), and* Patriotic Gore *(on the literature of the American Civil War). He was also a novelist, playwright, and, as he proves here, an occasional excellent student of popular culture. This notoriously cranky highbrow had an affection for lowbrow entertainment (he was expecially fond of magicians), but he did not park his critic's sensibility at the door, as this appreciation of* The Gold Rush *proves.*

The fundamental device of American moving-picture humor is what is technically known as the "gag." A gag is a comic trick, the equivalent in cinema action of the spoken gag of the stage. When Buster Keaton on a runaway motorcycle knocks the ladder out from under a house painter and goes off with the bucket of paint on his head, or when a clothesline, strung between two houses, on which Harold Lloyd is escaping, is cut at one end by an enemy and Harold still clinging to it, swings into a room below where a séance of spiritualists are awaiting a materialization, this is a movie gag. Inventing such tricks is today one of the principal professions of the film industry. In Hollywood, the gag-writers of the comic stars are among the most influential and the most envied members of the community; for without them the stars would be nothing. There are moments when Buster Keaton gives evidence of a skill at pantomime which his producers do nothing to cultivate; but one may say of these comics in general that they hardly need to be actors any more than Baby Peggy, Rin-Tin-Tin, Strongheart or Silver King.

The one performer of Hollywood who has succeeded in doing anything distinguished with this primitive machinery of gags is, of course, Charlie Chaplin. In the first place, he is, I believe, the only comic star in the movies who does not employ a gag-writer: he makes everything up himself; so that, instead of the stereotyped humor of even the best of his competitors, most of whose tricks could be interchanged among them without anyone's knowing the difference, he gives us jokes that, however crude, have an unmistakable quality of personal fancy. Furthermore, he has made it a practice to use his gags as points of departure for genuine comic situations. Thus in his latest picture, *The Gold Rush*, there is a cabin—with Charlie and his partner in it—which is blown to the edge of a cliff while the occupants are asleep. This in itself is a gag like another: for any other screen comedian it would have been enough to startle the audience by showing them the little shack rocking on the dangerous brink and then, by acrobatics and trick photography, to follow this with similar shudders. But Chaplin, given his gag, the same kind of thing as Lloyd's clothes-line, proceeds to transport his audience in a way of which Lloyd would be incapable, by developing it with steady logic and vivid imagination. Charlie and his companion wake up: the panes of the shack are frosted; they do not realize what has happened; Charlie sets out to get breakfast, but whenever he moves to the side of the room where his heavy companion is lying—the side hanging over the abyss—the house begins to tip. He puts this down, however, to dizziness—he has been drunk the night before—and goes resolutely about his business. But when his companion—the gigantic Mack Swain—gets up and begins to move around, the phenomenon is aggravated: "Do you have an illusion that the floor is tipping?"—"Ah, you notice that, too, do you?" They jump on it to see if it is standing solid; but as Charlie is jumping on the overhanging side while Swain is holding down on the other, they do not at once find out what is wrong, and it is some time before the fatal combination—both men on the projecting side— almost sends them over the cliff. They rush back to the safe side of the room, and Charles goes to the door—which has been frozen tight in the night—to see what is going on: after a struggle, it suddenly flies open, and he falls out into the void, only saving himself by a clutch at the sill. His companion rushes down to save him, but by the time he has pulled him in, their double weight has set the cabin sliding: it is anchored now only by a rope which has caught fast to something not far from the cliff. Charlie and his companion, abject on their bellies, try to crawl up the terrible floor, now at an angle of sixty degrees. At first, though the eyes of his companion are popping, Charlie remains cool and sensible. "Just go easy! A little at a time." But no matter how little they attempt, every movement makes the cabin slip. And so on, through a long passage of pantomime.

Conversely, however, the gag is sometimes resorted to by Chaplin to break up the non-farcical sequences—ironic or even pathetic—that are becoming more frequent in his comedies. Thus the love story in *The Gold Rush* is, on the whole, treated seriously, but from time to time enlivened by such low comedy incidents as that in which Charlie accidentally saturates his bandaged foot with kerosene and then has it set on fire by a match dropped by one of the ladies. In these sequences, it sometimes happens—as in parts of *The Pilgrim*, his previous film—that such gags in the straight situations produce a jarring effect. They seem to be introduced in order to hold Chaplin's old public, who expects their full allowance of "belly laughs." He has never dared desert this public, who first saw him for the same sort of entertainment that they find in Fox and Christie comedies. Yet in proportion as his reputation has grown with the sophisticated audience and the critics, his popularity has hardly gained—it has not even, perhaps, held its own—with this original popular audience, who do not seem to feel any difference between Chaplin himself, on the one hand, and his imitators and rivals, on the other. They seem, in fact, to be coming to prefer the latter. Buster Keaton and Harold Lloyd have, in a sense, carried gagging far beyond Charlie Chaplin. Their films have more smartness and speed; they cultivate more frightening mechanical devices. With their motorcars, their motorcycles, their motorboats, their airplanes, their railroad trains, their vertiginous scaling of skyscrapers and their shattering cataclysmic collisions, they have progressed a long way beyond Chaplin, who has made no attempt to keep up with them, but continues with the cheap trappings and the relatively simple tricks of the old custard-pie comedy. For Chaplin is even more old-fashioned than the old-fashioned Mack Sennett movies; he is as old-fashioned as Karno's Early Birds, the unusual music-hall turn in which he originally appeared and which was at least a school for actors, not for athletes.

What turn Charlie Chaplin's career will take is, therefore, still a curious problem. He is himself, I believe, acutely aware of the anomaly of his position. In the films, he seems hardly likely to play an important role in the artistic development of the future. His gift is primarily the actor's, not the director's or artist's. All the photographic, the plastic development of the movies, which is at present making such remarkable advances, seems not to interest Chaplin. His pictures are still in this respect nearly as raw as *Tilly's Punctured Romance* or any other primitive comedy, and it is only when the subject is sordid—as in *Pay Day*, with its crowded city streetcars taking people home after work and its suffocating slatternly city flat—that the *mise en scène* in Chaplin's comedies contributes in any way to their effectiveness. The much-praised *A Woman of Paris* was handicapped particularly, it seemed to me—since it did not have Chaplin as the central figure—by this visual lack of taste. It was intended as an attractive, a serious picture, yet, for all the intelligence he brought to directing it, he allowed it to go out as if naked in its flat light and putty make-up. He is jealous of his independence in this as in other matters. He is very unlikely to allow himself to be written for, directed or even advised. If he is not carrying along his old public, he will unquestionably in time have to give it up; but whether he will then simply retire from the screen or try something altogether different, it is impossible to predict. In the meantime, it may be that his present series of pictures—*The Kid, The Pilgrim* and *The Gold Rush*—with their gags and their overtones of tragedy, their adventures half-absurd, half-realistic, their mythical hero, now a figure of poetry, now a type out of the comic strips, represents the height of Chaplin's achievement. He could scarcely, in any field, surpass the best moments of these pictures. The opening of *The Gold Rush* is such a moment. Charlie is a long adventurer, straggling along after a party of prospectors among the frozen hills: he twirls his cane a little to keep his spirits up. On his way through a narrow mountain pass, a bear emerges and follows him. Any ordinary movie would, of course, have had it chasing him about for as long as he could work up gags for it. But Charlie does not know that the bear is there: he keeps on, twirling his cane. Presently the beast withdraws, and only then does Charlie think he hears something: he turns around, but there is nothing there. And he sets off again, still fearless, toward the dreadful ordeals that await him.

September 2, 1925

1957. Years later, on visits to London, I went to the Christmas pantomime and realized that the bear of *The Gold Rush* was one of the many things that Charlie Chaplin had borrowed from the British popular theater. There is always, in the pantomime, a scene in which the comedians are lost in a forest, and there used to be always a bear—though in the winter of '53–'54 a space man was substituted—which is following them but hides when they look around. Eventually, however, they must face the bear: it was Chaplin's original touch never to allow the traveler to see the bear at all. In the meantime, the pantomimist Chaplin—contrary to my expectations of 1925—had quite sloughed off the old vagabond and emerged on the speaking screen in characterizations wholly new: the contemporary Bluebeard of *Monsieur Verdoux* and the old music-hall comedian of *Limelight*. Though the last of these takes us back to the music hall, it is no longer to the music-hall devices as material for Hollywood comedy. Chaplin has outgrown these, and he now recreates the music hall, makes it one of the subjects of a work of art. The sequences in which Chaplin's hero is seen in his professional act, have something poetic, daemonic. They are among the high points of Chaplin's career. As funny as any of his earlier scenes, they are also intensely emotional. The clown with a breaking heart is as ancient as any of the stock situations which

Chaplin has never hesitated to exploit; but the result is, as usual, astonishing: the nightmare of the deadpan accompanist, whose music keeps slipping off the stand while the comedian diverts the audience by primitive clowning tricks that are at once unashamed and embarrassing; the sudden and mad climax in which the aging comic produces a small violin and fiddles feverishly till he falls into the orchestra. The accompanist here is Buster Keaton, who had passed into eclipse in Hollywood but was invited by Chaplin to take part in this film and is perfect in the uncanny atmosphere of this music hall of Hell. Not long afterwards—in February, 1954—I saw Buster Keaton perform at the Cirque Médrano in Paris, and was confirmed in my opinion of twenty-eight years before that Hollywood had not made the best of him. He is a pantomime clown of the first order, and his act at the Cirque Médrano—a presser's boy, morose and detached, attempting to deliver a dress suit while the circus is going on—seemed to be the best thing I had seen him do. His loss of reputation in the United States and his appearance in an engagement abroad is only another example of the perversion and waste of talent for which Hollywood has been responsible. Who could ever, in 1925, have believed that Charlie Chaplin would escape from it—having always been his own manager—and take his place among his age's first artists? But see my later note on this subject.

Dorado Eldorado

G. Cabrera Infante (1929–2005), an exile from Castro's Cuba, was widely regared as his native land's finest novelist. Before the revolution, in the late fifties, he reviewed movies under the pseudonym G. Cain. They are generous in spirit, passionately personal, alert to the essential surrealism of movies, and deliciously readable. They are collected in A Twentieth Century Job, *a work that deserves to be more widely read.*

The Gold Rush (United Artists) is the key to Charles Chaplin. Perhaps the most perfect of his silent movies — don't forget that *City Lights* as well as *Modern Times,* in which Chaplin still refused to speak, were sound films — it has kept its comic qualities intact after thirty-two years. Now, Chaplin has given it a sound track and has added to it a subjective narrator (the narrator uses his voice so that the characters 'speak' through him) and has composed a brief score for it. 'Now' is 1942, when Chaplin decided to rerelease his old film. It happened like this: Chaplin showed his silent movie to some of his children's friends, and he counted the laughs that the oldest of his silent gags still had for the new generation. He reasoned that the rest of humanity might well think the same. For this new sally of the Tramp (whom he had already

From A *Twentieth-Century Job* by G. Cabrera Infante, published by Faber & Faber in 1991.

decided to leave behind, lost on the primrose path along which he disappears at the end of *Modern Times*), Chaplin chose his most perfect film, the one he considers his masterpiece, *The Gold Rush*.

The Gold Rush was selected some years back as the second of the ten masterworks of the cinema. *The Battleship Potemkin* came in before. The former film was the first of the great hits of Chaplin and his first feature film. None of his other movies has enjoyed the success which *The Gold Rush* had. The little fellow departed in search of gold and found it at the box office, in a buoyant America, enjoying the most fabulous economic boom of its history. It was 1925. Two years before, Chaplin made the only film in which he did not participate as an actor, *A Woman of Paris*. This time one is not dealing with a comedy but with a dour drama. The performer is Edna Purviance, Chaplin's favourite actress. *A Woman of Paris* introduced true psychological elements into the cinema, observed with a realist's eye: Chaplin stretched his affection for detail to the point that no one would recognize in him the easy-street comedian of the films by Mack Sennett, but rather the maniacal perfectionist Erich von Stroheim. (It is said that for one scene in a cabaret, Chaplin had a set with four walls built. In one of them he had had a hole drilled through which the camera peered with its monocle: in the scene, real waiters served a real meal to the rhythm of a real orchestra—which would not be heard in the film. Adolphe Menjou, sipping real champagne, looked out of the corner of his eye at the heroine like a true libertine.) Over the bitter and sour ending of *A Woman in Paris*—which he always regretted later—Chaplin superimposed the noisy humour of the little fellow who waddles through the snow with his impossibly big shoes, who suffers hunger and cold, who is confused with a tasty chicken and who ends up a millionaire: it is not strange that the film has a happy end. A reporter interviews the millionaire Chaplin, and for a photo he is made to wear again the beggar's uniform. But he falls down a staircase instead, as far as the third deck: there he bumps into his lost girlfriend. The reporter comments: 'Say—this will make a great story—and with a happy ending!' and Chaplin, now his own narrator, affirms: 'And so it was: a happy ending.'

It has been said that *The Gold Rush* is an autobiographical movie. To which one would have to add that all the cinema of Chaplin is autobiographical. *The Kid* is his infancy in the East End of London; *The Circus*, his beginnings in music hall by the hand of Karno, garrulous producer of pantomimes; *City Lights* is the rescue of many of his celebrated actresses, from anonymous obscurity to the hideous clarity of fame: not a few were blinded again; *Modern Times* is the individualist creator, trapped by an unending assembly line called Hollywood and being driven mad by it (Chaplin himself suffered a grave mental crisis once) and rescued by falling in love; *The Great Dictator* presents the little Jew with a moustache crushed by the Nazis, an image that Hitler, with the same moustache, would have enjoyed fitfully (*Monsier Verdoux* in some ways escapes from this chart, perhaps because Orson Welles provided the story); *Limelight* is an admitted autobiography and a new version of *City Lights*, with the story of an old comic who no longer makes people laugh; to complete the sketch, Chaplin gave his clown a Spanish name, Calvero, in memory of his maternal grandmother. As one can see, it is not only Federico Fellini who supports his work with props from his life.

Like all the films of Chaplin, *The Gold Rush* is a madcap parody. Not only of adventure movies and of literature in a wild state as in Jack London but of the true tragedy of the search for gold by the countless prospectors of the Yukon, who risked life and limb in pursuit of a new El Dorado. To accentuate the similarities and thereby to split the difference, Chaplin begins his movie with a long thin line of men scaling a snowy mountain. With the laborious bustling of ants, the men show up dark against the snow, dwarfed by the mountain, mad under the sky—and the scene has nothing funny about it. But immediately an impossible precipice is seen ahead, and who comes up walking along the fearful and narrow ridge, risking his life by sheer ignorance? The Little Fellow, that's who. If on firm and sure ground he maintained a precarious balance, here he shows his scorn for danger by marching along as if on the widest avenue. But he does not fall. Miracles of gravity? Elie Faure, the art critic, has another theory: 'Hopping now on one foot, now on the other—those so sad and absurd feet—he represents the two poles of thought: one which is called conscience and the other desire. Hopping on one foot and the other, he seeks spiritual equilibrium, and after having found it for an instant he loses it immediately after . . .' Now the desire of Chaplin is to get

rich from one day to the next and of course he doesn't have the re-
motest consciousness of the danger that he defies. Like Mr Magoo,
another ineffable spirit, it is this innocence which saves him. Now it
is no longer the instincts which preserve the species. In Chaplin's new
species it will be its seraphic soul. If there is some drama in his life, it
is that of the good man: his existence is badly tolerated by the wicked
and he will never be understood. It is this which permits him to win
in the end.

The Little Fellow arrives at a cabin. A wicked man inhabits it, but
like Little Red Riding Hood, the Little Fellow doesn't see the danger
and, at the wolf's mouth, only asks: Can I come in? The mean
denizen of the cabin, a doer of iniquity, tries to hurl the Little Fellow
into the snow and cold and hunger: to his death. But the elements are
on the side of the Little Fellow: a strong wind prevents Chaplin from
moving from his place. As much as he tries he doesn't succeed in ad-
vancing in his attempt—forced by the circumstances of a strong
man—to abandon the cabin. When all is already lost, the elements
vanquished by evil, avenging chance arrives. Another big man, but a
good-hearted one, installs himself in the cabin and the Little Guy
stays with him, the two opposing forces, good and evil, neutralized,
equilibrium achieved.

The whole film is full of similar scenes, all of Chaplin is perme-
ated by this primitive philosophy. But there is more. Chaplin has
said: 'I have not tried to flatter the audience, but neither have I ever
tried to impose silence on them.' He doles out the philosophy lesson,
the critique of customs, and fills the film with guffaws: the sweet sap
of laughter mixed with some salt tears. The romance of Chaplin is
that form of solitary love which has even mortified someone as self-
sufficient as Elvis Presley: the one-sided love affair. At a dance, the
Little Fellow falls in love, at first sight, with the pretty, lissome Georgia. Georgia does not love the Little Fellow, she only makes fun of
him gently, with affection. The Little Fellow asks for nothing more:
his love is enough to cover the two: it is a wide sheet for a wedding
bed with just one pillow. The sentimental scenes are managed with
a kind of romantic detergent very near—or perhaps beyond—soap
opera, and they show that Chaplin owes to Griffith everything that
he does not owe to Max Linder and to Mack Sennett. Among the

tears of weeping there are the tears of laughter and *The Gold Rush* is turned into one of the most complete pieces of humour which the cinema has given us.

Proofs:

a) The unforgettable scene of the dance of the rolls, one of the most beautiful from the silent days and a frank example of the poetry of movement.*

b) The slapstick or pure comic incidence of the weapon which pursues the terrified non-belligerent: a shotgun obliges Chaplin to seek out the nearest refuge, while his two cabin-mates fight over the gun. But always the shotgun pursues Chaplin anxiously. The comedian will repeat this scene in *The Great Dictator*. On this occasion it is an animated cannonball.

c) Chaplin is dancing with Georgia. His pants fall down. He picks up an odd piece of rope and continues dancing. He notices that an enormous dog is slowing up his dance: the rope was holding the dog. Suddenly, a cat passes by . . .

d) Chaplin is earning a living shovelling snow. The snow that he removes from this door falls in front of the house next door. His clients grow. The snow keeps falling in front of the house next door. But now Chaplin doesn't dare advertise himself as a snow-sweeper: the house whose entrance the snow has covered is . . . the jail. (This scene was repeated with another reading in *City Lights* in the celebrated sequence of the street sweeper who has just finished cleaning up, irritated, the turds of a horse and now runs away after seeing with horror that down the street comes an elephant.)

e) Chaplin and his friend (brilliantly played by the late Mack Swain) are dying from hunger, on Thanksgiving Day to boot. For the dinner Chaplin only has one shoe, his right one. He has cooked it with culinary expertise and lovingly ladles the broth over it, as the most appetizing turkey. He serves it. Carefully he extracts the body of the boot and underneath there remain the nails, like the metallic

---

*This new print of *The Gold Rush* was shown in widescreen format, so that the dance of the rolls could hardly be seen. This would have greatly bothered Chaplin, who always avoided close-ups, because 'in my work the expression of the hands and the legs counts as much as that of the fact.'

spines of an unknown fish. Chaplin gobbles up the laces, which he has first rolled up on his fork, as if he were eating spaghetti. Now he sucks the nails with delight, like the bones of a tasty chicken.

f) His friend, still hungry, goes off his rocker and imagines the Little Fellow transformed into a hen ready for the oven. He chases him with his shotgun, but when he is just about to kill the hen, he sees that it is only the still starving Charlie.

g) And a long string of impractical jokes on which the best beads are these: Chaplin takes a bent nail and holds it with his little finger so that Swain can snap it as if breaking the wishbone of a yardbird, to make a wish for providence; Chaplin buries the shotgun to keep his friend, whom he has not entirely been able to convince that he is not just a hen, from killing him; when he has buried it, he turns his back on it and throws snow on it with his feet, just like a hen; Chaplin pretends to be frozen so that any kind soul may feed him but when he is carried inside and he is given tea he instantly comes out of his stupor to pick up two or three extra lumps of sugar and thus be able to drink a too bitter tea; Chaplin is now a millionaire on board a ship when he comes up behind a man smoking a cigar, the man throws the cigar away and Chaplin, in spite of his rich clothes, from the force of habit cannot resist the impulse to pick up the butt and take a puff. All the life preservers on the ship have different names.

Finally, a new coat of paint on this old picture which has seemed to disturb many people: the narration. *The Gold Rush* is now narrated by Chaplin, and it is precisely this which transforms it into a key film: the one that truly shows what Charles Chaplin the author thinks about Charles Chaplin the character: what Chaplin thinks about Charlie. Now Chaplin has been transformed into a spectator of himself and thanks to the distance which time gives, has seen the raggedy rags bum from a lucid perspective. Here is what the *cronista* has seen about what Charles Chaplin has seen. The tramp is a poor wretch: this ultimate vision is contained in a single moment of the narration. Observing the dance scene as a narrator and describing it blow-by-blow from his choice seat near the trampled ego of the tramp in the corner, whose pants are about to fall down in patches, whose shoes are soleless, and who weighs less than 100 pounds thanks to hunger, Chaplin tells how

Georgia, to show her utter contempt for Jack, has picked out the most deplorable-looking tramp in the dancehall . . . the Little Fellow, who can't believe his luck . . . Georgia, addressing herself to her boyfriend to pique him says: 'You see, I'm very careful whom I dance with' . . . The tramp is still a gentleman, like his pants come down in the world, but who keeps his anachronistic medieval customs and his costume in a society that is hostile and therefore cruel. Chaplin does repeat and repeat during the movie, each time he mentions the tramp, the phrase 'the poor little fellow'. In that sentence there is nothing disparaging, or ironic, or reproachful. At most there is a faint hectoring meaning, which impels him to keep letting his character live in spite of the inclemency of the weather, of the time and of men. It is this survival more than a revival which definitively separates the Little Fellow from Don Quixote—and draws him near to the *déclassés* of the twentieth century, to the remnants of the old world in a brave new world, to an émigré from Victorian morality and bourgeois customs, to a character of another Charles, Charles Dickens.

The Circus

One of his friends said that a good part of the fascination that Byron exerted on so many people who came in contact with him arose from the power he had of a certain dangerous intimacy.

I have often thought of that observation with regard to Charlie Chaplin. When you talk with him you sense at the very start an impulse to make the connection between the two of you direct and alive, a hunger that the moment should be pure and glowing, and the exchange between you and him open like a passage in art.

As we talk, I always have a sense that there is much that is not coming into what is said, facts, if you like, that are overcrowded, and facts that are so stressed and illuminated as to become different from what they might be for anyone else who knows them. But I never think of this as false, or that the truth is being distorted. I am convinced that it is a high and passionate sincerity that fills this conversation of Charlie Chaplin's, sincerity such as only an imagination like his could come at. I mean that, where exchange and *rapport* between two people, even those who trust each other, is often halting and half-divined, however true it intends to be, this moment between Charlie Chaplin and me, so evolved from his imagination and so driven with the necessity to express himself, has in it a great completeness and absorption; the thing between the two people involved is alive for both, and therefore full of its own truth. He will speak of his personal affairs, of events and of persons that delight, embitter, or destroy him,

From *The New Republic*, February 8, 1928, by permission of the *New Republic*.

with a warmth, sting, despondency, exact poetry, or gay wit that is meant to make me see them in the liveliest degree possible, and that, therefore, seeks to engage me through the regions where my response would be most likely and natural. He does not take his color from me, but from my color he takes what he needs to express himself to me. He says what he wants me to believe of what he is telling me and, at the same time, I can see that it is what he himself wants to believe of it through me.

To that talk he gives himself with a fluency and precision and rich-mindedness that must be rarely equaled. The soul of it is shy, but the blood excited; the points are quick and telling; the word sense is remarkable; the variety ranges from a beautiful, warm elevation and eager enthusiasm to the devil's own Rabelaisian articulation; and one of its secrets is that it cannot do without you.

This complete and shining persuasion and perfect conviction of sympathy and contact could not happen without a sharp air of frankness, of saying anything called for. It needs the sense of a sort of universal lyric candor by which whatever is said seems to be free of the speaker, no longer personal, as moving and alive to the one who hears as to the one who speaks. In Byron this dangerous frankness came from pride, passion, and a vehement sense of his inability to present to the world a just picture of himself, to do "himself justice," as Lady Blessington said. In Charlie Chaplin, shot about by a restless, intense, and fertile mentality, quivering, sensitive, hurt in his early years, proud, egotistical, loving what is gentle, warm, and laureate in life, imprisoned in a mask, this power of frank intimacy was made possible only by an immense success in the world, as life itself was made possible to him by success.

I remember four years ago one afternoon we were talking about this picture of The Circus that has not arrived at a public showing. I had spoken of the end of The Pilgrim, that place where, after the kind official had got him to the Mexican border and he could run for his life and so keep out of jail, Charlie must stop to pick a flower and turn back to present it before he sets out down the road to the vague freedom ahead of him. It was one of the best motivations in modern drama, I said. "Well, you see, he just wanted to give, he felt at the moment that he must give," Charlie Chaplin said. One of the most tragic and touching and wittiest, I said. He remembered tears had come in his eyes when he had thought of it, he said. Then he began to speak of *The Circus*, the clown idea, the comic images of action that should express what he wanted to express. Incident after incident, motive after motive were working out in his head, and everything was seen, at that stage, not as some action or gag, but as ideas, pictures, states of feeling, ironic poetry, poignant finalities; and about them Charlie Chaplin, tracking out his conception of the play, lighting his way from point to point in the design of it, was clear and shrewd like a fine artist, never soft, but bitter and deep like a poet. The only thing extraneous to the dramatic idea was the necessity he felt for engaging me in it for the moment, and this in a way was part of the idea after all, or was so, at least, for so long as he was talking to me of it.

I mention this conversation about *The Circus* because it may serve to dispose of such people as like to flout what they call Charlie Chaplin's esthete critics, and because of those who try to deride all attempts to assert profound meanings for these Chaplin films, and all attempts to turn their details into significant symbolism—which last I, for one, should never do; they are too perfect images, too aptly expressive and too final to be mere symbols. By a perfect image I mean a motive, an action, a personage or event that parallels a thing in nature, a hill, a tree, the wind blowing; it can be taken simply in itself, it carries for the simplest person, and carries with it its elemental idea, which it is inseparable from. But at the same time it is capable of the whole idea; it can exist with or without amplification or comment; it can hold as much meaning as you put into it.

The Circus, as we see it at the Strand, is, for the most part, purer in the old-style Chaplin that *The Kid* was or *The Gold Rush*. The acrobatic ability is the same as always, the flitting unreality of the figure and the elusive music of the movement, the poignant, shy motivation, the way of mocking life and breaking its heart, the astonishing effect of brevity and completeness in single incidents, the uncanny accuracy of effect where exactness is wanted, as, for example, where in front of the sideshow the supposed dummy figure fools the officer and knocks the man on the head at regular intervals till he falls over. The affair with the conjurer's table, where Charlie stumbles on to the forbidden button and lets loose the birds, rabbits, pigs, geese, balloons and so on, and in dismay tries to put them back while they fill the world around him—as we, all our lives, are loosing wings and absurdities and small bestialities that surprise and dismay us, flying about our heads and wriggling under our fingers—this motive is the most boldly imagined that I remember in any Chaplin film.

There are two things that, though easily understood, perhaps, as privately compensatory and as easily condoned, are regrettable, and need either to go farther and be more complete in their own kind or to come out of the next Chaplin venture. One is the less abstract general make-up, the entire mask of the face and figure, including the movement and pantomime now and then. The other is the conscious and elaborate pathos that appears two or three times, most of all in the scene near the very end, where the circus wagons have all passed, taking along with them the beloved girl, who has been given to the other man by Charlie, and we see him sitting alone, the paper torn from one of the clown properties, with the sole star on it, on the ground at his feet. Such effects as this will Charlie Chaplin's pathos to a wider public, no doubt, and so may serve to add to him a slightly different sort of popularity. But the whole world, often unconsciously perhaps, has already felt his pathos in its truest kind, and the scene mars what has just gone before in *The Circus*: he has no need of that sort of fact.

Meanwhile remain the directness and finality of those conceptions and those images that express them—the figure with the pile of plates running from the mule that is also so interested and hostile; the ghastly tightrope walking with the monkeys climbing up over him, stripping off his elegance and crazy exaltation; the turns in the mirror maze; the flights with the trapeze belt; and that constant tipping of his hat, at an insult, an order, an audience's applause, a race with the thief, as if always there must be that little leaping up to happiness and what is sweet in life, always the rebuff, always that foolish leaping up again.

Seeing *The Circus* more than once, and thinking on this art of Charlie Chaplin's that I see in it and of him also, I think of how much went to the creation of a single movement, a single perfect invention or motive or image, even a pause; exactly as so many centuries went to the development of an organ like the eye, or as so many forces, seasons, wind, rain, and so much of the chemistry of dust, went to the half-lights in the depths of a flower. I wonder if art is always like this, if it is something out of the memory, a voice of something past, the immortal come to us out of death; I wonder if art is like the return of a soul to its old life, of a ghost to its memory.

STANLEY KAUFFMANN

The Circus

Stanley Kauffmann (b. 1916) has been reviewing movies for The New Republic *since 1958. He is the author of seven novels, innumerable plays, and several collections of his movie pieces as well as a very affecting memoir,* Albums of Early Life. *His standards are high, his style sober, and his value—in an era when movie criticism grows increasingly trivial—becomes ever more impressive. This essay, a tribute to one of the delights of his childhood, is perhaps more warmly affectionate than many of his reviews.*

I saw Charlie Chaplin's *The Circus* in 1928, the year it came out, and loved it. I saw it about twenty years later, at a private showing, and loved it. I saw it again recently, in its first commercial release in more than forty years, and loved it again. Obviously the "I" was vastly different each time. One proof of Chaplin's genius is that the same film had the same fundamental effect on three different people, and this is not an egocentric proof because there must be millions who have had similar experiences with his pictures. But with *The Circus*, the experience is particularly striking—even more touching—because with the last two viewings, I've known that it isn't one of Chaplin's very best.

Naturally, that is strictly a relative statement.

In this film the Tramp is hanging around sideshows, is chased by a cop, and flees—into the main ring of a circus. The audience there, which was bored by the clowns, laughs heartily at this chase. The ringmaster-owner hires the Tramp to make him a clown, but the Tramp can't learn the traditional skits. He is fired, is again chased into the ring—by a donkey—and again convulses the audience. This time the wily ringmaster hires him as a prop man and arranges to have him chased into the ring at every performance. The Tramp is a hit but doesn't know it. The bareback rider, who is the daughter of the ringmaster and whom the Tramp loves, finally opens his eyes to his success. But when he learns that she is in love with someone else, the Tramp loses his ability to be funny. He brings the two lovers together, then lets the circus go on without him.

The Circus is slim, and part of the slimness is purely dimensional— it is Chaplin's shortest feature after *The Kid*. But there is also internal slimness: the story lacks drama and progression, and the supporting characters are not well-developed. The girl—played by Merna Kennedy, the most pallid of his leading ladies—lacks the gamine vitality of the waif in *Modern Times* or the complexity of the dance hall girl in *The Gold Rush*. (I saw the latter again recently and noted once more how subtly Chaplin assumes that we know she is a prostitute, without ever saying so, and proceeds to build the Tramp's pathos on the substructure of that assumption.) The only mildly colorful character here is the ringmaster, the girl's father, who in some books is called her stepfather. His brutality to the girl is stock villainy, but his handling of the circus has cynical verity.

Still, if *The Circus* lacks drama in its story, the dramatic structure of its comedy episodes is marvelous; and if the characters are thin, the thematic implications are not.

As for the first, Chaplin only occasionally uses an isolated gag. For instance, when he is dusting things in the circus one day, he takes the magician's goldfish out of the bowl, wipes them off, and puts them back. But, for the most part, the comic incidents are part of a knitted structure that grows to considerable size from a quite small beginning. I'll trace one example.

A pickpocket lifts a fat wallet and a watch from an old man in the sideshow crowd. The old man discovers the theft, and the pickpocket quickly shoves the stolen goods, unobserved, into the pocket of the Tramp, whose back is toward him. The starving Tramp is now (1) an innocent thief and (2) the unwitting professor of the means to end his hunger.

That is the simple beginning; now see what happens. In front of a hot dog stand, the Tramp steals bites of a hot dog held by a baby over his father's shoulder. This would be funny anyway, but we know that the Tramp has enough money in his pocket to buy the whole hot dog stand. While he is gazing longingly at the franks, the pickpocket approaches and tries to lift back the loot. This time a cop catches him with his hand in the Tramp's pocket and restores the loot to the "rightful" owner.

Amazed at his luck, the Tramp orders about a dozen franks. While he waits, he pulls out "his" watch grandly and looks at the time—just as the old man passes whose watch it really is. When the old man sees the Tramp also pull out his wallet, he calls a cop. The Tramp runs. Meanwhile the pickpocket has escaped from *his* cop. In a wonderful tracking shot the Tramp and the pickpocket run toward us side by side at full speed, each one with a cop behind him. Then the Tramp raises his hat to the pickpocket in salute, and they split in different directions.

But they meet again in a funhouse to which they flee, where Chaplin hilariously mimics a life-size mechanical doll and where there are marvelous optical tricks in a mirror maze. (Did Orson Welles remember this scene when he made *The Lady from Shanghai?*) At last the cop chases him into the circus ring and, after further complications with a magician's apparatus, into a new life. The Tramp escapes, returns the wallet and watch *en passant*, then hides in a chariot and sleeps. Next day he is discovered and hired.

All this exploded out of a tiny capsule: the pickpocket putting his loot in the Tramp's pocket. After that, all that was needed was the insanity of strict logic. But it is not "mere" logic, it is a dramatist's, including by implication everything that has gone before. The progress is not linear but cellular.

The theme of the film is a contrast between life and art. The Tramp is funny as a man. He is unfunny when he tries to amuse in a circus skit. His funniness is in his spontaneous being; consciousness kills it. There is one brief period during which he knows he is being funny, after the girl tells him he has been a hit for some time. With that confidence he can continue; but he loses that confidence as soon as he learns she doesn't love him, and he cannot "make" funny again.

Chaplin was always fascinated with this confrontation of a funny *man* with a theatrical environment in which people are trying to make emotion. In one of his earliest shorts, *A Film Johnnie* (1914), he follows some actors into a studio and bursts open several contrived scenes with the reality of his being. In one of his last features, *Limelight* (1952), he is still concentrating on the dividing line between facing audiences with comic equipment and facing life with comic bravery. At the end of *The Circus*, in one of the loveliest shots in any Chaplin film, he stands on the circus grounds as the wagons roll away one by one. Finally alone, he sits, and we see he is in the middle of a circle that was marked on the ground by the circus rings. The theater has once again become the world.

Chaplin has added a score for this new release, which is adequate though full of sudden cutoffs, and he includes a song, sung by himself at the beginning — "Swing, Little Girl" — as Merna Kennedy dangles idly in a trapeze. In best kindness, let us say that the song is an echo of a bygone age. But then so is the courtliness with which he treats the girl he loves or the pickpocket from whom he's parting. So complete is the magic with which this chivalry envelopes him that it gives him a physical magic: his wing collar is always neat and clean whether he is in a circus, an alley, the Alaskan gold rush, or sleeping by a roadside. To my knowledge, no one has ever objected to the impossibility of this haberdashery — nor do I: which is one more proof of the persuasion of genius. We *want* Chaplin to be as he is for our sakes, ducking with polite aplomb and clean collar the outstretched hand of the monster policeman of the universe. Hart Crane understood this. When he wrote "Chaplinesque," he spoke of Chaplin as "we":

> We will sidestep, and to the final smirk
> Dally the doom of that inevitable thumb
> That slowly chafes its puckered index toward us,
> Facing the dull squint with what innocence
> And what surprise!

ALEXANDER WOOLLCOTT

Charlie—As Ever Was

If he is remembered at all today, it is as the model for Sheridan Whiteside, the acerbic drama critic in the often revived Kaufman-Hart comedy, The Man Who Came to Dinner—*a role he often played, with considerable relish, in touring companies. In his day, however, Alexander Woollcott (1887–1943) was a force to be reckoned with in American culture: he had been a* New York Times *drama critic, a* New Yorker *columnist, a best-selling author, and, most famously, a regular on* Information Please, *a hugely popular radio quiz show on which the audience posed difficult questions to a panel of certified "intellectuals." Woollcott's public persona was "high camp" long before Susan Sontag popularized the term—affected, precious, yet often whimsical and sentimental. In this piece, however, his worst stylistic characteristics are largely hidden as he offers a good account not only of* City Lights *but of the universality of Chaplin's hold even on figures as eccentric (and annoying) as Woollcott himself was.*

A great statue is being unveiled. It is a group of three heroic figures in marble, hidden now under a canvas covering that is like a gigantic tea-cozy. At the tug of a rope, when the right moment comes, these swaddling clothes will fall away and the sculptor's work will greet the sun and sky. For this right moment a mighty, milling multitude waits in the square. Waits while the band plays and the pennants flutter. Waits while the fat governor falls all over himself shaking hands with the more aggressively prominent and hatchet-faced club-women who come simpering into the speakers' stand. Waits while huge bouquets and floral horseshoes are duly hoisted into view. Waits while the dedicatory speeches (fortunately inaudible) are squawked into the microphone.

At last the breathless moment comes. Everyone rises. The military guard of honor goes into a catalepsy of attention. The band lets out a blare of triumph. The rope is pulled. The canvas shivers and drops to the ground. The statue emerges in its splendor. And in the lap of the central figure, on the knees of Columbia herself, a little tramp lies curled up in the comfort of a nap, a homeless waif now grossly intruded upon in his snug refuge, even as he was sleeping the sleep of the pure in heart.

In all officialdom there is consternation unutterable. But from the milling multitude—of which you and I by now are part—comes a fond roar in recognition of this bantam tramp now tipping his hat disarmingly. This *soigné* ragamuffin, who is so visibly sorry to have disturbed the nice celebration, is no stranger. Not he. We recognize his battered but cherished derby, his jaunty bamboo stick, his absurd black patch of a mustache, his monstrous shoes, and the desperate, defiant elegance of his shabby clothes. It is Charlie, Charlie—as ever was. Charlie—with the odds, as always, against him. Charlie—God bless him!

Revisiting us as a comet might. Returning after four years of loitering on the other side of the moon. Bringing to a sore and anxious world a gift of healing laughter and quickening, cleansing, inexplicable tears. A gift comparable, let us say—there is really no good analogy anywhere—to the sweet melodies that Franz Schubert left behind him when he visited this earth. Or comparable—and this is nearer—to the tale a jolly old pedagogue told to some wide-eyed children on a river's bank one afternoon and then put into a book which he signed Lewis Carroll.

Off and on during the next two years, in sundry towns the world around, you may come upon the new Chaplin picture which, for no good reason, is called *City Lights*. It began in February of this year a spasmodic series of releases, and in the town where I happen to live, during the week after its first showing, no one talked much of anything else. A couple of our banks had closed their doors and a few of our judges were hastily leaving town, but as men met on the street the first word between them would be "Have you seen it?" And the question needed no elaboration.

It is a great brotherhood, the Chaplinites. There has been nothing in the world quite like the sheer fraternity of his following since the novels of Charles Dickens were new. When *David Copperfield* was first appearing a few chapters at a time, each monthly installment bound as a slim green pamphlet, there would be a considerable dropping around to any house in the neighborhood that had received one. "Have you read it?" men asked each other in London, when the earliest editions of *A Christmas Carol* were issuing from the press. And the answer would be, "Yes, God bless him, I have." I remember my grandmother telling me how she used to wait each month for the installment of *David Copperfield*, and how it was at a neighbor's house, one afternoon late in 1850, that someone read her the fateful paragraph, just off the boat from England, which reads:

> He led me to the shore. And on that part of it where she and I had looked for shells, two children—on that part of it where some lighter fragments of the old boat, blown down last night, had been scattered by the wind—among the ruins of the home he had wronged—I saw him lying with his head upon his arm, as I had often seen him lie at school.

She caught up her shawl and ran home through the twilight with the news, the heart-breaking news, that Steerforth was dead.

Now, as one neighbor to another, as I might call across the fence from my back yard to yours, I here report on the latest installment of a saga told in another idiom by another Charles. This other Charles learned his humanity also in the same streets of London through which he, too, once wandered ragged and hungry as a child.

It has often been said of Charles Dickens (not quite accurately, by the way) that, though he created scores of immortal characters, there was not a gentleman in the lot. It must be said of Charles Chaplin that he has created only one character, but that one, in his matchless courtesy, in his unfailing gallantry—his preposterous innocent gallantry, in a world of gross Goliaths—that character is, I think, the finest gentleman of our time.

In the latest chapter of this gentleman's adventures he has his full share of the anguish of this world. This time his vagrant steps bring him across the pathway of a blind girl who must sell flowers all day long on a street corner. At first sight he is sick with love and pity and from that moment he must needs be her knight-errant, emptying her flower basket with his lavish purchases and luxuriating in the stolen sweetness of her romantic belief that he is some rich and handsome gallant who will one day carry her off on his milk-white steed.

To pay the overdue rent of her tenement home and to buy the surgery that will restore her sight he steals and goes to prison. It is a pretty forlorn knight-errant who creeps out of jail some months later. The shabby elegance is in tatters. The once incorrigibly cheerful face has lost its fine defiance. Newsboys pelt him with their bean-blowers and he can only drag himself along. Then he sees her—her sight restored, her flower-basket expanded into a resplendent shop, her loveliness become radiant. She is the work of his hands—the oblivious work of his loving hands. And at the sight of the little hobo she cries out: "Did you ever see such a spectacle?" and goes into gales of laughter.

As the picture was originally made, Charlie gave one terrified look at this toppling of the tower his dreams had built, then tipped his eternally propitiatory hat and, with this secret locked forever in his heart, went shuffling off into eternity. But now a pang of pity sends her flying after him with a flower for his preposterous buttonhole and a bit of silver for his hunger. As her hand touches his, by a sense far quicker than her new-found sight, she knows him. And the end of the chapter is just the incredulous wonder in his eyes as he looks at her. You do not need sound effects to make you hear the thump of his heart against his ribs, and the glory that shines round him is not made by any lights that electricians can devise.

The picture, of course, is a history of his struggles to fend for her. For her sake he is decoyed into the prize ring for a couple of nightmare rounds that constitute as mad a ballet as ever which danced on a blasted heath in the dark of the moon. For her sake he goes to work as a street-cleaner. His fastidious displeasure at the goings-on of a single horse lends point to his nimble avoidance of the next street, down which a pack of mules chance to be jogging. He seeks refuge around the corner, only to be confronted there with a sight that discourages him utterly. A moment later the plausible cause of his discouragement lumbers into view. It is an elephant.

But his great hope is pinned to the singularly intermittent generosity of a rollicking old sport who, when in his cups, has a maudlin passion for Charlie, but on sober reflection next day cannot recall ever having seen the fellow before. Thus is Charlie again and again lifted to the stars only to be cast down next morning. The distaste with which the recovering Mæcenas discovers his erstwhile protégé in bed with him cannot be expressed in such poor things as words. And a moment later Charlie, who in last night's debauch had been promised motor cars, a home for life, the kingdoms of the earth, finds himself out on the doorstep in the morning sunlight with nothing to show for his recent dizzying good fortune except one banana, salvaged from the wreck of his hopes as he was in the act of being thrown out by the butler. Well, at that, a banana is something. You can imagine how smartly he peels it as he steps forth once more to make his fortune, somehow imparting to the homely process of peeling a banana the elegant nonchalance of a duke drawing a monogrammed cigarette from a platinum case.

Some will rejoice most in the moment when the sadism of an Apache dance so outrages our Charlie's sense of chivalry that, with dignity but firmness, he kicks the Apache in the stomach. Other will chuckle reminiscently over the episode of the spaghetti course, when Charlie must eat endlessly because his fork has caught up by mistake an interminable paper streamer. But I suppose *City Lights* will be remembered longest for the mishap of the penny whistle. You see, at a party, he is blowing it in a resolute attempt to partake of the general gayety. When some jocund reveler slaps him on the back he swallows the whistle. Thereafter he is most unhappy. The newcomer does not rest easy within him. He begins to hiccup and, at each surge, the whistle within lets out a little, persistent cheep.

This grows embarrassing. Guests draw away from him. A baritone, who is determined to sing, cannot get started. Always his impressive preliminary pause is disturbed by the whistle invisible. Finally, with the feelings of a leper, Charlie staggers out into the garden to be alone in the moonlight with his unhappiness. Just when he thinks he has conquered it, he hiccups again. A taxicab responds, and when it is silently waved away, the driver departs cursing. Another pause. Another hiccup. Several collies respond. When Charlie comes back to the party, he is followed by all the dogs in the neighborhood.

All of which is pretty comical, and each audience in which I have (with the aid of a shoe-horn) imbedded myself for a glimpse of *City Lights* has rocked with laughter—your correspondent doing a tidy bit of rocking himself. Mr. Chaplin's comedic gift is at high tide. Quite as if he thought of *City Lights* as a gauntlet thrown down to all of Hollywood, he has taken pride in cramming this cake with the richest plums of his invention. Yet when, as has occasionally happened in the past fifteen years, someone says to me (just for something to say, I suppose) that this or that new-risen comedian is "funnier than Chaplin," I am always taken by incurable surprise. But only because I never think of the dauntless Charlie as a figure of fun. Or at least not as primarily a figure of fun. Primarily Charlie is innocent courage, gallantry—the unquenchable in mankind—taking on flesh and walking this earth to give us heart.

And if Chaplin, of whose incomparable art and winged imagination this insouciant tatterdemalion is the creature—as authentic a creation, mind you, as Falstaff or Don Quixote—if in our time he is the ultimate clown, it is because he is an artist whose craftsmanship is at once as sinewy and as exquisite as Heifetz's, and whose secret of the sorcery of motion is the same that transformed Pavlowa into thistledown. I would be prepared to defend the proposition that this darling of the mob is the foremost living artist. There could be no conceivable need to defend the proposition that he is the foremost living actor. It so happens that he drifted into the movies as a medium, and whenever the world's first actor makes a picture that matches the best work he has done—*City Lights* belongs in the gallery of immortals with *The Kid* and *Shoulder Arms* and *The Pilgrim*—why, surely some such immoderate fandango in the streets as this discourse involves is, as they say, indicated.

But just as no one can rely on the grandfather's clock in the hall who does not keep in mind that the creaky old timepiece is always about half an hour fast, so, perhaps, you ought to know something of the predilections of your oracular correspondent. For one thing, I suppose I should break down at this point and admit that if there is one thing I cannot abide in this raucous age it is the transitory monstrosity known as the talkie. This aversion is essentially undebatable, just as I could never explain to the manufacturer who put out a Venus de Milo with a clock in her stomach that he had, to my notion, got hold of a bad idea. His dashing invention won first prize in the Bad Taste Exhibition held in New York twenty years ago, and yet it seems to me, as I look back on it, no uglier a piece of fancy work than this idea of a talking photograph.

I have made this avowal thus far down on the page, not to be furtive about it, but only because it does seem to me irrelevant. Charlie is Chaplin, and nothing can be proved by him. The fact that the public has clasped to its multitudinous bosom this movie without a single spoken syllable in all its crowded length is no proof that the talkie is doomed or even on the wane and no proof that any other player would be thus accepted at his face value.

So much for *City Lights*. So much for Charlie. Please think of my testimony as one of thankfulness. I sometimes wish I had lived in my grandfather's time instead of today. The pattern of life was less complicated then. This was a cleaner, greener land, and a man who took to the highroad might breathe, instead of gasoline vapors, a forgotten boon called air. But there are times when I would not swap places with my grandfather, and one of those times is when there is a new chapter of the Charlie saga to be seen in town.

I wrote that last sentence in the present tense. But that was bravado. For there is no use pretending that we can count on such chapters as an endlessly recurrent phenomenon. Indeed, there must, I think, fall across each screen on which *City Lights* is shown a shadow not cast by any of the properties or puppets of the Chaplin lot. It is the shadow of a foreboding, an uneasy feeling that in this visitation we are seeing our Charlie for the last time.

Well, that is as may be. At all events, his like has not passed this way before. And we shall not see his like again.

GEORGE JEAN NATHAN

The Chaplin Buncombe

George Jean Nathan (1882–1958) is another great intel-
lectual figure of his day who is now not much more than
a footnote in our cultural history. Founder (with H. L.
Mencken) of The American Mercury, *he was in the*
1920s "virtually literary dictator of New York," to borrow
a phrase from an antique literary encyclopedia. As a
critic his work was marked by an air of elitism, scorn for
the popular arts, and a belief in "art for art's sake." He
particularly despised the movies—which may partially
account for the negative tone of this consideration of
City Lights *in particular, Chaplin in general. Alas, the*
Little Tramp did not measure up to Eugene O'Neill,
whose work Nathan particularly championed.

1. Charlie Chaplin is a superior clown.
2. Charlie Chaplin is the most famous product of the Hollywood studios.
3. Charlie Chaplin is an international favorite.
4. Charlie Chaplin often combines with his humor the effective touch of pathos.
5. Charlie Chaplin is one of the few really expert pantomimists that the screen has developed.

From *Passing Judgements* by George Jean Nathan (New York, 1934).

1. *True.*
2. *True.*
3. *True.*
4. *True.*
5. *True.*

1. Charlie Chaplin is a great artist.
2. Charlie Chaplin is a genius.
3. Charlie Chaplin is a great actor with infinite possibilities as a tragedian.
4. Charlie Chaplin is a great movie director.
5. Charlie Chaplin shows himself in the preparation of his pictures to be a highly imaginative scenarist and a skilful musician.
1. *Eliminate the adjective and heavily qualify the noun.*
2. *Bosh.*
3. *A limited actor with no possibilities as a tragedian.*
4. *Competent but certainly not great.*
5. *A sometimes moderately imaginative scenarist and a very shabby musician.*

Now that we have had his picture, "City Lights," believed by Chaplin himself to mark the pinnacle of his talents in the various directions above named, some such critical stock-taking of his gifts and resources may be undertaken. Since he devoted three solid years of effort to the picture, it may—even without Chaplin's word for it—be held as a standard of more or less final judgment. In what light does it disclose him? It discloses him as still the ingratiating clown with a comedy routine that remains exactly the same as that displayed in his very earliest pictures. Its humor, edited by him, consists chiefly in a series of ancient "gags," such as the jocosity implicit in a stab in the seat, in the eating of paper streams under the impression that they are spaghetti, in the adjustment of the thumb to the nose, in the accidental falling backward into a body of water and splashing around therein, in an inopportune attack of hiccoughs (on this occasion embellished with a whistle), in the pursuit of a cigar butt, and in the propulsion from a house of an unwelcome guest at the point of a toe. Its musical accompaniment, save for a few moments' burlesque of the talking pictures, amounts to nothing more than a cheap para-phrase of such past popular tunes as "Valencia" and the like. And its remarkably original and imaginative thematic thread of pathos—so lavishly praised by the journalistic enthusiasts—is discovered to be the long familiar motif dear to Max Maurey's Grand Guignol and the sentimental novelists and playwrights of a bygone day: the blindness which imagines it beholds beauty and, with the return of vision, finds to its own and another's heartache only the commonplace and the sadly ugly.

Through all this, Chaplin moves as he has always, without much variation of any kind, moved. He is still the fundamentally proficient zany that he was years ago, but so inelastic is his technique that his every movement, every grimace, every gesture, every eye-lift is fore-tellable a second or two ahead of itself. Every now and then in his career—or at least since he abandoned the high silk hat he used in his first picture and put on the funny little derby—he has hit upon a jolly or tender bit of stage business that has lent to his performance a momentary superficial aspect of novelty. But, in the main, his antics, often winning though they are, have followed a more or less established pattern.

The funniest moment in "Easy Street" was not Chaplin's, but the scene wherein a monstrous thug, walking down the street with a girl after committing murder, arson, mayhem and what not, suddenly reflects that he is walking on the wrong side of the lady and chevalier-like quickly changes his position. Certainly half the pathos touched with humor in "The Kid" was due to the performance in that picture of the then little Jackie Coogan. The monkeyshines of the fire department, rather than the tricks of Chaplin, constituted the most comical moments in "The Fireman," and the audience's loud shouts of mirth over the spectacle of Chaplin hanging on to the hut toppling over the precipice in "The Gold Rush" were evoked not by Chaplin but by a hired dummy. It would be interesting for a better memory than mine to plumb the various films further and determine just how much of their real humor or pathos was directly attributable to Chaplin's performances or to those of others. What is to be credited to Chaplin as a scenario-compiler or a director is apparently not always properly to be credited to him as an actor.

In "City Lights," Chaplin had a rich opportunity to make use of sounds, both for their own valuable collaborative effect and in the way of travesty, which he did not take advantage of. After the first few moments with their imitation of the talking screen's voices in terms of musical instruments—a fetching idea—there was no use of sound that was not stale and obvious. The imagination shown by René Clair, the French director, in "Under the Roofs of Paris," in such a situation, say, as that wherein the increasing volume of an approaching train accompanies the mounting anger and desperate combat of the two gangsters, was nowhere visible in the Chaplin film. The musical invention and humor divulged by the director of such a German picture as "Two Hearts in Waltz Time" were completely absent, as was the murderous talking picture burlesque of even some such third-rate Mack Sennett film as "A Hollywood Hero."

The newspaper hallelujah chorus, perhaps not altogether oblivious of the size of the advertisements and the consequent glee of the advertising departments, proclaimed "City Lights" and Chaplin—I quote literally—in the following terms: "superb," "incomparable," magnificent," "a dazzling pattern of comedy and pathos," "a great genius," "an artist without a peer," "killingly funny," "a very brilliant film," etc., etc. The picture and Chaplin were not any of these—and by a long shot. I should sum up the situation rather by saying that the picture was one of the poorest that Chaplin has made and that Chaplin himself, while still the best clown that the movies have bred, and while a pantomimist above the ordinary, is no longer, because of endless repetition, anything like so amusing as once he was. In plain fact, he is frequently a bore.

I V

A Mid-Life Crisis

Everybody's Language

Yes, he's that Winston Churchill (1874–1965) — Britain's wartime prime minister and one of the great figures of twentieth-century world history. In 1935, however, he was out of power and no longer a member of His Majesty's cabinet, making his living as an author, lecturer, and journalist. He and Chaplin met on one of the actor's trips to London, and thereafter Churchill always visited Chaplin when he was in Los Angeles. As you can see in this piece, Churchill was another writer who harbored high, traditional ambitions for Chaplin, but with greater shrewdness about where his strengths lay than his more literary supporters (see Stark Young's essay) demonstrated.

In a room in St. Thomas' Hospital, London, a man lay dying. He had had a good life — a full life. He had been a favorite in the music halls. He had tasted the triumphs of the stage. He had won a measure of fame as a singer. His home life had been happy. And now death had come for him. While he was yet in the prime of manhood, with success still sweet in his mouth, the curtain was falling — and forever.

From *Collier's*, October 26, 1935, by permission of Curtis Brown Group Ltd., London.

The other windows of the hospital were dark. In this one alone a light burned. And below it, outside in the darkness, shivering with cold and numbed with fear, a child stood sobbing. He had been told that there was no hope, but his wild heart prayed for the miracle that could not happen, even while he waited for the light to go out and the compassionate hesitations that would tell him his father was no more. The dying man and the child outside the window both bore the same name—Charles Chaplin.

Destiny shifts us here and there upon the checkerboard of life, and we know not the purpose behind the moves. His father's death brought a safe, comfortable world crashing about Charlie Chaplin's head, and plunged his mother, his brother and himself into poverty. But poverty is not a life sentence. It is a challenge. To some it is more—it is an opportunity. It was so to this child of the theater. In the kaleidoscopic life of London's mean streets he found tragedy and comedy—and learned that their springs lie side by side. He knew the problems of the poor, not from the aloof angle of the social investigator, but at firsthand. They were his mother's problems—and his own. But the very struggle of life gave a new zest to common things. And upon the margin of subsistence human nature has few reticences. It reveals itself far more clearly and fully than in more sheltered surroundings. So daily Charlie's keen eyes noted some new aspect of the exposed expanse of life around him.

In somewhat similar circumstances, many years before, another boy had found, amid the rank luxuriance of London life, a key to fame and fortune. He also had been desperately poor. He also had missed much that should be the birthright of every child. But the alchemy of genius transmuted bitterness and suffering into the gold of great literature and gave us the novels of Charles Dickens.

THE BEGINNINGS OF GENIUS

Between these two there is, I think, an essential similarity. Both knew hardness in childhood. Both made their misfortunes steppingstones to success. They developed along different lines, chose different mediums of expression, but both quarried in the same rich mine of common life and found there treasure of laughter and drama for the delight of all mankind. Mark Twain, left fatherless at twelve, had substantially the same experience, though in a different setting. He would never have written Huckleberry Finn had life been kinder in his youth.

So we need not regret the shadows that fell over Charlie Chaplin's early life. Without them his gifts might have shone less brightly, and the whole world would have been poorer. Genius is essentially a hardy plant. It thrives in the east wind. It withers in a hothouse. That is, I believe, true in every walk of life. The reason the historic English families have produced so many men of distinction is that, on the whole, they have borne great responsibilities rather than enjoyed great wealth. Their younger sons, especially, have usually had to make their own way in the world, to stand on their own feet, to rely on their own merits and their own efforts. I am glad that I had to earn my living from the time that I was a young man. Had I been born heir to millions I should certainly have had a less interesting life.

Naturally and inevitably, once school days were over, the youthful Charlie Chaplin found his way on to the stage. And when he was twenty-one he signed a contract which took him to the Untied States and Canada with the Fred Karno Comedy Company. This American tour was, in some ways, as important to the development of the Chaplin that we know as were his early days in London. It was one of the great formative experiences of his career. We in England like to think of Charlie Chaplin as an Englishman, but America gave a new direction, a new edge to his quality. It opened to him new fields of character and circumstances.

Twenty-five years ago, when the young actor crossed the Atlantic, life in the States was more fluid perhaps than it is today. Its forms had not set. Personalities were more important than conventions. Democracy was not only a political institution but a social fact. Class distinctions mattered comparatively little when the hired hand of today was so often the employer of tomorrow, and the majority of professional men had paid for their university training with the work of their hands.

A PURELY AMERICAN TYPE

Even poverty wore a different face in America. It was not the bitter, grinding destitution Charlie had encountered in the London slums and which has now, thanks to the extension of social services, largely disappeared. In many cases it was a poverty deliberately chosen, rather than imposed from without.

Every cinema-goer is familiar with the Chaplin tramps, but I wonder how many of them have reflected how characteristically American are these homeless wanderers. In the dwindling ranks of the English tramps one finds all sorts of people—from the varsity graduate whose career has ended in ruin and disgrace, to the half-imbecile illiterate who has been unemployable since boyhood. But they all have one thing in common—they belong to the great army of the defeated. They still maintain the pretense of looking for work—but they do not expect to find it. They are spiritless and hopeless.

The American hobo of twenty-five years ago was of an entirely different type. Often he was not so much an outcast from society as a rebel against it. He could not settle down, either in a home or a job. He hated the routine of regular employment and loved the changes and chances of the road. Behind his wanderings was something of the old adventurous urge that sent the covered wagons lumbering across the prairie towards the sunset.

There were also upon the highways of America, in the old days of prosperity, many men who were not tramps at all in the ordinary sense of the term. They were traveling craftsmen, who would work in one place for a few weeks or months, and then move on to look for another job elsewhere. Even today, when work is no longer easy to secure, the American wanderer still refuses to acknowledge defeat.

REDISCOVERING PANTOMIME

That indomitable spirit is an integral part of the make-up of the screen Charlie Chaplin. His portrayal of the underdog is definitely American rather than British. The English workingman has courage in plenty, but those whom prolonged unemployment has forced on the road are nowadays usually broken and despairing. The Chaplin tramp has a quality of defiance and disdain.

But the American scene as a whole has influenced Chaplin—its variety, its color, its animation, its strange and spectacular contrasts. And the States did more than this for the little English actor; they provided the opportunity for which, without knowing it, he had been waiting. They introduced him to the ideal medium for his genius, the motion picture.

It was a sultry day in July, 1913. A bored film magnate, Mr. A. Kessel, was strolling along Broadway. Pausing at Hammerstein's Music Hall to chat with the manager, he heard roar upon roar of laughter. The sound interested him. It had been a long time since anyone had made him laugh.

"I expect it's that young Chaplin that's causing the cackle," said the manager. "He's pretty good."

So in went Mr. Kessel to see the Fred Karno Comedy Company perform A Night in a London Music Hall and to investigate young Chaplin.

Soon he was laughing with the rest of the audience. But when Mr. Kessel laughed in a place of public entertainment, his mirth meant business. Round he went to the back, was ushered into Chaplin's tiny dressing-room, and at once proceeded to offer the Englishman seventy-five dollars a week to play in Keystone comedies. It was more money than he had ever earned before, but Charlie said "No."

That only made Mr. Kessel more determined. He raised his bid to one hundred dollars a week. Still Charlie said "No." For the moment the film magnate left it at that. But now he was no longer bored. He had a new interest in life. He wanted Chaplin.

Presently he returned to the attack. This time his offer was one hundred and fifty dollars. Charlie still hesitated, but in the end he accepted. And so to Hollywood and the beginning of the most astounding career in cinema history.

It is Mr. Chaplin's dream to play tragic roles as well as comic ones. The man whose glorious fooling made *Shoulder Arms* a favorite with war-weary veterans of the trenches wants to reinterpret Napoleon to the world. There are other characters, as far removed from those in which he won preeminence, which he desires to portray.

Those who smile at these ambitions have not appreciated Chaplin's genius at its true worth. No mere clown, however brilliant, could ever have captured so completely the affections of the great public. He owes his unrivaled position as a star to the fact that he is a great actor, who can tug at our heartstrings as surely as he compels our laughter. There are moments, in some of his films, of an almost unbearable poignancy.

It is a great achievement, and one possible only to a consummate actor, to command at once tears and laughter. But it is the laughter which predominates, and Mr. Chaplin is perfectly right in desiring an opportunity of playing straight tragedy. Until he does so, his pathos will be regarded as merely a by-product of his toothbrush mustache and the ludicrous Chaplin walk.

I believe that, had it not been for the coming of the talkies, we would already have seen this great star in a serious role. He is the one figure of the old silent screen to whom the triumph of the spoken word has meant neither speech nor extinction. He relies, as of old, upon a pantomime that is more expressive than talk. But while the silence of Charlie Chaplin has lost none of its former magic, would Mr. Charles Chaplin, in a role of a kind completely unfamiliar to his audiences, and of which they would almost certainly be highly critical, be able to "get away with it"?

Frankly, I do not wonder that he hesitates, just as he did when Mr. Kessel offered him his first film contract. But he would be taking no greater risk now than he did then. So I do not think that he will hesitate forever. Pantomime, of which he is a master, is capable of expressing every emotion, of communicating the subtlest shades of meaning. A man who can act with his whole body has no need of words, whatever part he plays.

It is the supreme achievement of Mr. Chaplin that he has revived in modern times one of the great arts of the ancient world—an art the secret of which was as completely and, apparently, as irrevocably lost as that of those glowing colors, fresh and vivid today as when they were first applied, which were the glory of the van Eycks.

PANTOMIMES IN ANCIENT ROME

The golden age of pantomime was under the early Caesars. Augustus himself, the first of the Roman emperors, is sometimes credited with its invention. Nero practiced it, as he wrote poetry, as a relaxation from the more serious pursuits of lust, incendiarism and gluttony. But the greatest pantomimes—the name in Ancient Rome denoted the performers, and not the art of which they were the exponents—gave their whole lives to acting in dumb show, till they had mastered the last potentialities of expression in movement and gesture.

When Christianity triumphed, the pantomimes fled. Their favorite subjects were too frankly physical for the Fathers of the Church, and they were not sufficiently adaptable to seek new ones in the shadow of the Cross. But the subjects were there, had they realized it. Chaplin showed that in *The Pilgrim*. You remember the sequence in which, as an escaped convict disguised in clerical attire, he finds himself in the pulpit, and tells the story of David and Goliath? It is a wonderful piece of mining, in which we follow every detail of the drama.

It was by accident that Chaplin rediscovered the art which, nineteen hundred years ago, cast its spell over the City of the Seven Hills. As a youth he was a member of a variety company touring the Channel Islands, home of a sturdy race to whom the King of England is still the Duke of Normandy. The islanders, speaking mainly the Norman-French patois of their ancestors, could not understand the Cockney phrases of the players, whose best jokes fell flat.

At last, in desperation, the company decided to try to get their effects by action and gesture. A single performance under the new conditions revealed Charles as a mime of genius and also showed him how powerful was the spell which this acting without words could cast over an audience. From that time he developed his natural gift for pantomimic expression and so unconsciously prepared himself for the day when the whole world should be his audience.

GESTURE MORE EFFECTIVE THAN THE VOICE

But the full flowering of his art came only after he was launched on his film career. He adapted his technique to the cinema and as he grew to appreciate at once the limitations and the possibilities of the screen, his mastery of the new mode of acting was perfected. He had realized that, as he himself had put it, "people can be moved more intensely by a gesture that by a voice."

American films generally were then in a highly favorable position. They were simpler, more direct than the best of the continental pictures, and consequently met the needs of a far wider audience. Had their producers and stars learned from Chaplin and the Europeans, the silent screen might have defied the talkies. The sound picture would have come just the same, but it would not have scooped the pool.

If we are ever to realize to the full the art of the cinema, I believe that it may be necessary deliberately to limit the mechanical aids we now employ so freely. I should like to see films without voices being made once more, but this time by producers who are alive to the potentialities of pantomime. Such pictures would be worth making, if only for this reason, that the audience for a talkie is necessarily limited by the factor of language, while the silent film can tell its story to the whole of the human race. Pantomime is the true universal tongue.

There are thousands of cinemas throughout the world which have never yet been wired for sound, and which constitute a market for non-talking pictures. Nor is it safe to assume that this is a shrinking market. There are many countries which lack the resources to make their own talkies. There are millions of people whose mother tongue will never be heard in any cinema and who understand thoroughly no other speech. As the standard of life rises throughout Asia and Africa, new cinemas will be built and a new film public will be created—a public which can be served most effectively by means of pantomime.

The English-speaking nations have here a great opportunity—and a great responsibility. The primitive mind thinks more easily in pictures than in words. The thing seen means more than the thing heard. The films which are shown amid the stillness of the African tropical night or under the skies of Asia may determine, in the long run, the fate of empires and of civilizations. They will promote, or destroy, the prestige by which the white man maintains his precarious supremacy amid the teeming multitudes of black and brown and yellow.

I hope that we shall not have to wait another four years for the next Chaplin picture. But it would be worth waiting for if he built up a team of actors and actresses who could use pantomime effectively. He has already shown his power of inspiring others by his production of A Woman of Paris and the grim realism with which the hardships of the Klondike pioneers were portrayed in The Gold Rush. And I see no reason why, if he can train such a company, he should not realize his ambition of playing the victor of Arcola. I think he might give us a picture of the young Napoleon that would be one of the most memorable things in the cinema.

Our difficulty in visualizing him in such a role is that we think of him as he appears on the screen. We think especially of his feet. Napoleon never had feet like that.

Neither has Chaplin. The feet are a "property"—the famous walk is the trick of a clever actor to suggest character and atmosphere. They are, in fact, the feet and walk of an ancient cabman, whom the youthful Charlie Chaplin encountered occasionally in the Kennington Road, in London. To their original owner they were not at all humorous. But the boy saw the comic possibilities of that uneasy progress. He watched the old man and copied his movements until he had mastered every step in the dismal repertoire and turned it into mirth.

The same power of observation, the same patient thoroughness, could be used—and would be used—to give us convincing characterizations of serious roles. Charlie Chaplin's feet are not a handicap; they represent an asset—the power to convert the thing seen into the thing shown.

And the real Chaplin is a man of character and culture. As Sidney Earle Chaplin put it, when interviewed at the tender age of five: "People get a wrong impression of Dad. It's not good style to throw pies, but he only does it in the films. He never throws pies at home."

I believe, therefore, that the future of Charlie Chaplin may lie mainly in the portrayal of serious roles in silent, or rather, non-talking films, and in the development of a universal cinema.

He need not ignore sound entirely. His pictures can be wedded to music. Natural sounds may be introduced. But these effects would be accessories only—the films could be shown—without any serious weakening of their appeal, in cinemas which were not wired for sound.

A TRAIL TO BLAZE

If Mr. Chaplin makes pictures of this kind, I think that he will not only increase his already great reputation, but he will blaze a trail which others will follow, and add enormously to the range of cinematic art.

It is a favorite cliché of film critics, in discussing talking pictures, to say that we cannot go back. In effect, they suggest that, because technical progress has given us sound, all films must be talkies and will continue to be so forever. Such statements reveal a radical misconception of the nature of progress and the nature of art. As well say that, because there is painting in oils, there must be no etchings; or that because speech is an integral part of a stage play, dialogue must be added to ballet. To explore the possibilities of the non-talking film, to make of it a new and individual art form, would not be a retrograde step, but an advance.

There are many brilliant and original minds associated with the cinema today. But there is no one so well equipped for this experiment as Mr. Chaplin. Possibly no one else would dare to make it.

I wish him good luck—and the courage of his own convictions and his own magnificent powers. But I hope also that he will not forget the world's need of laughter. Let him play in tragedy by all means. Let him display to us the full extent of his histrionic genius. But let him come back—at least occasionally—to the vein of comedy that has been the world's delight for twenty years.

Chaplin at Mid-Passage

*Max Eastman's (1883–1969) journey through political
life was almost archetypal. Founder of* The Masses, *in
the teens of the twentieth century the most important
American radical journal, his opposition to U.S. partic-
ipation in World War I, led to his trial for sedition.
Thereafter he became a Stalinist, a Trotskyite, and, finally, of all things, an editor of* Reader's Digest. *Along
his wandering way he was a poet, a critic, and a general
intellectual gadabout. Among his many books was* Enjoyment of Laughter, *a study of humor, from which the
following material is drawn. It is, as Eastman himself
was, surprisingly good-natured — a description not often
applied either to ideologues or to studies of comic theory. Eastman, incidentally, was a good and faithful
friend to Chaplin and wrote well and lengthily about
him in his autobiography,* Enjoyment of Living.

Charlie Chaplin is not an intrinsically comic character. He conveys,
on the contrary, when you meet him, the impression of a being that,
although slight and almost miniature, possesses a kind of perfection —
a grace, poise and agility both of body and speech, that you are not

moved to improve upon. I once heard an enamored woman sum up the impression—in words that Charlie will not like too well: "He is so exquisite that you feel like wrapping him up carefully and taking him home and setting him on the mantelpiece." Moreover, Chaplin is an extremely serious person, so serious that he will talk your very head off—he will lecture you into a sound sleep—if you get him on one of his favorite topics, like Social Credits or the fluctuations of the gold standard. Instead of a funny man, he is a man of humorous imagination, the most original, perhaps, since Mark Twain, and also a consummate actor. He can imagine and act like a funny man—like almost any funny man, for the little tramp that has become identified with his person in the public mind is but one of an endless repertory of such roles that he has at his command, if he were bold enough to show them. But in his own person he is impressive rather than funny. And it is this fact that sets him apart, and makes the word comedian seem a little inadequate to describe him. He is a poet of humor.

In Chaplin's comedies then, more than in others, we enjoy the representation, and not the actuality, of a comic person. In them we take one step toward the purely imaginative enjoyment of the ludicrous, and we see all the more clearly what the ludicrous is. The little tramp's shoes are too big; he can not manage his feet; his pants do not fit; he has a habit of getting in wrong wherever he goes. So much so, that at moments we feel more like crying than laughing. His humor, as we say, comes close to pathos. Or in the words of Milt Gross: "He's sotch a dolink, wot one minute he makes you you could rur from leffing und gradually in de naxt minute it becomes so sed, wot it could make you you should cry—is werry appalling to de emulsions."

This particular way of appealing to the "emulsions" is, of course, a very object-lesson in our theory of humor. If the same character and situation which were provoking us to comic laughter can by a mere movement of the wrist, the flexing of an eyebrow or a muscle round the lips, be made a cause for tears, it is clear that objectively the comic and the painful are the same. The character and situation remain unchanged, but we of a sudden have become serious. The opposite shift of feeling, described in the phrase "laughs it off," is equally good evidence of the correctness of our view.

I found Charlie Chaplin not only conscious of the distinction between pictorial humor and its point, but disposed to take a stand in favor of its having, in America in the future, a little more point.

"It seems to me," he said, "that there are two different kinds of laughter. Superficial laughter is an escape. The waiter comes in and the duck isn't cooked properly, and you pick it up and throw it at him—yes, and by God, he throws it back! That's an escape. It's a break in the monotony of normal conduct. That's superficial humor, slapstick. Subtle humor shows you that what you think is normal, isn't. This little tramp *wants* to get into jail. The audience thinks at first that he's ridiculous. But he isn't. He's right. The conditions are ridiculous. If I make them laugh that way, it's what I call subtle laughter.

"Modern humor frightens me a little. The Marx Brothers are frightening. Thurber, Stewart, Joe Cook, Benchley—yes, all of them. They say, 'All right, this is how we live and we'll live that way.' They go in for being crazy. It's a soul-destroying thing. They say, 'All right, you're insane, we'll appeal to your insanity.' They make insanity the convention. They make humor a premise. Acquiescence in everything disintegrating. Knocking everything down. Annihilating everything. There's no *conduct* in their humor. They haven't any attitude. It's up-to-date, of course—a part of the chaos. I think it's transitional."

. . . In Charlie Chaplin's film *The Immigrant* . . . while the shop steams into port he hangs over the rail retching and squirming in what seems a very death agony of nausea—hangs so far over, and stays so long, that only those really addicted to the sufferings of others can keep on laughing at this old gag, and then suddenly comes up in triumph with a fishline and a big live fish. That fish, and that instantaneous and total change of roles between the actor and the audience, are greeted with a roar of laughter. And yet the joke is wholly on the audience. They thought they were indulging a tendency to enjoy the sufferings of others, but found instead that the actor was playing a trick upon that very tendency.

I wish the defenders of the derision theory, as well as the Freudians, would go to see this picture, and hear an entire theaterful of people enjoy the sudden frustration of their sadistic impulse with more gusto and a louder laugh than they accorded to its satisfaction.

Charlie Chaplin himself rejects the idea that "there is hostility in all laughter." "Of course they are often sympathetic with me while they laugh!" he exclaims. And I think that exclamation worth more than quite a long volume of professorial apologies for laughter.

BROOKS ATKINSON

Charlie Chaplin

From 1924 until 1960, Brooks Atkinson (1894–1984) was the New York Times *drama critic and thus the most important voice in determining whether a play would live or die on Broadway. During World War II he served as a war correspondent for the* Times, *winning a Pulitzer Prize for his reporting from the Soviet Union. His was a gentlemanly critical voice, though he never suffered foolishness gladly, and he was more open to new voices than people in positions like his often are. Considering that his reviews had to be dashed off in the hour between a play's conclusion and his newspaper's deadline (he always wrote in longhand), they have a patient literacy that wears quite well. He only rarely wrote about film, but this piece about* Modern Times *(and his lifelong admiration for Chaplin) is an excellent example of Atkinson's modestly worn virtues.*

To be genuinely critical one must be in part detached. No matter how congenial the subject, one must be objective enough to retain some general perspective. Toward Charlie Chaplin, however, I am wholly idolatrous. Nothing said here will be half so judicial as the two pungent and enthusiastic bulletins Frank Nugent has posted in honor of the current *Modern Times*. But Mr. Nugent, who has exclusive rights to all screen pabulum in this newspaper, has given me permission this morning to prattle away about the beloved vagabond whose tottering image I first saw on a wrinkled screen more than twenty years ago. On Saturday evenings some itinerant impresario used to show films in the local hall of our Massachusetts town to the rag-time accompaniment of a facetious piano. All the boys used to go, racing noisily up the wooden stairs to the balcony in the hope of getting into the first row of seats. The colored and comic slide, "Ladies will kindly remove their hats," was the signal that at last the show was on. It lasted until almost ten o'clock, leaving just time enough to run to the butter-and-egg store for the family provisions before the crochety manager locked the door for the night.

In those days there was no such thing as a bad movie show. Every one enjoyed every film every Saturday night. But one night cross-eyed Ben Turpin, who was a familiar figure, appeared in the company of a ragged little tramp, who was new to us, and they fled the cops and floundered over the landscape in an epic style that was more hilarious than anything we had ever seen before. The laughter was titanic. No one knew the name of the clown who was making Ben Turpin look like old Sober-sides, for it was not the fashion then to pay much attention to the names of screen performers. But for some inexplicable reason his image was vivid. When it next appeared in a film entitled *The Janitor* he was already an old friend who improved upon acquaintance, and Charlie Chaplin was an easy name to remember, particularly when we begin to see it everywhere on bulletin boards and in store windows. From that time on we made it our business to see every Chaplin picture that appeared, and for the next few years they came out with grateful rapidity, although they were likely to be much too short for our taste. To the best of my knowledge I have seen every Chaplin film at least once, including an obscure Keystone comedy made before he assembled the costume and created the character of the tramp. To judge by the revivals that occasionally turn up in the "grind houses" off Broadway he has never been a better actor than he is today. There was some pretty crude stuff in those early films, although we all liked it well enough at the time.

To an idolator he can do no wrong. Some of the films have been better than others, and at least one of them, *The Idle Class*, was indisputably bad. Especially in those early, rushing days some of the gags were malodorously stale, for Charlie had to learn his business amid the helter-skelter of rapid producing. But the character he gradually created out of his imagination and his genius for pantomime is now so perfectly wrought that the merits of the films are of subordinate importance. Like Puck, Ariel and Mickey Mouse, Charlie Chaplin is unearthly—a figure in the dance, a masquerade. In well-balanced plays that arrive at an emotional conclusion, like *Shoulder Arms* and *The Kid*, the character is doubtless most satisfying and useful. But the joy, pathos and sentiment a Chaplin film arouses are chiefly evocations of character, unfettered and free; they are not to be imprisoned in a plot. The most we can hope for is a story pattern that does not confine the agile pantomimic dance of the little man with the hard hat and mustache.

Those of us who have been sitting at Charlie's knee, lo! These many years, have been uncomfortably aware of his restless longing for profundity. He has the clown's respect for intellect. *Modern Times* begins ominously with a sociological prologue which indicates that the little tramp is about to hand down a judgment on mankind. Whereupon you see him at work in an inhuman factory, gradually going mad from the monotony of labor at the moving belt. If you have an eager eye for social comment, you may see in some of the other episodes a suggestion that Charlie broods o' nights. But if he is offering *Modern Times* as social philosophy it is plain that he has hardly passed his entrance examinations, his comment is so trivial. As a matter of practical fact, the "modern times" of the title are only the dour background of an indifferent and hostile world that comically exaggerates the unworldliness of the little tramp. To be fully articulate he has always needed hostility—ferocious foremen, brutish police, villainous thugs; and the industrial tyranny of factory discipline, savage machinery and unemployment are an excellent environment to set off the pathos and comedy of the little tramp who does not belong. Like the scene in which he unwittingly carries a red flag at the head of a parade of bellicose strikers, the social significance of the new film is more technique than philosophy.

As an actor he has never been more brilliant. He is the master of pantomime who found in the silent screen the perfect medium for his genius. In these modern times of the audible screen he still realizes that the little tramp will lose immortality if he speaks in the tongue of common men. At the age of forty-six Charlie's roller-skating is full of exuberance and ecstasy; in the scenes of joy his tottering clown's gait is on tiptoe with lyric rapture. Put him in an austere line of ordinary men, as in a jail yard, where he spends a good deal of time, and the buoyancy of his spirit makes him instantly distinguished. He cannot be assimilated. Charlie is the footloose vagrant who has the instincts of a gentleman; he is courteous, elaborately proper, kind, chivalrous, generous and his manners are instinctively elegant. Even his vulgarity is daintily acted. His career as an actor has been marked by a steady refinement in the art of the character he created. In the course of two decades every man has to revise or discard many things he once believed, for only the true things endure. One of the durables is Charlie Chaplin. I have never had to change my mind about the funny little tramp who scampered across a screen that Saturday night in a rapt town hall.

V

The Late Features

Modern Times

Graham Greene (1904–1991) was, of course, the world-famous novelist. But before he attained his deservedly high status as both a writer of well-crafted "entertainments" (mostly in the espionage genre) and of more serious works (chiefly about guilt-ridden Catholics), he served for five years (1935-1940) as movie reviewer for The Spectator *in London. His work in the field was excellent, witty yet commonsensical in the best English manner. He was—quite famously—successfully sued for libel by Shirley Temple when he implied in one of his pieces that there was something Lolita-ish in her appeal. He was not necessarily wrong, but shortly thereafter he decamped to try his hand at more imaginative literary forms.*

I am too much an admirer of Mr. Chaplin to believe that the most important thing about his new film is that for a few minutes we are allowed to hear his agreeable and rather husky voice in a song. The little man has at last definitely entered the contemporary scene; there has always before been a hint of 'period' about his courage and misfortunes; he carried about with him more than the mere custard-pie of Karno's days, its manners, its curious clothes, its sense of pathos and

From *The Graham Greene Film Reader* (New York, 1972), by permission of ICM Talent.

its dated poverty. There were occasions, in his encounters with blind flower-girls or his adventures in mean streets or in the odd little pitch-pine mission halls where he carried round the bag or preached in pantomime on a subject so near to his own experience as the tale of David and Goliath, when he seemed to go back almost as far as Dickens. The change is evident in his choice of heroine: fair and featureless with the smudged effect of an amateur water-colour which has run, they never appeared again in leading parts, for they were quite characterless. But Miss Paulette Goddard, dark, grimy, with her amusing urban and plebeian face, is a promise that the little man will no longer linger at the edge of mawkish situation, the unfair pathos of the blind girl and the orphan child. One feels about her as Hyacinth felt about Millicent in *The Princess Casamassima*: 'she laughed with her laugh of the people, and if you hit her hard enough would cry with their tears'. For the first time the little man does not go off alone, flaunting his cane and battered bowler along the endless road out of the screen. He goes in company looking for what may turn up.

What *had* turned up was first a job in a huge factory twisting screws tighter as little pieces of nameless machinery passed him on a moving belt, under the televised eye of the manager, an eye that followed him even into the lavatory where he snatched an illicit smoke. The experiment of an automatic feeding machine, which will enable a man to be fed while he works, drives him crazy (the running amok of this machine, with its hygienic mouth-wiper, at the moment when it has reached the Indian corn course, is horrifyingly funny; it is the best scene, I think, that Mr. Chaplin has ever invented). When he leaves hospital he is arrested as a Communist leader (he has picked up a read street flag which has fallen off a lorry) and released again after foiling a prison hold-up. Unemployment and prison punctuate his life, starvation and lucky breaks, and somewhere in its course he attaches to himself the other piece of human refuse.

The Marxists, I suppose, will claim this as *their* film, but it is a good deal less and a good deal more than Socialist in intention. No real political passion has gone to it: the police batter the man at one moment and feed him with buns the next: and there is no warm maternal optimism, in the Mitchison manner, about the character of the workers: when the police are brutes, the men are cowards; the little man is always left in the lurch. Nor do we find him wondering 'what a Socialist man should do', but dreaming of a steady job and the most bourgeois home. Mr. Chaplin, whatever his political convictions may be, is an artist and not a propagandist. He doesn't try to explain, but presents with vivid fantasy what seem to him a crazy comic tragic world without a plan, but his sketch of the inhuman factory does not lead us to suppose that his little man would be more at home at Dneipostroi. He presents, he doesn't offer political solutions.

OTIS FERGUSON

Hallelujah, Bum Again

*Otis Ferguson (1907–1943) is the best film critic most
people have never heard of. He reviewed for* The New
Republic *from 1934 until early 1942. His style—
cheeky, jazzy, highly personal—obviously influenced
Agee, Manny Farber, and, I'm convinced, Pauline
Kael. So did his attitude, which was ironic but never
condescending. He took movies as he found them and
was not much interested in reforming them or turning
them into a high art form. In general I prefer his criticism to that of those he influenced, because of its lack
of pretense and its lightly worn intelligence—and because he had fewer prejudices and blind spots. He had
been in the navy as a young man, and after the United
States entered World War II he shipped out with the
Merchant Marine. He was killed, at age thirty-six,
when his ship was bombed in the Bay of Salerno. His
best qualities are on display in this consideration of*
Modern Times.

Modern Times is about the last thing they should have called the
Chaplin picture, which has had one of the most amazing build-ups of
interest and advance speculation on record. Its times were modern

From *Film Criticism of Otis Ferguson* (Philadelphia, 1971).

when the movies were younger and screen motion was a little faster and more jerky than life, and sequence came in 40-foot spurts, cut off by titles (two direct quotes here are "Alone and Hungry" and "Dawn"); when no one, least of all an officer of the law, could pass a day without getting a foot in the slack of his pants, when people walked into doorjambs on every dignified exit, stubbed toes everywhere on the straightway, and took most of their edibles full in the face; when tables and chairs were breakaways, comedy was whiskers, and heroes maneuvered serenely for minutes on abysses that were only too visible to the audience. It is in short a silent film, with pantomime, printed dialogue, and such sound effects as were formerly supplied by the pit band and would now be done by dubbing, except for Chaplin's song at the end. And not only that: it is a feature picture made up of several one- or two-reel shorts, proposed titles being *The Shop, The Jailbird, The Watchman, The Singing Waiter.*

Part of this old-time atmosphere can be credited to the sets. The factory layout is elaborate and stylized, but not in the modern way or with the modern vividness of light and shadow; the department store might have been Wanamaker's in its heyday; the "dance" music is a cross between Vienna and a small-town brass band, twenty years old at least; the costumes are generally previous; and as to faces and types, Chaplin has kept a lot of old friends with him, types from days when a heavy was a heavy and Chester Conklin's moustache obscured his chin (still does). Above everything, of course, is the fact that the methods of silent days built up their tradition in group management and acting—in the first, a more formal explicitness, so that crowds gather jerkily from nowhere, emphasized players move stiffly front and center, the camera does less shifting; in the second, actors tend to underline their parts heavily and with copious motion (see the irate diner, see the hoity-toity wife of the parson, see Big Bill and the rest).

Modern Times has several new angles, principally those of the factory and the occasional off-stage reports of strikes and misery (the girl's father was shot in a demonstration). But they are incidental. Even in taking René Clair's conveyor-belt idea, for example, you can almost hear Chaplin, where Clair directed a complex hubbub, saying to one of his old trusties: You drop the wrench, I kick you in the pants, you take it big, and we cut to chase, got it? It has the thread of a story: Chaplin's meeting up with the orphan girl, very wild and sweet, and their career together. For the rest it is disconnected comedy stuff: the embarrassing situation, the embroilment and chase, and the specialty number, *e.g.*, the roller skates, the completely wonderful song-and-dance bit, the Chaplin idyll of a cottage and an automatic cow, beautiful with humor and sentiment. These things and the minor business all along the way—in jails, cafeterias, with oil cans, trays, swinging doors, refractory machinery—are duplicates, they take you back.

But such matters would not call for discussion if all together they did not set up a definite mood, a disturbing sense of the quaint. Chaplin himself is not dated, never will be; he is a reservoir of humor, master of an infinite array of dodges, agile in both mind and body; he is not only a character but a complex character, with the perfect ability to make evident all the shades of his odd and charming feelings; not only a touching character, but a first-class buffoon and I guess the master of our time in dumb show. But this does not make him a first-class picture maker. He may personally surmount his period, but as director-producer he can't carry his whole show with him, and I'll take bets that if he keeps on refusing to learn any more than he learned when the movies themselves were just learning, each successive picture he makes will seem, on release, to fall short of what went before. The general reaction to this one anyway is the wonder that these primitive formulas can be so genuinely comic and endearing.

There has been a furor here and there in the press about the social content of *Modern Times*, and this could be skipped easily if Chaplin himself were not somehow confused (see his introduction to the film) over its worth as corrective comment. Well, the truth is that Chaplin is a comedian; he may start off with an idea, but almost directly he is back to type again, the happy hobo and blithe unregenerate, a little sad, a little droll. Whatever happens to him happens by virtue of his own naïve bewilderment, prankishness, absurd ineptitude, and the constant support of very surprising coincidence. He couldn't keep a job or out of jail anywhere in the world, including the Soviet Union—that is, if he is to be true to the Chaplin character.

And Chaplin is still the same jaunty wistful figure, pinning his tatters about a queer dignity of person, perpetually embarked on an elaborate fraud, transparent to the world but never very much so to himself. He brings the rites and dignities of Park Avenue to the gutters of Avenue A, and he keeps it up unsmilingly until it is time to heave the pie, to kick the props out, to mock with gestures and scuttle off, more motion than headway, all shoes, hat, stick, and chase. With him it is all a continuous performance, played with the gravity, innocence, and wonder of childhood, but with ancient wisdom in the matters of sniping cigar butts and tripping coppers into the garbage pile. He is pathetic with the unhappiness of never, never succeeding—either in crossing a hotel lobby without at least one header into the spittoon or in eating the steaks, chops, and ham and eggs that are forever in his dreams; and yet he somehow cancels this or plays it down: when the ludicrous and debasing occurs, he picks himself up with serenity and self-respect, and when it is time for heartbreaks he has only a wry face, a shrug, some indication of that fall-to-rise-again philosophy that has made hoboing and destitution such harmless fun for his own special audience, the people of America. His life on the screen is material for tragedy, ordinarily. But on the screen he is only partly a citizen of this world: he lives mostly in that unreal happy land—you see the little figure walking off down the road toward it always into the fade-out—where kicks, thumps, injustice, and nowhere to sleep are no more than a teasing and a jolly dream (Oh, with a little pang perhaps, a gentle Woollcott tear) and the stuff a paying public's cherished happy endings are made of.

The Great Dictator

From 1939 to 1989—a round fifty years—Dilys Powell
(1901–1995) was film critic for the London Times, a
tenure unsurpassed by any critic, in any of the arts, in
British journalism. Even though she worked for what
was then England's most influential newspaper, which
made her the country's most influential movie voice,
she was widely beloved not only by her readers but by
the film community as well. That's because she was
witty without being cruel, intelligent without being
overbearing. She was as sensible (and long-wearing) as
a good pair of English walking shoes. This review of
The Great Dictator shows this plainspoken woman at
her best.

War, says the voice of the commentator as *The Great Dictator* opens,
war on the Western Front, war in 1918; and 1918 it is, with Chaplin as
a German soldier chased by a mad shell, Chaplin dropping a hand
grenade down his own sleeve, Chaplin flying a plane upside-down;
the photography is 1918, the make-up is 1918, the fun is 1918, everything is 1918 except—Chaplin speaks. He speaks in a normal English
voice; an agreeable but not a memorable voice; the voice not of a

From *The Dilys Powell Film Reader* (Oxford, 1992), by permission of Carcanet Press.

comic, but of a pleasant little chap worried rather than scared by the incidence of mad shells, elusive hand grenades and recalcitrant planes. But nor for long. The years whiz by; and now it is nearer 1940 than 1918, and Chaplin as Hynkel, Director of Tomania, is driving down an avenue embellished by the statuary of the New Order, statuary in which even the Venus de Milo has an arm for giving the Nazi salute; he is conferring with his gallant Garbitsch and his stout Herring, he is addressing his loving people in a crazy German-sounding gibberish, he is shouting and screaming and frothing and wheedling about the Jews and the British and democracy and the inalienable rights of the heroic and suffering Tomanians. And somewhere in the city Chaplin as a little Jewish barber, the same little man who suffered the unwelcome attentions of the mad shell, is returning to his shop in the Ghetto after years in a hospital where he has heard nothing of the glorious march of the new Tomania.

After nearly thirty years then, of playing one character in one set of clothes, Chaplin takes on a double role. The subject of the film is thus new to him, or shall we say it is a new and advanced branch of his old subject, the dictatorship of the powerful and cruel over the humble and the dispossessed? He delivers his assault on the mighty not indirectly only, through the medium of the comical oppressed, but directly as well, through the medium of the comical oppressor; the attack is a split attack. In another way, too, the film is a split film; it darts between satire and realism; at one moment the comic Chaplinesque fight, at another the wholly uncomic sadism of the Storm Troopers, at one moment the Dictator robustly ridiculed, at the next the burning Ghetto, the sobbing women. Only the presentation, both of satire and of realism, is not new; the camerawork, though it emerges from the primitive simplicity of the first sequences, never reaches the standards we have come to expect today. Chaplin is still the Great Dictator in the cinema; he makes his own laws; the film is his own film, connived, elaborated, controlled by his single imagination.

But how superbly he does the things which lie within the compass of his comic genius! The screaming dictator tearing off Herring's decorations (down to his trouser-buttons), or posing for an infinitesimal second to despairing sculptors and painters before stamping off to strum on the harmonium; the little barber attending to a customer to the rhythm of rhapsody from the Tomanian radio, and straightening his tie at the mirror of the man's bald head; the dictator dancing a parody of a bubble-dance with the world, the little barber drawing lots for the task of blowing up the palace, finding the fatal coin in *his* piece of pudding, surreptitiously swallowing it, taking a confident second mouthful of pudding, finding a coin in that too, swallowing again, swallowing coin after coin until as he hiccups the cash chinks treacherously together. But it would not be just to imply that Chaplin is a one-man band; the touching charm of his scenes with the Jewish working girl (very well played by Paulette Goddard), would be refutation enough, and so would the farcical interplay with Napaloni, the rival dictator (Jack Oakie). Indeed there are moments when Jack Oakie, loud, beaming, the very portrait of a cheerful, boisterous ruffian, holds the screen, and deserves it.

All the scenes between Chaplin and Oakie are brilliantly contrived and played: the train drawing up at the wrong end of the platform, Napaloni bawling from the window, 'You gotta de carpet, you puttem down!'; Madame Napaloni arrested by the police for trying to get into the same car with her husband; the two dictators, while waiting reporters are assured of the cordiality of the meeting, brawling at the buffet and throwing the nearest thing to a custard pie. The comic invention throughout has the old Chaplin touch. The serious interludes, the domestic scenes in the Ghetto, even the moments of brutal realism, though there are poor and dull patches, did not offend me by their contrast with the satirical farce of the rest of the story; indeed, I was moved by much of this as I have not been moved by the more ambitious horrors of the straightforward propagandists. But for me the film contained one major error: the final speech in which the little barber, mistaken for the Dictator, speaks to the people in the serious tones of an orator appealing for humanity and brotherly pity. This finale is so blatantly out of harmony with what has gone before as to nullify much of the effectiveness of the preceding two hours.

OTIS FERGUSON

Less Time for Comedy

There will be some to whom a systematic four- or five-year advance build-up on each picture is going to make *The Great Dictator* a disappointment. That will be too bad, because it is a good picture, and this time something new in Chaplin. There will be others, however, who will find the symbiosis of comedy and earnestness an unhappy state of union, detrimental to both; and I think these people will be right. For the world's first funny man to prove that he too can write a *New Republic* editorial, but several years later, is something rather less than the dog who walked on his hind legs, because this is the place in the act where he was supposed to do "dead dog."

Through Mr. Chaplin's characteristic reticence you know what the picture is all about, of course. One Charlie is Hitler; the other is a Jewish barber in Hitler's Germany, an amnesia victim left over from the World War. Paulette Goddard is a Waif. Jack Oakie is a Mussolini briefly, and good while he's there. And both Charlie's talk. Everybody knows all about these facts because the secret was guarded so hard for so long.

What nobody suspected is that the Hitler Charlie, the new Charlie of authority, double-talk, and complete confusion, actually steals the show. This was hardly by design. All the old luggage of slapstick and pathos and after-my-laughter-came-tears is in the ghetto sequences, with people being bonged over the head with a skillet and

From *Film Criticism of Otis Ferguson* (Philadelphia, 1971).

Chaplin with the stick and that crazy-ballet walk of his and the girl being waifed right and left and the Keystone cops in storm-trooper uniforms piling all over the place.

The Great Dictator opens on some pretty dated nonsense in the war zone and the kind of lighting and movie action they used in *Shoulder Arms*. What's new is the acting, the new and different character, a mixture of sharp mimicry and the devices of absurdity. And as we might have expected from the wonderful double-talk song in *Modern Times*, Chaplin is as acute and perfect verbally as he is in pantomime: he has the splenetic and krauty fustian of the German orator as exactly as Hitler himself. When he says "Democracy shtoonk. Liberty shtoonk," he crowds out over his collar to the precise degree, and he never misses an opportunity to go from the normal English of the story into this hortatory gibberish, booting his lieutenants around and scaring the devil out of everybody, including himself. And the old reliable panto at the same time too, so that his version of the Nazi salute is a blend of pomp and monkeyshine that leaves them in the aisles, and his dance with the globe is one of the triumphs of all satiric dancing, for point, grace, and perfection.

The whole thing is worked out with a great deal of care for many effects, some of which are on the gag side, some not. The dictator can never quite get a pen out of the patent inkwell to sign documents with, for example; or he gets tied up in his cape, or the train he is meeting stops at the wrong place (this, the arrival of Napolini of Bacteria, is one of the highlights, together with the review of the troops that follows). On the other side there is great business with affairs of state, the dapper and ominous figure whipping around from audience to conference to portrait sitting, half a minute for each. There is a character called Herring (Henry Daniell) and a character called Garbitsch (Billy Gilbert), who is always demonstrating a new and invincible device that doesn't work—as when the parachute inventor takes off and they watch him crash to the sidewalk below: "Far from perfect," the dictator says incisively. The two dictators end up trying to bluff each other, and we go back to the story of Charlie the barber, which has been going on intermittently.

When this is funny it is funny as always, in the shop, on the street, around the chimney pots, with some of the oldest Chaplin favorites still peeping through. But it is also tragic because a people is being persecuted; these Jews are straight characters, not the old cartoons; and the laughter chokes suddenly and is reluctant to start again. Chaplin likes to pull out all the stops on sentimental passages, but this thing is too near and meaningful. It isn't that a comedian should be denied indignation and kept clowning forever; it is that old thing in all art of the demands of unity, of a complete and sustained mood or tone. He was always a funny figure against the rude world, but the gulf between a kick in the pants and a pogrom is something even his talent for the humorous-pathetic will not cross. And his unrelieved six-minute exhortation to the downtrodden of the world, look up, stand up, etc., is not only a bad case of overwriting but dramatically and even inspirationally futile.

These things must be reported, though that other burning question of whether the satire is actually effective, and to what extent, will get small play here. You could remember that the size of policemen's feet was never seriously affected by all the skylarking of the Keystone lot; but you could also remember that a man's heart being in the right place is a good thing to witness, and that laughter is one of the great and joyous healers of the spirit, whatever the recent crop of solemn buffoons have to say about its social waste. And again as always where there is a Chaplin picture, there is laughter here, warmth and grace too. I think it will do you good, just for what is there, let alone that this is still Chaplin the Great, and growing at his age.

A lot of people don't have time enough for comedy these days, and it is getting so you wince every time someone in a film trifle says the word democracy; it means they are going to pull out with a heavy speech. *Arise, My Love* is the latest to capitalize on the situation in Europe. It is the old girl-reporter framework with angles, such as idealism. Mitchell Leisen did another one of his bright comedy jobs through most of it, and got action in too; the dialogue really jumps; there is a nice boy-girl angle; Claudette Colbert, Ray Milland, and a well-placed cast breeze through it.

But there is that need to milk the headlines, which is not so much a bad thing in itself as a poor excuse for shooting around story complications; and when they start talking with too much feeling and punk poetry about the little fellows in Spain (a safe subject now; when it would have done some good it was too hot to touch), Poland, Norway, France, without really caring a damn or devoting enough of the picture to making it real, it gets embarrassing. This is the story of a condemned Loyalist aviator, pardoned by a ruse, chasing the newspaper career girl to Paris, almost running away home with her, and then going back to fly in Poland. It came to a good enough end in about an hour and a half; but twenty minutes later they were still making speeches and all they needed was the American flag in *The Time of Your Life* and a new arrangement of "The Parade of the Wooden Soldiers." You can save time by getting out when it becomes clear that the boat the two are on is the *Athenia,* by a device heisted from *Cavalcade,* though in this instance the lovers don't die—just the picture. Can I help you with your coat?

Monsieur Verdoux

James Agee (1901–1955) a legendary critic, wrote reviews for The Nation and Time *simultaneously in the 1940s. He was also the author of a Pulitzer Prize–winning novel,* A Death in the Family, *and of a poetic and highly regarded work of journalism about Southern sharecroppers in the Great Depression,* Let Us Now Praise Famous Men. *In addition he wrote poetry and screenplays. It was a lot of work to cram into a mere forty-six alcoholic and otherwise disheveled years. He loved the movies, of that there can be no doubt, but very often he did so neither wisely nor well. He often exalted mediocre talents and dismissed larger ones. That is not the case in this remarkable essay about* Monsieur Verdoux. *Agee had loved Chaplin from his boyhood, even considering him something of a surrogate father figure after his own father died; but he did not meet him until a tumultuous press conference a day after the disastrous New York premiere of* Verdoux. *Alone of the assembled journalists, Agee rose to defend Chaplin. Later they became friends, and Agee even wrote a perfectly awful screen treatment in which he tried to interest Chaplin. This tortured, three-part article is a rather desperately reasoned defense not so much of* Verdoux *but of its intentions. It is also a critic's fawning love letter to an artist he loved beyond reason. As such,*

From *The Nation*, May 31 and June 14, 1947, by permission of *The Nation*.

it is one of the more remarkable documents in the history of movie criticism.

I

Although I have been granted extra space, and propose to discard most other considerations for brevity's sake, I can say here only a few of the things that I feel need to be said about Mr. Chaplin's new film. I can only hope that these notes may faintly suggest the frame-by-frame appreciation, the gratitude, and the tribute which we owe this great poet and his great poem; and may help some readers to enjoy more of what he has done than they otherwise might.

The skeletal story: Henri Verdoux, a French bank teller of the thirties who has lost his job in a depression, works out a business of his own whereby he can support his crippled wife (Mady Corell) and their little boy. He becomes a professional murderer of women of means. He courts them, marries them, finesses their little fortunes into his possession; murders them and eliminates their corpses; plays the market with the whole of his profits. We see him at work on four such women. One is going up in smoke when Verdoux first appears. One is a socially prominent widow (Isobel Elsom) whom he woos industriously through most of the film; she takes him for a boulevardier. One is a sour old small-town dame (Margaret Hoffman) whose money he cajoles by stop-watch and whom he promptly murders; she thinks he is a globe-trotting civil engineer. One is a half-daft ex-tart (Martha Raye) who has hit luck in a lottery. She takes him for a sea captain. His efforts to kill her are almost the only passages of pure slapstick in the film.

A very busy little man—his business dashes him all over France and from top to bottom of society—Verdoux can visit his true home seldom. Even when he does he is likely to mix business with the pleasure. He learns from a druggist friend (Robert Lewis) about a new poison, painless and untraceable. He picks up a friendless young woman (Marilyn Nash) to try it out on, but spares her when he realizes that she, like himself, "could kill for love." When he meets her later, by accident, he cryptically brushes her off. Late in the film, long after he has retired from business, they meet again. But just then and there he is recognized by relatives of a former wife. After showing how effortlessly he could have escaped, he deliberately puts himself in the way of arrest. The film ends with the famous scenes in which Verdoux hears his sentence and explains himself, more or less, to the court and the world; pays his equally cold respects to journalism and to God; and walks to the guillotine.

Disregard virtually everything you may have read about the film. It is of interest, but chiefly as a definitive measure of the difference between the thing a man of genius puts before the world and the things the world is equipped to see in it. There is room neither to analyze nor to argue much about this peculiar criticism; yet in all conscience a few points must be mentioned. The ruck of these reviewers have said, for instance, that the film isn't funny; is morally questionable; is in bad taste; that Chaplin should never have stopped playing the tramp; that Raye steals her scenes with Chaplin; that Chaplin is no good at casting, writing, directing, producing; that he should have hired people, for all these jobs, who knew the techniques which have been developed since talkies began. Some brief replies:

Not funny. Not much of it is, unless you have an eye and mind for the far from cliché matters which can be proved and illuminated through poetically parodied cliché; an appetite for cold nihilistic irony; respect for an artist who subdues most of his outrageous fun to the grim central spirit of his work.

Morals. For later discussion. I could take more seriously those who have objected on these grounds if any of them had shown himself capable of recognizing an act of moral and artistic heroism when he saw it. Not one did.

Taste. *Verdoux* is in bad taste if death is, as so many Americans feel; and if it is in bad taste to treat a serious matter seriously, and to make comedy cut to the bone.

The tramp. Very young children fiercely object to even minor changes in a retold story. Older boys and girls are not, as a rule, respected for such extreme conservatism.

Raye. Verdoux cannot properly get many of the big laughs; that is what Raye is there for. She does her job beautifully, and Chaplin feeds her and foils her beautifully. One of the finest aspects of his miraculous performances is his quiet skill and graciousness, in these and many other scenes, as a feeder, a sardonic ringmaster, an inspired emcee.

Casting. Raye's mere presence disproves that. So does Marilyn Nash; name one trained actress who could give that role, besides her lovely demeanor, her exactly right spirit, vitality, and freshness. So does every player and bit player in the cast. Chaplin is the most perceptive, imaginative, exact man alive, at casting; these reviewers are less so.

Writing. Verbally most of *Verdoux* is inferior to its visual achievements—that is to say, it is only one of the most talented screen plays ever written. Chaplin also wrote the story and its subtleties; designed one of the few really *formed* movies in years; invented at least twenty-five characters who live very keenly both as social types and as individuals; and reproduced, just as cleanly and quietly, that entire grand façade of a society which was germane to this theme. (The significant omissions are farmers and industrial workers; the world of *Verdoux* is the world of gain, gotten ill, by chance, by heritage, by crime.)

Directing. He directed this film—all the people mentioned and successes suggested above, and still others as great and greater, handling a munificent complex of characters, ideas, milieux, and tributary styles and tones with all but perfect visual wit and expressiveness and with an all but unblemished grace, force, and economy. For directing as brilliant I refer you to his own *Modern Times* and to Dovzhenko's *Frontier*; there has been none since.

Production. Is criticized as stingy, and as unlike France. Instead, it is a manifesto against a kind of vulgarity in which Hollywood is drowned—the attempt to disguise emptiness with sumptuousness. It looks handmade, not machine-turned. Like the casting and acting and directing it is poetic, not naturalistic, though naturalistic elements are finely used poetically. Verdoux's France is a highly intelligent perhaps paraphrase, far more persuasive of its place—half in the real world, half in the mind—than most films are of their supposed place, foreign, native, or imaginary.

New techniques. They are on the whole weakened derivations from styles developed before sound came, in Russia, Germany, and, in this country, by Chaplin among others; virtually nothing has been done with sound. Such as the new style is, it can be used decently; that is proved by *The Best Years of Our Lives*. But in the average well-made movie, such as these reviewers praise, it signifies just this: the art of moving pictures has been so sick, for so long, that the most it can do for itself is to shift unceasingly from one bedsore to the next. Chaplin, by contrast, obviously believes that if you can invent something worth watching, the camera should hold still and clear, so that you can watch it. That is still, and will always be, one of the best possible ways to use a camera; Chaplin is the one great man who still stands up for it.

To be sure, you have to be competent to see what he puts before you; and thanks to the depravities of the latter-day "style," most of us have spoiled eyes. We cannot appreciate swiftness and uninsistence; nor the bracing absence of fancy composition and prettiness; nor Chaplin's genius for "mood" when that is important (the first great shot of Verdoux's closed garden); nor for atmosphere, authenticity, and beauty in mock formlessness (some wonderful loose group shots, full of glass, gravel, gray sky, pale heads, and dark clothing, at the garden party); nor for visual wit (the astoundingly funny long shot of the lake, with the murder boat almost imperceptibly small). We are just smart enough to recognize a cliché; never enough to see how brilliantly a master can use it. So we sneer at Chaplin's frequent use of locomotive wheels, charging ever more desperately across the screen, this way and that, to mark another business trip or return; saying that he tries thus, unimaginatively, to bind together his formless continuity. But in fact these wheels do a lot at once. They are in the best sense economical; they are cumulatively funny; they cumulatively express Verdoux's ever more frantic busyness; and they wind the film up like a tight spring.

II

Chaplin's performance as Verdoux is the best piece of playing I have ever seen: here, I cannot even specify the dozen or so close-ups each so great and so finely related and timed that withdrawn and linked in series they are like the notes of a slow, magnificent, and terrifying song, which the rest of the film serves as an accompaniment. I could write many pages, too, about the richness and quality of the film as a work of art, in fact, of genius; and as many more trying, hopelessly, to determine how Chaplin's intellect, instinct, intuition, creative intelligence, and pure experience as a master artist and as a showman, serve and at times disserve one another: for intellectually and in every other kind of self-exhaustion this seems incomparably his most ambitious film. And since the film is provocative of so much that cannot be examined as fun, I wish I might also use the many thousands of words I would require to do it adequate honor, purely as fun. And all the more because I love and revere the film as deeply as any I have seen, and believe that it is high among the great works of this century, I wish I might discuss at proper length its weaknesses as a work of art and of moral understanding. I have reluctantly chosen, instead, to suggest a single aspect of its meaning, which seems to me particularly important. And this itself, I fear, I may have reduced beyond usefulness.

Chaplin's theme, the greatest and the most appropriate to its time that he has yet undertaken, is the bare problem of surviving at all in such a world as this. With his usual infallibility of instinct he has set his story in Europe; Europeans are aware of survival as a problem, as we are not. As rightly, he has set aside the tramp, whose charming lessons in survival are too wishful for his purposes, for his first image of the Responsible Man, and of modern civilization. (For Verdoux embodies much of the best that can be said of modern civilization, whether democratic-capitalist, fascist, or communist: whatever he may lack in the way of conscience, he does have brains; and whatever crimes he commits, they are committed, or so he believes, out of compassionate love and in uncompromising discharge of responsibility.) The tramp is the free soul intact in its gallantry, innocence, eagerness for love, ridiculousness, and sorrow; we recognize in him much that is dear to us in ourselves. Verdoux is so much nearer and darker that we can hardly bear to recognize ourselves in him. He is the committed, dedicated soul, and this soul is not intact: we watch its death agonies. And this tragic process is only the more dreadful because it is depicted not gravely but briskly, with a cold savage gaiety; the self-destroying soul is rarely aware of its own predicament.

The problem of survival: the Responsible Man. Chaplin develops his terrible theme chiefly as a metaphor for business. But the film is also powerful as a metaphor for war: the Verdoux home as an embattled nation, the wife and child as the home front, Verdoux as expeditionary force, hero in the holiest of causes, and war criminal. But it is even more remarkable and fascinating as a study of the relationship between ends and means, a metaphor for the modern personality— that is, a typical "responsible" personality reacting to contemporary pressures according to the logic of contemporary ethics.

In the terms of this metaphor the basic cast is small. Verdoux, his wife, and their son are differing aspects of a single personality. Verdoux is the master, the intelligence and the deep unconscious; he has estranged his soul and his future. He has made the assumption that most people make, today—one of the chief assumptions on which modern civilization rests. That is, that in order to preserve intact in such a world as this those aspects of the personality which are best and dearest to one, it is necessary to exercise all that is worst in one; and that it is impossible to do this effectively if one communicates honestly with one's best. Accordingly the personality which, until the world struck that living down, lived in poverty and docility, but happily, is broken and segregated.

The wife and child are shut away in a home which is at once a shrine and a jail; and there, immobilized, and cut off from the truth, they virtually cease to exist as living objects of love; they become an ever more rigid dream. For when the worst and the best in the personality are thus segregated, and the worst is thus utilized in the nominal service of the best, it is inevitably the good which is exploited; the evil, which thinks of itself as faithful slave, is treacherous master; and evil, being active and knowledgeable, grows; and good, rendered motionless and denied knowledge, withers. Like most men obsessed with the world's ruthlessness, Verdoux carries his veneration of innocence to the extreme; he is determined that it shall never be touched, shall never change (the song of how many million homesick soldiers: "We want to find everything at home just as we left it"). But change is inevitable, and uncontrollable. Ruthlessness and the murderous adoration of static innocence enlarge each other; and the ruthless man becomes the more ruthless because he has broken all communication with innocence. And innocence itself is altered. At the moment Verdoux tells his wife that they own their home at last, she dares to remember sadly that they were happier when they were poor. Her face shows the terrible intuitive guilt that comes of all that is uneasily apprehended, untold, and unasked. Small wonder that she has become a cripple; the wonder is that she continues to breathe. Passiveness was forced on her, truth was destroyed, love was undermined, her own love became pity, as surely as her husband's, and in pity and in fear she failed to question what was being done. As is so often true, it was not she who wanted to be so well provided for; that was her husband's desire, the one desire he might hope to satisfy; so she let him satisfy it.

As for Verdoux, he is irreparably committed. All the heart he has left prevents his confessing to his wife, and prevents his changing trades. He could only have chosen his course through defect of love—vengefulness and self-pity masked as pity, pity masked as love; the love-destroying, monstrous arrogance it requires to make the innocent answerable for your guilt—and the constant necessity of deceiving love has damaged love still more profoundly. Like many business men who feel unloved, or incapable of full enough love, he can only propitiate, and express, his love by providing for his family as handsomely as possible. (He can desire this of course, rather than the bare subsistence his wife prefers, only because he respects the standards of the world he thinks he despises. During his docile years, remember, he served at the high altar of modern civilization, breathing year in and year out The Bank's soul-dissolving odor of sanctity, all day, every day, touching the sacred wealth he must never dare touch with his conscious desire. When he was thrown out of his job, this ruthlessness released the tremendously impounded ruthlessness in him.) But that is never well enough to satisfy him—and only *his* satisfaction really counts, in this household—for his wife and child scarcely exist for him except as a self-vindicating dream, which he must ceaselessly labor to sustain, improve, perfect, be worthy of. A vicious cycle is established. Only through the best good-providing possible can Verdoux at once express his love, quiet his dying intuition that his love is defective and that he is wrong even in the little that he believes to be right, sustain the dream that is all that remains of love, require of himself ever more obsessive industriousness in crime, and silence his wife.

As good, by his will, is ever more stonily immobilized, evil becomes ever more protean in disguise and self-disguise, ever more mercurial in its journeyings. (The personality is also a constant metaphor for modern civilization—in which, for one instance, creative power is paralyzed except in the interests of gain and destruction; in those interests it is vigorous as never before.) Verdoux cannot bear to sit still, to stop work, long enough to realize his predicament. He cannot feel "at home," at home. He has to act his roles as perfect husband and father, dearly as he wants merely to *be* both, just as he acts all his other roles. All that he loves is saturated in deceit; and he in self-deceit as well. He gets home seldom, apparently never longer than overnight; the divided spirit can only assert its unity, even its illusion of unity or its desire, in twilight contemplation or in dreams; and the pressure of business is always on him. The pressure of business indeed! Verdoux's family is almost lifeless; such piteously cherished life as it retains, he is hopelessly estranged from. All that requires his intelligence, skill, and vitality, all that gives him life, is in his business. He is the loneliest character I know of: he can never be so desperately lonely as during these hours among those dearest to him, when he must deceive not mere victims, or the world at large, but those he loves. The only moments during which this appalling loneliness is broken during which he ever honestly communicates, however briefly, with other human beings, are those few moments during which he can know that his victims realize they are being murdered. No doubt he loves his wife and child—there are two of the most heart-stopping, beautiful close-ups ever made, to prove that—but in the fearful depths into which he cannot risk a glance he loves only their helplessness; and deeper, only the idea of love; and that only because it consecrates his true marriage, which is to murder.

III

(Monsieur Verdoux *has been withdrawn and will be re-released only after a United Artists' build-up which will, I hear, try to persuade people that they will kill themselves laughing. I will take care to notify readers of this column of its return, and of changes, if any are made. I am grieved to be so late—or early—with this review, but not very; this film has too long a life ahead of it. It is permanent if any work done during the past twenty years is permanent.*)

The most mysterious line in the film, Verdoux's reference to having "lost" his family, becomes clear if the three are seen as members of a single personality. The wife whom segregation and deceit so inevitably paralyzed was dying a slow death from the moment she became uneasy and failed with her own kind of misguided tenderness, to beseech her husband's confidence; and the child could not long have survived his mother.

With their death Verdoux all but dies himself. He becomes old, bent, sore, stiff, not only through heartbreak or because all that he most cherished in his nature is destroyed, but because their death has deprived him of the one motive he would recognize for his criminality. The third meeting with Miss Nash, for all its handsome prospects, revives him only to an old man's charming glimmer; but as soon as danger once more requires work of him and, after showing how effortlessly he might escape, he casually surrenders himself to society's vengeance, he limbers up and shines like a snake which has just cast its winter skin. All that remains now is memory and the pure stripped ego, the naked will to survive which discovers, with ineffable relief, that there is no longer any point in surviving.

With his soul dead at last, it is no wonder that Verdoux asserts himself so proudly, in the courtroom and death cell, in terms of his dream of himself. He would have explained himself less proudly and with greater moral understanding to his wife, but he had successfully avoided that possibility, at the cost of their marriage and her life. His dream of himself is urgently challenged only once, by the girl whose life he spares; and he successfully resists that challenge in the strangest and, I think, most frightening scene ever filmed.

I had expected this film to be the last word in misogyny; but although there is a good deal of it about, Verdoux's handling of his victims is in general remarkably genial and kindly. The one really hair-raising moment of that sort is the chance second meeting with the girl, the scene in which he brushes her off. After all, Verdoux risks nothing against the poor frumps he kills or tries to kill, except his life. But the girl is infinitely more dangerous. She is the one human being with whom he holds in common everything he regards as most important. Both have known love as passionate pity for the helpless, both could kill for love; both would be capable of maturer love, if at all, only with their own kind. The girl is much closer to Verdoux than his own wife, or his murdered wives; in sparing her he has betrayed both his marriage and his vocation. Since he is above all else a family man and an artist, she threatens the very structure of his soul. But the deranged and deadlocked will which has made and sustained Verdoux is never so strong or so ruthless as when it faces the threat of cure; and I know of no moment more dreadful or more beautifully achieved than that in which Verdoux veers from the girl, the sun on his suddenly shriveled cheek, and mutters in the shriveled, almost effeminate little voice of more than mortal hatred and terror: "You go on about your business."

But *why* does Verdoux become a murderer? One good answer is: why not? Verdoux is a business realist; in terms of that realism the only difference between free enterprise in murder and free enterprise in the sale of elastic stockings is the difference in legal liability and in net income. And if the film is regarded as a metaphor for war, we may blush to ask Verdoux *why*; or if it is regarded as a metaphor for the destruction of the soul, murder is almost too mild a vocation. Yet we may still ask why, and wonder why Chaplin's only direct statements, most of which are made through Verdoux, are so remarkably inadequate. Verdoux, to be sure, is grandly in character in holding "society" accountable and in absolving the individual; but is this all that Chaplin knows? If so, he is as surely a victim and dupe of evil as Verdoux or the civilization he excoriates, and all that goes deeper in the film is achieved intuitively, as if in a kind of waking dream. If he knows better, then he is gravely at fault, as artist and moralist, in making clear no more than he does, still worse in tossing the mass-audience so cynical and misleading a sop; and one of the purest and most courageous works I know of is, at its climax, pure and courageous only against the enemy, not in the face of the truth. For the answers to why and how criminality can be avoided, we can look inward more profitably than at the film; for all that is suggested in the film is operant in each of us.

If Chaplin had illuminated these bottom causes more brightly than we can see them in ourselves, *Verdoux* would be a still greater work of art than it is. But in proposing so richly suggestive an image of process and effect in the world and in the personality, and in proposing it so beautifully, the film, with all its faults, is one of the few indispensable works of our time.

It even contains and implies the beginning of the answer. Good and evil are inextricable, Verdoux insists. But his fatal mistake was in trying to keep them apart. If the film is regarded as a metaphor for the personality, and through that metaphor, as a metaphor for the personality as the family as business as war as civilization as murder, then this is certain: if the man and wife had honored their marriage with more than their child, the murders would never have been committed, the paralysis would never have imposed itself or would have been dissolved, and the wife and child would never have been shut into that exquisite tabernacle of a closed garden, but all three would have lived as one in that poverty for which the wife was forlorn, in the intactness of soul and the irresponsibility of that anarchic and immortal lily of the field, the tramp, the most humane and most nearly complete among the religious figures our time has evolved; whom for once in his life Chaplin set aside, to give his century its truest portrait of the upright citizen.

DWIGHT MACDONALD

Monsieur Verdoux

*In his long journalistic career, Dwight Macdonald
(1906–1982) was many things—a writer for* Fortune;
*publisher, editor, and pretty much the sole writer of a
little magazine called* Politics; *a staff writer for* The
New Yorker. *Politically, too, he shifted ground on several occasions—being at one time or another a Trotskyite, a pacifist, a self-described anarchist. But his interest in film began in college and was abiding. He
wrote about movies in many venues, most notably as*
Esquire's *film critic in the 1960s. He had a particular
love of the silent film classics and was thus highly
knowledgeable about Chaplin. This piece, which was
among other things was a belated response to Agee's
long essay, is notable for its brisk common sense about
Verdoux. He writes with respect for Chaplin's accomplishments, but he was not, for a moment, taken in by
this effort.*

The Broadway premier of *Monsieur Verdoux,* Chaplin's first talkie, took
place in 1947. It was not a success: the audience was unsympathetic, at
times audibly, and the daily reviewers were hostile, except for Archer
Winsten of the New York *Post* and, less expectable and more important,

From *Dwight Macdonald on Movies* (Englewood Cliffs, N.J., 1969).

Bosley Crowther of the *Times*. It was taken off after six weeks and, a few months later, was also withdrawn from national distribution. It didn't reappear on American screens until last summer [1966], when it was the popular hit of the Plaza Theatre's Chaplin revival series. For here at last the serious movie public, which has grown so rapidly of late, could see this "banned masterpiece" which the late Robert Warshow had celebrated in an essay in *Partisan Review* (reprinted in his posthumous collection, *The Immediate Experience*) as "a great work of irony," comparing it to Swift, and the late James Agee, in a three-part review in *The Nation* (reprinted in *Agee on Film*, v. 1), had called "one of the best movies ever made," saluting "this great poet and this great poem," and later adding, after six months' reflection: "Beside it every movie since *Zéro de Conduite* and *Modern Times* is so much child's play." Since these were made in 1933 and 1936, the Plaza stretched around the block, and the re-reviews were enthusiastic, or, at worst, respectful. You can't fight City Hall. Or the Cultural Establishment.

There was something else working for *Verdoux* last summer. While "banned" was mythical (since it was Chaplin's decision, from no more lofty a motive than pique, that had denied *Verdoux* to American distributors for seventeen years), it was true that its failure in 1947 was in large part due to certain pressures. Chaplin was unpopular because of the Joan Barry paternity suit (which he won, but only after the public had seen that their beloved Charlie, the "little man," was a libertine) and, more important, because of his alleged Communist sympathies. As Chaplin's *Autobiography* makes clear, and all the more since he is—as throughout that remarkable exercise in self-concealment— obviously trying to explain away things rather than to explain them, his fellow-traveling was prompted by nothing more sinister than vanity and a sentimental feeling for what he, like many others in Hollywood then, thought was the cause of the underdog. It was a case for Freud, not Marx: a symbolic compensation for guilt feelings about his wealth rather than any wish to subvert the capitalist system that protected it. Groups like the American Legion, however, as simpleminded as he, picketed *Verdoux* (which, in a simpleminded way, satirized capitalism, war, and religion—so that the film was as objectionable as its creator) and, supported by the usual pack of moralistic wowsers, intimidated exhibitors.

But I wonder if the coolness of the 1947 audiences toward *Verdoux* can be explained wholly by the pressure of wowsers and patrioteers. Maybe moviegoers just didn't like *Verdoux* and maybe they had some good reasons not to. Looked at simply as another movie seen in the dark privacy of a theatre without either highbrow critics or lowbrow legionnaires breathing down the back of one's neck, how does *Verdoux* strike one? That is, me.

I've seen it twice: in 1956 at the National Film Theater in London, and in 1964 at New York's closest replica of that useful institution, except for the Thalia seven blocks farther up Broadway, Daniel Talbot's New Yorker Theatre. My 1956 reactions were published in *Encounter*:

> *Monsieur Verdoux* is really two films, one a sentimental melodrama, the other a comedy in the old Chaplin style that burlesques the melodrama. What makes it confusing is that Chaplin shifts gears between the two without apparently knowing he is doing so. He will be strutting around in a comic scene with Martha Raye, flourishing his moustaches in an exquisitely shaded parody of the stock-company notion of a boulevardier, and in the next scene, with a pretty street waif as his foil, he will be playing the part straight, hamming it up with innocent relish. It is unsettling to see an actor brilliantly taking off the conventional rhetoric of his trade one moment and the next employing it seriously, especially since Chaplin's serious rhetoric expresses a vain and foolish concept of himself—as the tragic man-of-the-world, disenchanted, elegant, sensitive, the gallant protector of the weak who, to make the bogus diamond shine all the more brilliantly, are usually crippled or blind. In the film after *Verdoux*, the disastrous *Limelight*, this mawkish exhibitionism goes right over the edge [and, as of 1965, his *Autobiography* shows us what was at the bottom of the abyss: not much one likes to see].
>
> There is even a third film here, that bursts into the last part with shattering banality, a "message" drama, the message being that a man is a hero if he kills wholesale (like Napoleon or Hitler), but a murderer if he does it retail, an irony that was probably first observed by some ur-Montaigne of the time of Belshazzar. It was a sad day for Chaplin when the intellectuals convinced him he was the Tragic

Clown, the Little Man. From a parodist he graduated into a philosopher, but since his epistemology was all instinctive, even physical (his eyebrows, fingers, teeth "know" precisely, instantaneously, how to behave in order to mimic a clergyman, a banker, a dandy, a tramp), it didn't help him in his new role. The nature of reality, which he understood intuitively as a mime, became opaque to him when he tried to think about it, and where he once danced lightly he now stumbles into bathos and sentimentality.

Rereading the above, after seeing *Verdoux* again last year, I think it on the whole accurate. The comic parts were as good as ever: Verdoux counting one widow's stack of bank notes with light-fingered professional speed; his amorous lunges at another as they sip tea on her sofa, upsetting her and himself but never his cup and saucer which, like a mad gyroscope, he keeps on the same level no matter where the rest of him is; the acrobatics at the wedding to keep out of sight of Martha Raye. And how could I have omitted *her*, the indestructible widow whose raucous sprawling vulgarity is the perfect foil to Chaplin's desiccated gentlemanliness, the messy life principle winning out over the neat little merchant of death? It is Chaplin's one triumph in casting, script and direction. But the rest! (And it should be remembered that "the rest" is more than half the film, closer to two-thirds, and that it is the distinctive part—the slapstick and pantomime are good but no better than Chaplin had been giving us since his first Keystone comedies in 1913—and also the part that the critics admire especially.) The rest looked even worse than it had eight years ago. The banality and pretentiousness of the script, as in the two long scenes with the waif-girl-of-the-streets (who for once isn't blind or crippled, except as an actress) with lines, delivered tremolo by Chaplin-Verdoux, like, "Is a little kindness such a rare thing?" and "In the sunset of our lives, we need love." The first of these scenes may be read in the *Autobiography*. Apparently Chaplin is proud of it. One exchange may give the flavor:

"GIRL (*quizzingly*): You don't like women, do you?

"VERDOUX: On the contrary, I love women . . . but I don't admire them.

"GIRL: Why?

"VERDOUX: Women are of the earth … realistic, dominated by physical facts.

"GIRL: (*incredulously*): What nonsense!"

Her last comment may be explained by the fact, established earlier, that she has been reading Schopenhauer. "Do you like him?" asks Verdoux. "So-so." "Have you read his treatise on suicide?" It seems she hasn't. He's one up.

He's always one up. His wife is a paralytic, his boy is six, not big enough to worry about, his closest friends are a little chemist and his mountainous wife, both of them, for some reason, aggressively ugly, the women he preys on are (except for Miss Raye) easy game, the police are so stupid that he has trouble giving himself up to them, and in his final not at all *mauvais quart d'heure* in the death cell he scores off everbody, the jailer, the priest, even his own lawyer. He gives the priest a specially hard time. "I've come to ask you to make your peace with God." "I am at peace with God, my conflict is with man." "Have you no remorse for your sins?" "Who knows what sin is, born as it was from Heaven, from God's fallen angel, who knows what mysterious destiny it serves?" The priest doesn't know, so Verdoux tops his own line: "What would you be doing without sin?" Chaplin records all this, and more, in the pages of his *Autobiography* concerning his interview at the Breen Office, which made many foolish objections to the script—all of which Chaplin parries with ease—and one sensible one, "That's a lot of pseudo-philosophizing," which he disdains to answer. They ask him why he didn't give the priest "some worthwhile answer" to the "What-would-you-be-doing-without-sin?" topper, and he indulgently promises to "think up something for the priest to answer." If he did, I don't remember it. That priest just doesn't shine when he's up against Chaplin-Verdoux. He can't even get away with what one would think a puncture-proof exit line: "May the Lord have mercy on your soul." "Why not?" Verdoux shoots back quicker than Bob Hope. "It belongs to Him." (When a Breen official fatuously complained, "You don't talk to a priest like that," Chaplin, or Verdoux, upstaged him: "That line is said introspectively. You must wait until you see the film." I've seen the film and I don't understand how an actor can say a line "introspectively"; Chaplin didn't succeed anyway.) No wonder they instantly hustle Chaplin, I mean Verdoux, out to the guillotine. They were afraid he'd write his autobiography: *God Is My Straight Man*. One heaves a sigh of relief as that proud little figure walks slowly up the fatal courtyard to his destiny, erect, defiant, and smug to the end, and the camera draws back and back and those blessed words, surcease and anodyne, drawn radiantly on the screen, "THE END."

Chaplin's direction is no better than his script. The photography is by an old Hollywood hand named Roland Totheroh, and looks it. Except for Miss Raye, the actors seem to have been selected by taking the first candidates sent up from Central Casting; they're not good even as extras, nor are there any of those familiar bit-part players that are often in Hollywood movies better than the principals; there are, in short, no faces that were familiar up to 1947 or that have become familiar since then, for obvious reasons in both cases. It must have been a cheap film to cast. The opening scene gives it to you right in the eye: a family group—they are beginning to wonder what has become of Aunt Mathilde—of stiffly nervous actors who walk around and overplay without making connection with each other, or with the spectator; clumsily directed and tritely photographed. Neither realistic or stylized, *Verdoux* is amateurish without freshness. Hollywoodish without technique. It comes to life only when Chaplin is onstage, and even then only when he is parodying his boulevardier and not in the longer stretches when he is trying to impress us as a philosopher ("Have you read Schopenhauer's treatise on suicide? . . . It's the approach of death that terrifies"). As Chaplin's script is only a device to show him off (and not so much as an actor but, worse, as an actor's narcissistic dream of his "real" self), so his direction reduces all the other performers to stooges—no wonder he didn't bother much with casting—except for the indestructible Miss Raye. His directorial eye finds nothing interesting in the inanimate world either, which is reduced to a conventional background for his own performance. I can recall few films in which there was so little to *see*. Since it is a movie, Chaplin thinks he has to show us realistic interiors and real landscapes and cityscapes, but they are botched in so routinely, with so little sense of what they look like, that they might as well be those painted backdrops of a park or a street, bordered with local advertisements, in front of which vaudevillians used to do their turns. In fact, *Verdoux* would have been better, not good but better, if Chaplin had had the imaginative daring to realize that a series of such backdrops was all he needed for his drama; it would at least have had an original, and appropriate, style—and I daresay some pop scenic designer will steal the idea if he hasn't already thought of it himself. (Think what a wrench would be given to Albee's *Tiny Alice*—and any wrench would be an improvement—if it were played against such appropriately flimsy specimens of the sign-painter's art, complete with ads for painless dentists, discothèques and psychoanalytic parlors, instead of expiring under the weight of that massive Belasco-type set!)

The closest *Verdoux* comes to visual style is a shot of the Eiffel Tower (to show us we are in Paris), supplemented, as a transitional device, by close-ups of revolving locomotive wheels (to show us we are leaving, or returning to, Paris). Economical but a little familiar. "Vorkapich Effects" they used to call them in the old, innocent Hollywood of the thirties, after a Yugoslav technician named Slavko Vorkapich who was rumored to have worked with Eisenstein. A modest Prometheus, Mr. Vorkapich brought to the hinterland this small spark of montage—other Vorkapich Effects included calendar leaves blowing off one by one to indicate the passage of time, shots of frenzied brokers intercut with newspaper headlines to indicate the 1929 market crash, and a series of quick-cut newsreel shots of soldiers going over the top, huge guns firing, mines exploding in No Man's Land, etc., to indicate that World War I had occurred. At this very moment, Mr. Vorkapich is in full course at the Museum of Modern Art, an institution that keeps abreast of the times, especially in its Film Department, with a series of ten weekly illustrated lectures under the general title, *The Visual Nature of the Film Medium*, with subtitles ranging from "To Hold, As't Were, a Moving Mirror up to Nature" (camera movement), up to the grand finale: "Aesthetics of Film Content" (. . . transcending the literal meaning of the shot. . . . The objective correlative . . . dynamic images on the screen suddenly come to life in their own ineffable way).

To get back to *Monsieur Verdoux*: why did, and do, many intelligent critics evaluate it in terms that make recognizable the account I have given above? Who is right on the main point—is it a good movie?—cannot be settled definitively here, or anywhere, or ever, since it's an argument about values, not facts; each viewer must decide for himself which evaluation best explains what he saw on the screen. But some peripheral answers to the problem are possible. An editorial in the Summer 1964, issue of *The Seventh Art* takes an historical view. The editors think better of *Verdoux* than I, though not much. After describing "the brain-washing effects of reputation—Chaplin's . . . Agee's, Warshow's and The New York *Times*'" on the 1964 audiences as "merely the reverse of what occurred in 1947," they suggest that, whether or not *Verdoux* failed in 1947 because it was ahead of its time, as has been argued, it "has come to us now five years too late." (I doubt it would ever have arrived on schedule by my timetable, but let it pass.) "The objections raised initially," they continue, meaning the brilliantly if not convincingly, stand. The film's strong points—its gallows humor, its acerbic cynicism—these virtues have been exploited and possibly exhausted by the theatre of the absurd and its progeny. Not only does much of the technique seem dated now, the humor of the film has also passed its prime and has become, in one way or another, banal."

This seems reasonable, as far as it goes. But I think something simpler, and more fundamental, than period and fashion may also be involved: that the appeal of *Verdoux* may be political rather than cinematic, that those who find it important may be reacting to it more as a tract for the times, an indictment of the hypocrisies of capitalism than as a work of art. Robert Warshow, for instance, writes of it almost entirely in psychological and sociological terms, as was his custom. (Anyone interested in movies or popular culture will find *The Immediate Experience* brilliant and original, but he mustn't expect much aesthetic criticism, or much interest in it.) James Agee was, of course, a professional critic, but in the twelve pages devoted to *Verdoux* in his collection (Huston's *The Treasure of the Sierra Madre* is a poor second, with six pages) it is notable how defensive and often equivocal he is about it as a movie and how enthusiastic when he analyzes, as he does at length and with subtlety, its social and political meanings—or what he says they are; I found his glosses much richer than the text. He does defend on page 254 the casting, the script, the direction and even "the production," by which he seems to mean that perfunctory *mise-en-scène* I objected to above, but briefly, vaguely, evasively. The scrupulous honesty that was one of his most admirable traits makes him add, under *New Techniques*: "They are on the whole weakened derivations from styles developed before sound came, in Russia, Germany and this country, by Chaplin among others; virtually nothing has been done with sound." (And this was 1947, fifteen years after Clair and six years after *Citizen Kane*.) He also defends Chaplin's routine use of the camera and even those locomotive wheels, the former thusly: "Chaplin . . . obviously believes that if you can invent something worth watching, the camera should hold still and clear, so that you can watch it. That is still, and will always be, one of the best possible ways to use a camera: Chaplin is the one great man who stands up for it"; and the latter thusly: ". . . we sneer at Chaplin's frequent use of locomotive wheels, charging ever more desperately across the screen. . . . But in fact these wheels do a lot at once. They are in the best sense economical; they are cumulatively funny; they cumulatively express Verdoux's ever more frantic busyness; and they wind up the film like a tight spring." The defense of Chaplin's static camera reminds me of the paradoxical reflex by which Miss Susan Sontag defends bad movies (by, say, Godard or the Smiths) precisely on the grounds they *are* so courageously boring, so defiantly sloppy; as to those wheels, I saw no increasing desperation in their revolutions (in fact I thought Chaplin, with his usual economy—financial, not artistic—had simply used the same shot over and over), and I suspect that Agee's response is an example of his chief weakness as a critic: his directorial imagination which sometimes remade the movie inside his head as he watched it, so that what came out on his page was often more exciting than what had appeared on the screen.

Why is Agee so unconvincing about *Verdoux* as cinema and so persuasive about it as satire? I think the film struck home to him emotionally because of its anti-bourgeois "black" humor and because of his admiration for Chaplin and his generous indignation at the 1947 campaign of calumny.

"I love and revere the film as deeply as any I have seen," he wrote in *The Nation*, "and believe that it is high among the great works of this century. I wish I might discuss at proper length its weaknesses as a work of art and of moral understanding." I should have thought a three-part review might have been enough.

A great strain must have been put on Agee's fine intelligence by the pressure of his personal feeling for *Verdoux*, his love and reverence (not critical categories), and the contrary pull of his perception of its artistic defects. He was too honest, too serious, to gloss over the conflict by omitting either term. In this *Time* review, positive thesis and negative antithesis seesaw back and forth, as in the following excerpts, in which I have italicized the negative antithesis.

"Monsieur Verdoux *has serious shortcomings both as popular entertainment and as a work of art. But whatever its shortcomings*, it is one of the most notable films in years.... *It has its blurs and failures.* Finely cut and paced as it is, *the picture goes on so long* . . . that the lazier-minded type of cinemagoers will *probably get tired. Chaplin overexerts, and apparently overestimates, a writing talent which*, though vigorous and unconventional, *weighs light beside his acting gifts. As a result, a good deal of the verbal and philosophic straining seems inadequate, muddled and highly arguable*—too highbrow for general audiences, and *too naïve for the highbrows.*"

One sentence in Agee's review, however, is not antithetical: "At a time when many people have regained their faith in war under certain conditions and in free enterprise under any conditions, he has ventured to insist, as bitterly as he knows how, that there are considerable elements of criminality in both." That this is one of Chaplin's intentions I grant, and a noble one it is. But wasn't it Herbert Hoover who once described Prohibition as "an experiment noble in purpose"? That Agee, and others whom I respect, take the will for the deed in *Verdoux* is a lapse that is explicable in such intelligent persons—for to call a badly flawed movie great because of its theme and its creator's intentions is like saying an orator is eloquent but inarticulate—only on the hypothesis that they are really interested in something else, something outside my province as a film critic, something that doesn't appear on the screen.

ANDREW SARRIS

Monsieur Verdoux

Andrew Sarris is the crucial figure in bringing the au-
teur theory *to America. His belief in the director as the*
most significant figure in the creation of movies has of-
ten been challenged but never repudiated. His tone
about the great directors has, it seems to me, changed
over the years, becoming warmer and more affectionate
toward them. This is particularly evident in his writings
about Chaplin.

I

If this were the most fitting of all possible worlds, Chaplin would
have dedicated the current revival of *Monsieur Verdoux* to the late
James Agee in the generous spirit of Renoir's dedication of the restored *La Règle du Jeu* to the late André Bazin. Agee's extensive
comments on Chaplin's "comedy of murders" appeared originally
in the *Time* of May 5, 1947, and the *Nation* of May 31, June 14, and
June 21, 1947, and are reprinted in a new paperback entitled *Agee on
Film—Reviews and Comments* by James Agee. I do not entirely
agree with Agee's position on *Verdoux*, but I admire the force and lu-
cidity of his arguments. Not only has he prevailed posthumously

From the *Village Voice*, July 16 and 23, 1964, courtesy of the *Village Voice*.

over the negative critical consensus of his time but he has kept *Verdoux* alive and legendary through seventeen years of nonexhibition.

What, then, is left to say about Verdoux after Agee? As Anna Maganani replies in *The Gold Coach* when asked if she misses her lovers: "a leetle." Time, no less than seventeen years' worth, has altered the context of Chaplin's ironic conceits. Back in 1947 *Monsieur Verdoux* was disconcerting not merely to the rabble of the right but to the prevailing liberal optimism about the perfectibility of man. Agee was most perceptive about this latter aspect of his Zeitgeist: "At a time when many people have regained their faith in war under certain conditions and in free enterprise under any conditions whatever, he [Chaplin] has ventured to insist, as bitterly as he knows how, that there are considerable elements of criminality implicit in both."

Note, however, that *Verdoux* follows *The Great Dictator* by seven years, and yet recedes historically to the early thirties of *Modern Times*. The internal evidence of newspapers indicates crucial decisions in 1932. We see newsreels of Hitler and Mussolini like a recurring dream of *The Great Dictator* while the insanely logical world of Monsieur Verdoux collapses around him. When Verdoux taunts his judges about a future war, it is not clear whether he is predicting World War II fatuously or World War III fatalistically.

Why does Chaplin cling to the dead past for his background? To my mind, Agee never satisfactorily answered this question. Normally a retreat into the past indicates an artist's desire to distance his material from a rigorous moral accounting, but Chaplin and Verdoux are so inextricably linked that both creator and creature are implicated in each other's activities. I suspect that Chaplin's solipsism as an artist translates his personal bitterness into political malaise into personal bitterness. It is only natural that the world seems more wicked as we grow older. What is amazing about Chaplin is the mellowing process between *Verdoux* and *Limelight*. Perhaps it is not so amazing if we consider *Verdoux* as Chaplin's last dialogue with a drifting audience, and *Limelight* as his first soliloquy before a departed audience.

Even today *Monsieur Verdoux* will seem a failure to anyone who has taken half a dozen lessons in film technique. Things were much worse, however, back in 1947 when Chaplin was squeezed between the patrons of Hollywood illusionism on one hand and the partisans of Italian neorealism on the other. *Verdoux* is neither slick enough for the dream merchants nor sincere enough for the humanists, and this is not necessarily all to the good, as Agee seemed to suggest. There are distinct pleasures in both stylistic elaboration of a dream apparatus and the God-given ambiguity and accident of raw realism.

These pleasures are not to be fond in *Verdoux* or in the rest of Chaplin. What we get instead is the genius of economy and essentiality, and it follows that the most drab moments in *Verdoux* are also the most functional. Indeed, the opening exposition involving the family of a Verdoux victim is about as bad as anything I have ever seen in the professional cinema. Yet after repeated reviewings, the badness seems not only integral to Chaplin's conception but decidedly Brechtian in the bargain. Chaplin has stacked the deck shamelessly and crudely, but as soon as he makes his first entrance in his rose garden with his meticulous hands and pliers ravishing sweet nature, all is forgiven, particularly the smoking remains of his wife in the incinerator.

II

If 1947 audiences were too reluctant to laugh at the cruelty in Monsieur Verdoux, today's crowds may be too eager. We are becoming so oversatirized that our capacity for pity and terror is rapidly shrinking to bread-and-circuses dimensions. Perhaps all the sick jokes of the past decade have finally come home to roost in the nomination of Barry (Triumph of the Won't) Gauleiter (sic, sic, sic), and we'll all be laughing on the way to the concentration camp. I certainly hope not. However, aside from ultimate consequences, excessive risibility tends to obscure the distinction between jokes and japes. If people can laugh even slightly at the moronic slapstick of *Bedtime Story*, Chaplin might just as well regress to slipping on banana peels. The paradox here is that *Monsieur Verdoux* seems much greater as a popular failure than as a popular success. After all, Chaplin ends up thumbing his nose at his audience, a gesture performed with great difficulty when the audience insists on embracing the artist. It may be, as Cocteau once remarked, that it is the fate of iconoclasts to become icons. Then again, Chaplin's reputation may at last be filtering out of his audience all those who are not at least tolerant of his vaguely leftist and agnostic convictions.

There are some bad gags in *Verdoux*. The fat woman who falls asleep after dinner in the Verdoux cottage is incomprehensibly obvious and overdone. The business with Martha Raye's maid losing her hair is both ugly and uninspired, and the strenuous contrivances by which the poison is misplaced in the same episode are too farfetched for the logic of farce. The functional family of one of Verdoux's victims is a five-pronged ordeal on every occasion it is summoned to advance the plot, particularly when any comically exaggerated reaction is demanded.

Fortunately the great moments are far more numerous and infinitely more memorable. The hilarity I found richest and deepest was inspired not by the famous boat scene with Martha Raye but by that fantastic surprise when Chaplin comes dancing into Isobel Elsom's apartment with satyrlike abandon to embrace miss Elsom's fat, ugly housekeeper before discovering his mistake. The rest of the scene is drowned out by the convulsed audience as Chaplin commits a second gaffe with Miss Elsom's lady friend and then pauses in perplexity for Miss Elsom herself. Beneath the laughter is the most incisive expression of the pathos and tragedy of Don Juanism I have ever encountered. Until one has seen Chaplin in *Verdoux* one cannot fully realize how little has been done with sex and desire on the screen. We have had gigolos and foolish old women and May-December and December-December romances, but little of the pain and anguish that accompanies the perversion of romantic emotion.

There is a distant parallel, for example, between Chaplin-Elsom and Groucho Marx-Margaret Dumont. Groucho always treated Miss Dumont shamefully, too shamefully, in fact, for realism to intrude on comic fantasy. Deep down we have always known that Groucho is too much of a gentleman and Miss Dumont too much of a lady for anything irrevocably sordid to occur. Groucho's excessive rudeness is actually a form of gallantry, enabling Miss Dumont to withdraw from his bedroom without being deeply humiliated. Groucho takes the burden of outrageousness upon himself because he can afford to let people see through him. He has nothing to hide; his transparency is merely the means by which he deflates the pomposity of others.

Chaplin-Verdoux is more desperate. Despite his courtliness, he is no gentleman. He is a man. Unlike Groucho, he is not a fraud, however hilariously transparent. He accepts his part of the bargain. He seduces his old, ugly victims before he murders them, but he knows the day will come when he will be too old even for the last dregs of wealthy womanhood. It is a measure of Chaplin's incredible instinct for counterpoint that his ugliest victim (Margaret Hoffman) ignites the brightest flame of his poetic imagination. Gazing out the window upon a paper moon against a *papier-mâché* sky, he pauses in the trajectory of his murderous task to choreograph "this Endymion hour" with his eloquent body. His victim summons him to her doom, but the shot of his poetic universe is held. The murder, an act of imaginative schizophrenia, is performed musically offscreen.

Chaplin gets laughs along the way with his businesslike briskness. Whether he is counting his ill-gotten francs with the page-flipping technique of a bank teller or courting a victim by his timepiece or complaining to his adoring wife (Mady Corell) about the stresses and strains of business, Chaplin expertly performs all the scales of social parody. It is possible to deduce that he is attacking capitalism, war, business ethics, family solidarity, bourgeois morality. These are mundane matters for Chaplin's genius. Where he rises with the angels is in the self-revelation of his sexual relationships, particularly with man-eating Martha Raye, the supreme expression of the otherness of life forces in Chaplin's cinema. All the wiles of Verdoux are of course futile against Martha's luck and vitality. (The fiasco on the lake should make it impossible for *An American Tragedy* to be filmed ever again.) Verdoux is clearly appalled by Martha, a creature of force without style. However, Martha's extreme raucousness may be Chaplin's method, conscious or unconscious, of masking what he really finds objectionable in her, namely her perversity. Perversity doesn't go with pedestals. Chaplin's heroines almost invariably begin by loving outer handsomeness and end by perceiving inner goodness. A casual glance at dating couples on Saturday night should dispel that notion. Even granting that beautiful faces are screen metaphors for beautiful souls, Chaplin underestimates the range of choices involved in feminine free will. Women are too much an extension of his angst-ridden ego, too much an index of his moral sensibility, for him ever to acknowledge their ultimate separateness.

Where Chaplin indulges himself to some extent is in his overly abstract, overly philosophical dialogue. His relationship to Marilyn Nash's tall waif is expressed almost entirely in aphorisms of the I-am-an-optimist-you-are-a-pessimist variety. The beauty of these speeches derives from the effort of Chaplin's expressive face to determine hidden meanings, if any, from the echoes of the sound track. It is interesting that most critics have created the impression that the last line of Verdoux is, in reply to a priest's unctuously routine "May God have mercy on your soul," the metaphysically defiant "Why not? After all, it belongs to Him." The abstraction, it would seem, to end abstractions. However, Chaplin's last line is actually, "Wait, I've never tasted rum." Verdoux drinks the rum. He throws his chest out to the sunlight pouring into the cell as the door opens. The camera follows him through the door and then parks by the hall so that he may turn his back to the audience and show just a hint of the way the Tramp would have walked to the guillotine. The hint is sufficient for sublime recognition. In the end as in the beginning, Chaplin belongs to the things of this world—rum and sunshine—and not to the things beyond—souls and such.

THEODOR W. ADORNO

Chaplin Times Two

Theodor Adorno (1903–1969) was one of the leaders of the so-called Frankfurt School of social and philosophical thought in the last years of the Weimar Republic. The school, officially the Institut for Sozialforschung, was driven out of Nazi Germany, then settled in New York, where its members continued developing a highly sophisticated critique of all forms of totalitarianism. Adorno, who was also a musician and music critic, had a special interest in popular culture with particular attention to comedy and animation (he loved the early Betty Boop). He was never a lighthearted critic, but he did enunciate the notion, implicitly influential among many later critics, that the most interesting cultural work was to be found at the high end and the low, with the middle ground—which most commercial movies occupy—viewed contemptuously. His little piece about Chaplin, whom he admired with reservations, is a good small metaphor for his larger thoughts. It also shows that even the intellectual critics were not immune to the power of celebrity.

I. PROPHESIED BY KIERKEGAARD

In *Repetition*, one of earlier pseudonymous writings, Kierkegaard gives a detailed treatment of farce, true to a conviction which often leads him to seek, in the refuse of art, that which eludes the pretensions of art's great self-contained works. He speaks there of the old Friedrichstädter Theater in Berlin and describes a comedian named Beckmann[1] whose image evokes, with the mild fidelity of a daguerreotype, that of the Chaplin who was to come. The passage reads:

> He is not only able to walk, but he is also able to *come walking*. To come walking is something very distinctive, and by means of this genius he also improvises the whole scenic setting. He is able not only to portray an itinerant craftsman; he is also able to come walking like one and in such a way that one experiences everything, surveys the smiling hamlet from the dusty highway, hears its quiet noise, sees the footpath that goes down by the village pond when one turns off there by the blacksmith's—where one sees [Beckmann] walking along with this little bundle on his back, his stick in his hand, untroubled and undaunted. He can come walking onto the stage followed by street urchins whom one does not see.[2]

The one who comes walking is Chaplin, who brushes against the world like a slow meteor even where he seems to be at rest; the imaginary landscape that he brings along is the meteor's aura, which gathers here in the quiet noise of the village into transparent peace, while he strolls on with the cane and hat that so become him. The invisible tail of street urchins is the comet's tail through which the earth cuts almost unawares. But when one recalls the scene in *The Gold Rush* where Chaplin, like a ghostly photograph in a lively film, comes walking into the gold mining town and disappears crawling into a cabin, it is as if his figure, suddenly recognized by Kierkegaard, populated the

---

[1] "Friedrich Beckermann (1803–1866), famous German comic actor, from 1824 the leading actor of the Königstädter Theater for many years." (Note from Soren Kierkegaard, *Fear and Trembling and Repetition*, ed. and trans. Howard V. Hong and Edna H. Hong (Princeton: Princeton University Press, 1983), 367.)

[2] *Repetition*, 163–4.

cityscape of 1840 like staffage; from this background the star only now has finally emerged.

II. IN MALIBU

The fact that profundity is irritated by profound topics, that it would rather, according to Benjamin's phrase, latch onto that which is devoid of intention,[3] would be reckoned a good thing if only profundity, so self-satisfied and untrammeled by an object, would not then wear itself out. For the most part, profundity uses unhackneyed topics as a pretext for vagueness and banality, exploiting the apparent inability to resist of that which from itself sets forth no meanings and which possibly, to the extent of its immediacy, itself tends toward banality or stupidity just like the empty ideas on which it is sharpened by the clever mind. The link between mind and clown is as understandable as it is unfortunate. The children's darling is spared no demonology; one owes it to him to certify once again the laughter he arouses before decorating him with the trumpery of great categories, which hang more loosely and less amusingly on him than his traditional costume. At least he should be allowed a long and thorough grace period.

Psychoanalysis tries to relate the clown-figure to the reaction formations of earliest childhood, before any crystallization of a stable self.[4] As always the situation is the same: more information about the clown is to be found among children who, as mysteriously as they do with animals, communicate with his image and with the meaning of

---

[3] Cf. Benjamin, *The Origin of German Tragic Drama*, trans. John Osborne (London: Verso, 1977), 183–185: "If the object becomes allegorical under the gaze of melancholy, if melancholy causes life to flow out of it and it remains behind dead, but eternally secure, then it is exposed to the allegorist, it is unconditionally in his power. That is to say it is now quite incapable of emanating any meaning or significance of its own; such significance as it has, it acquires from the allegorist. . . . It may not accord with the authority of nature; but the voluptuousness with which significance rules, like a stern sultan in sadist that he humiliates his object and then—or thereby—satisfies it. And that is what the allegorist does in this age drunk with acts of cruelty both lived and imagined. . . . For the only pleasure the melancholic permits himself, and it is a powerful one, is allegory."

[4] Cf. Freud's discussion of the comic as the result of a "comparison between the ego of the grown-up and the ego of the child" in "Wit and Its Relation to the Unconscious" in *The Basic Writings of Sigmund Freud*, trans. and ed. Dr. A. A. Brill (New York: Modern Library, 1966), 795.

his activity, which in fact negates meaning. Only one capable in the language common to the clown and to children, a language distanced from sense, would understand the clown himself, in whom fleeing Nature bids a shocked adieu, like the old man in the illustration "Winter-ade":[5] Nature, so pitilessly suppressed by the process of becoming an adult, is, like that language, irrecoverable by adults.

Its loss demands silence, and especially in the face of Chaplin. For his precedence over other clowns, among whose number he proudly counts himself—as far as I know, their club is the only one to which he belongs—encourages interpretations which inflict more injury the higher they elevate him. In this way they move away from the conundrum whose solution is the only interpretive task worthy of Chaplin.

I do not wish to offend in this way. Only because I knew him many years ago would I stress, without any philosophical pretensions, two or three observations which might contribute to a descriptive account of his image [*zur ecriture seines Bildes*]. It is known how different Chaplin looks in private from the vagabond on the screen. However, this difference pertains not only to his soigné elegance, which as clown he in turn parodies, but to expression. This has nothing to do with sympathy towards a begging, abandoned and unshreddable victim. Rather, his powerful, explosive and quick-witted agility recalls a predator ready to pounce. Only through this bestial quality would earliest childhood have brought itself safely into wide-awake life. There is something about the empirical Chaplin that suggests not that he is a victim but rather, menacingly, that he would seek victims, pounce on them, tear them apart. One can well imagine that Chaplin's cryptic dimension, or precisely that which makes this most perfect clown more than his genus, is connected with the fact that he as it were projects upon the environment his own violence and dominating instinct [*sein Gewaltsames und Beherrschendes*], and through this projection of his own culpability produces that innocence which endows him with more power than all power pos-

---

[5] "Winter ade" ("Adieu, Winter") is the title of a children's song by Hoffman von Fallersleben (1798–1874), a 19th-century liberal and populist poet and philologist perhaps best known as the author of the old German national anthem, "Deutsch land, Deutsch land über alles." "Winter ade" is an ironic song of "sad farewell" ("Adieu, Winter!/ Parting brings sorrow./ But your departure is such/ That now my heart laughs").

sesses. A vegetarian Bengal tiger: comforting, because his goodness, which the children cheer, is itself in a compact with the very evil that in vain seeks to destroy him—in vain, for he had already destroyed that evil in his own image.

Presence of mind and omnipresence of mimetic ability also characterize the empirical Chaplin. It is well known that he does not confine his mimetic arts strictly to the films which, since his youth, he produces only over great intervals of time and in an intensely and openly self-critical spirit. He acts incessantly, just like Kafka's trapeze artist, who sleeps in the baggage rack so as not to ease off training even for a moment. Any time spent with him is an uninterrupted performance. One scarcely dares speak to him, not from awe of his fame—no one could set himself less apart, no one could be less pretentious than he—but rather from fear of disturbing the spell of the performance. It is as though he, using mimetic behavior, caused purposeful, grown-up life to recede, and indeed the principle of reason itself, thereby placating it. But this endows his incarnate existence with an imaginary element beyond the official artforms. If Chaplin the private citizen lacks the features of the famous clown (as though these features were under a taboo), he has all the more of the juggler about him. The Rastelli of mine,[6] he plays with the countless balls of his pure possibility, and fixes its restless circling into a fabric that has little more in common with the causal world than Cloudcuckooland has with the gravitation of Newtonian physics. Incessant and spontaneous change: in Chaplin, this is the utopia of an existence that would be free of the burden of being-one's-self. His lady killer was schizophrenic.

Perhaps I may justify my speaking about him by recounting a certain privilege which I was granted, entirely without having earned it. He once imitated me, and surely I am one of the few intellectuals to whom this happened and to be able to account for it when it happened. Together with many others we were invited to a villa in Malibu, on the coast outside of Los Angeles. While Chaplin stood next to me, one of the guests was taking his leave early. Unlike Chaplin, I extended my hand to him a bit absentmindedly, and, almost instantly,

[6] Enrico Rastelli (1896–1931), Italian juggler.

started violently back. The man was one of the lead actors from *The Best Years of Our Lives*, a film famous shortly after the war; he lost a hand during the war, and in its place bore practicable claws made of iron.[7] When I shook his right hand and felt it return the pressure, I was extremely startled, but sensed immediately that I could not reveal my shock to the injured man at any price. In a split second I transformed my frightened expression into an obliging grimace that must have been far ghastlier. The actor had hardly moved away when Chaplin was already playing the scene back. All the laughter he brings about is so near to cruelty; solely in such proximity to cruelty does it find its legitimation and its element of the salvational. Let my remembrance of this event and my thanks be my congratulations to him on his 75th birthday.[8]

---

[7] The actor described here was Harold Russell (b. 1914 in Nova Scotia), who in fact lost both his hands as a soldier during World War II. Acclaimed for his performance as one of the three returning veterans in William Wyler's *The Best of Our Lives* (1946), Russell became the only actor ever to win two Oscars for the same role: one for Best Supporting Actor, the other a special Oscar given "for bringing hope and courage to his fellow veterans." Russell made history again in 1992, as he became the first Oscar recipient to sell one of his awards, which he did in order to raise money to help cover his wife's medical expenses.

[8] The translator would like to thank the following people for their assistance: Charles Musser, Joanna Spiro, Michael Kerbel, Lance Duerfahrd, Dan Friedman, Patrick Noon, Richard Field, Carol Hightower, Alexander Ulanov, Christa and Jeffrey Sammons.

ROBERT WARSHOW

A Feeling of Sad Dignity

Born in 1917, Robert Warshow died in 1955—a tragically short life which produced only a short, posthumously published collection of essays and reviews, The Immediate Experience, *a book almost universally revered by the generations of critics that came after him. Most of the pieces in the book are about movies, but some of the best of them take up matters as diverse as* Krazy Kat *and the Rosenberg case. Had he lived, I suspect he might have become less a film critic, more a general cultural commentator. His affection for Chaplin is much more tempered than Agee's and much more pleasingly analytic. His study of* Limelight *is high in tone but also subtly personal and quite practical—a masterly performance.*

Beneath all the social meanings of Chaplin's art there is one insistent personal message that he is conveying to us all the time. It is the message of most entertainers, maybe, but his especially because he is so great an entertainer. "Love me"—he has asked this from the beginning, buttering us up with his sweet ways and his calculated graceful misadventures, with those exquisite manners so perfectly beside the point, with that honeyed glance he casts at us so often, lips pursued in

From *Partisan Review*, November–December 1954.

an outrageous simper, eyebrows and mustache moving in frantic invitation. Love me. And we have, apparently, loved him, though with such undercurrents of revulsion as might be expected in response to so naked a demand.

Does he love us? This is a strange question to ask of an artist. But it is Chaplin himself who puts it in our mouths, harping on love until we are forced almost in self-defense to say: what about *you*? He does not love us; and maybe he doesn't love anything. Even in his most genial moments we get now and then a glimpse of how cold a heart has gone into his great blaze. Consider the scene in *City Lights* when he tactfully permits the Blind Girl to unravel his underwear in the believe that she is rolling up her knitting wool; the delicacy of feeling is wonderful, all right—who else could have conceived the need for this particular kindness?—but it is he, that contriving artist there, who has created the occasion for the delicacy in the first place. No, the warmth that comes from his image on the screen is only our happy opportunity to love him. He has no love to spare, he is too busy pushing his own demand: love *me*, love *me*, poor Charlie, sweet Charlie. Probably he even despises us because we have responded so readily to his blandishments, and also because we can never respond enough.

If there was any doubt before, surely *Monsieur Verdoux* made things clear. It gives us the Tramp no longer defeated by his graces but suddenly turning them to account, master of himself and all around him. And what is this mastery?—Verdoux is a murderer. I know very well that Verdoux is not the Tramp, but he rises from the ashes of the Tramp. In their separate ways they both represent the private life of cultivation and sensibility in its opposition to society with its crowds and wars and policemen. If the Tramp had an unconscious (which is not possible), it might make him dream of being Verdoux, for Verdoux's murders are committed so that he can carry on his own idyll with his own Blind Girl; it is true that the idyll is utterly overshadowed by the murders, but this may tell us as much about idylls as it does about murder. *Monsieur Verdoux* is a cold and brilliant movie, perhaps more brilliant than anything else ever done in the movies, but we must make a certain effort of will to like it, for it gives us no clear moral framework, no simple opportunities for sentiment, and not even, despite Verdoux's continual "philosophical" pronouncements, any discernible "message," but most of all an unremitting sensation of the absence of love. The effort should be made. It is no part of Chaplin's function as an artist to love us or anyone, and I do not offer these observations as a complaint.

But if *Monsieur Verdoux* was a disturbing experience for Chaplin's audience, it must have been a truly painful one for Chaplin himself. Sweet Charlie had changed his public personality, or at any rate had thrown off its more agreeable disguises, revealing what he must have thought a more serious and in that sense more "real" aspect of himself. And the experiment was apparently disastrous; nobody loved him any more: the "true" Chaplin was repulsive. There was even an organized campaign against the movie, which, though it ostensibly concentrated its fire on Chaplin's personal and political behavior, could be successful only because *Monsieur Verdoux* was so forbidding. When this campaign culminated some years later in the Attorney General's suggestion that Chaplin, then in Europe, might not be permitted to re-enter this country, there were surprisingly few Americans who cared. We can say easily enough that this is a national shame: once again America has rejected one of her great artists. And Chaplin, no doubt, is only too ready to say the same thing; he has said it, in fact, as crudely and stupidly as possible, by his recent acceptance of the "World Peace Prize." But for him, who has asked so insistently for our love, there must be more to it than that; there must be the possibility that he has given himself away.

Limelight, made during these years of the great comedian's disgrace and completed just before his departure for Europe, is his apology and, so far as he is capable of such a thing, his self-examination. "The story of a clown who has lost his funny-bone," he called it while it was being made, and he has tried to live up to the candor of this description, presenting himself to us from the "inside" so that we may understand what has happened to him and perhaps give him again the love he has forfeited. Of course it remains a question, with him as with any artist, whether there *is* an "inside"; candor is one of the tools of art. Certainly he does not confess to anything, nor can one imagine what he might confess to if he did. But it is clear at any rate that he asks for clemency. He even brings his five children into court to sway the jury (the three youngest, though they appear for only a moment, would go far with any jury I was on). He makes little mocking references to his personal fortunes: "I've had five wives already; one more or less doesn't bother me." And he smiles at us sweetly as he has done so often in the past, but more gently now as fits his years; only once, in some "imitations" of flowers and trees, does he fully recall the archaic elfishness of the Tramp.

Now and then, it is true, he shows his teeth: as individuals, he tells us, we may possibly be lovable, but in the mass we are "a monster without a head"; Chaplin has the gift of stating such "insights" as if they have occurred to him for the first time, thus somehow redeeming them from banality. But most of the time he is rather humble, acknowledging at least the main point: that he cares for our applause. "What a sad business it is, being funny!" says the Blind Girl of this movie, and Calvero replies with a wry smile: "Yes, it is—when they don't laugh." Then he tries to explain more profoundly: "As a man gets on, he wants to live deeply. A feeling of sad dignity comes over him, and that's fatal for a comic." There is a moment when Calvero, in a dream of his past greatness, stands receiving the applause of an audience; then the smile fades, giving place to a fixed mask of the most extreme sorrow, the applause dies, the theater is empty. Again we are aware of a banality that somehow does not matter. The scene is false—how often we have been asked to believe that the sorrows of a clown are deeper than all other sorrows!—but Chaplin has lived with the falsehood and is committed to it. Besides, the statements of a clown are always false, his gestures excessive, his mask painted out of all credibility. *After all*, we are supposed to say, there is something very real in all this—but only "after all."

Perhaps, then, if Chaplin is actually trying to tell the truth, he is trying what is not possible to him, and that is why we find ourselves uneasy in his altered presence. But I don't think he has made that mistake. He is only trying to tell a clown's truth, and the "inside" of a clown, if it exists, must be as distorted as the outside—at any rate if he is a thorough clown. Chaplin is among the subtlest of artists, but he is not corrupted by subtlety. His gestures remain broad, his statements marvelously simple and clear, his ideas self-confidently crude. When

Calvero smells gas on entering his house, he looks first at the soles of his shoes to see whether he has stepped into dog's excrement. Even while he lectures on the Spirit of Life to the young girl he has saved from suicide, he remains primarily concerned with such distractions as the smell of kippered herring that has got onto his fingers—not exactly to underline what he is saying, though it has this effect, but simply because he knows a smell is always more arresting than an idea. And after all these past years of developing cinematic "art," Chaplin remains the most innocent of film technicians, using his camera only to seek the most direct means of exposition and his lighting only to illuminate; a clown's first task is to make his point unmistakably: if there is subtlety, it will come. What a world of sophistication has had to pass over Chaplin's head so that he may open this film with the epigraph, "The glamour of limelight, from which age must pass as youth enters. . . ."

Of course we would be wrong to take this epigraph entirely at face value. Chaplin often turns out to be more conscious of what he is doing than we suspect, and he has chosen to preserve the archaic tone. But with whatever reservations, he does certainly believe in what it expresses, in the "glamour of limelight"—which must mean the glamour of his own personality. It is true, perhaps, that he ought to be beyond that by now: we all know, don't we, that applause and "glamour" are not what really matter. But he is willing to admit he is not beyond it, just as he is willing to admit he can't keep his mind on the deeper questions of existence because of the smell of herring that clings to his hands. The joke is, of course, that we can't either: nobody ever gets "beyond" anything; that's probably the one joke there is in the world, and all the clowns have nothing to do but tell it to us over and over— no wonder they see no point in being anything but clear.

But though Calvero can never quite get away from the kippered herring, he keeps trying. Once awakened to the advantages of talking pictures, Chaplin in his last two movies has found it almost impossible to stop talking; it seems to have come upon him that he must bring forth all at once the stored-up wisdom of a lifetime. And like many who have thought to save their deepest statements for the last (Mark Twain is another example), Chaplin turns out to have nothing very illuminating to say; his true profundity is still in his silences. Verdoux, having discovered that men do not really live up to their moral ideas, not only drew the logical conclusion by becoming a murderer, but could not resist making little speeches about his discovery, continually poking us in the ribs for fear we might miss the point. In the end Verdoux turned out to be personally as vulnerable as his logic, and that saved the comedy, though one couldn't be sure how much of Chaplin had gone down with Verdoux. Calvero, quite as much a man of the world as Verdoux and sharing his slightly questionable elegance and half-baked independence of mind, is a more agreeable philosopher, preaching not murder but tolerance, vitality, and love. Yet his tone is not very different; like Verdoux, he is over-impressed with his ideas and must be always laboring the point. Now and then he strikes a real spark: "That's all any of us are—amateurs. We don't live long enough to be anything else." More often he can only make a good try: "Life is a desire, not a meaning." Dying, Calvero can leave us only with this: "The heart and the mind—what an enigma!" Is it this kind of thing the Tramp might have been wanting to say during those years of his silence?

I suppose it is, and I suppose it might have been better if we had never found out. But now that Chaplin has broken the silence, I confess I do not find these platitudes of his quite so distressing or inappropriate as, perhaps, I ought to. To be a clown is not an art of detachment. With whatever deliberation he may contrive his effects, in the end the clown must submit *personally* to humiliation, receiving a custard pie in his own face, falling on his own behind. Even though the fall is not so painful as it looks, it is still a real fall. Every clown, no doubt, dreams that because he has practiced the fall in advance it will not truly touch him, his essential being will remain upright; this is the source of that "tragedy" of a clown's life that we have heard so much about. But if he is a true clown, then his essential being is precisely what consents to the fall, and we who refuse to separate him from his role are more right than he is.

In *Limelight*, as in *Monsieur Verdoux*, Chaplin has got caught in this paradox. He has grown reluctant to submit directly to humiliation and is anxious to be accepted as something "more" than a clown; this is the "feeling of sad dignity" that he speaks of. It is true he also takes great pride in being a clown, but pride itself he uses as a means to deny his identity: we become aware of him suddenly as belonging to a "tradition." Of course there *is* a "tradition" and Chaplin is its highest embodiment, but when he presents himself in that role he has to that extent violated it. He is never more dignified, never less a clown, than in the scenes where he appears as a street singer, dressed handsomely in motley, passing a hat for pennies, thoroughly at ease because he has come back to his roots. "This is the only true theater," he says gesturing at the street and the world; the statement is true as it has always been, and he makes it with the authority that belongs to him, but there is something questionable in his making such a statement at all: it would come better from us who watch him.

Verdoux, despite his pretensions, was still basically a figure of absurdity, clearly unable to understand how one must get along; in his way he was just as "innocent" as the Tramp. Calvero, on the other hand, is not supposed to be in himself a clownish figure, he is just a clown by profession. In fact there must be such a division in Chaplin's personality; if there weren't, he would be insane. But his function as an artist is to demonstrate that in some fundamental sense the division is a false one; when he succeeds in obliterating it, as he was able to do entirely in the character of the Tramp and very largely even as Verdoux, he is closest to the kind of truth that most intimately belongs to him and most deeply implicates his audience. In *Limelight* he makes it very clear that he knows this. But, again, his knowledge is not what counts; a clown knows nothing, he only exists. Finding it necessary to make a direct examination of his problem as an artist, Chaplin is forced to repeat in the structure of the movie itself that division between reality and comedy, between dignity and drunkenness, which is the problem the movie deals with. The scenes of actual clowning are presented simply as stage performances, a kind of documentation of the case of the clown Calvero who has "lost his funny-bone," whereas the movie proper, so to speak, is only occasionally funny, and never very much.

The most disturbing thing about Verdoux was that one did not always know how much he was supposed to be accepted on his own terms, how much Chaplin himself was implicated in Verdoux's murders. With Calvero we are left in no such uncertainty: he is Charles Chaplin "in person" presiding at the telling of his own story and not for a moment relinquishing control. If Chaplin is willing in the role of Calvero to acknowledge his own sense of failure, it is only while making it plain that he will be the one to define what is meant by failure. If he has Calvero die breathing that lame little sentence about the enigma of the heart and the mind, it is not because he sees the sentence as dramatically appropriate, but because he thinks it expresses in itself a profound philosophical and poetic truth. The trouble is that it undeniably does, and there seems to be nothing in Chaplin's education or sensibility to tell him what the sentence lacks. And yet, whatever might be true of his education, has he not shown us over and over a sensibility a hundred times more delicate than our own?

Here we come back to that coldness of heart which seems to belong inextricably to Chaplin's genius. It must often have been said of him that he is an embodiment of childhood, and it is perfectly true. His perceptions have the eccentricity of viewpoint and the almost dazzling detailed clarity of a child's perceptions, and carry similar suggestions of unspecific and perhaps unintended depth. His feelings are as definite and as strong as a child's, and as irresistibly appealing. But like a child he is also imprisoned within the limits of his own needs and understanding, and can express no true relation with others. Precisely the lack of such a relation is what makes him a clown—the most childish kind of entertainer—and gives him his clown's subject matter. What is the Tramp but the greatest of all egotists?—an outcast by choice refusing to take the least trouble to understand his fellow men, and yet contriving by his unshakable detachment to put everyone else in the wrong, transforming his rejection of society into society's rejection of him. The Tramp can draw close only to those who are outsiders like him: children, animals, the Blind Girl—the maimed and the innocent. And in the end he is always walking away into the depths of the screen with his back turned. Verdoux, instead of protecting the lonely and innocent, preys on them, though the difference is not so absolute as it might seem: he is just as much a sentimentalist as the Tramp, as he demonstrates in sparing the life of one woman merely because he is touched by her history and because she has read Schopenhauer; and even for his victims he has a kind of icy kindness which might be one of the things that attract them.

Calvero, combining Verdoux's doubtful *savoir faire* with the Tramp's sweetness, is neither the victim of his world nor its victimizer, but a kind of benevolent observer with all the threads of life held loose in his hands. Though we come upon him when he is no longer successful as a performer, he has failed by becoming too good for his audience, too "dignified," not by falling below it. Besides, he is the only one who understands his failure, or if he doesn't exactly understand it, at least his tolerant acceptance of it takes the place of understanding. There has been a significant change in the role of the Blind Girl—this time not blind, of course, but lonely, defeated, and suffering from a functional paralysis of the legs. Having saved her from suicide and reluctantly taken her into his lodgings, Calvero in a few minutes of psychoanalysis discovers the cause of her paralysis and proceeds to cure it. Soon she becomes a ballet star. This moment of her success is when the Tramp would have found himself rejected. But now the girl makes a declaration of love—that declaration which the Tramp never had the courage to make for himself—and though Calvero lets himself be persuaded for a time, it is he who eventually refuses; he must be the one to decide who loves whom, and he has settled it that she belongs to the young composer (a part played by Chaplin's son). This is no very great renunciation, nor indeed is it presented as one. Calvero has simply avoided an entanglement as the Tramp always did, and he has bettered the Tramp by accomplishing this in such a way as to emphasize his own attractiveness. When he has gone away and the girl after many months finds him again to say she still loves him, he replies with magnificent candor: "Of course you do. You always will."

It is easy to believe him, too, for no one else in the movie is allowed to rival his charm and the mature strength of his presence, or even to become real. The girl herself, though she takes her place readily enough in the gallery of Chaplin's heroines, has less independent power than any who have preceded her. Chiefly, her function is to listen attentively, to offer herself as a passive object for his benevolence, and, since she is not actually blind, to look at him with adoration as once the Tramp would have looked at her; the looks Calvero casts back at her are looks of kindness. As for the young man, his function is to be young and nothing more. Calvero will give way to him because age must give way to youth, fathers must give way to sons, the "glamour of limelight" cannot last forever; that is the theme of the movie. But again Chaplin sets his own terms, and if he yields, it is only in principle: between the young man's stiff, un-differentiated "youth" and Calvero's lively and self-assured "age," there can be no real contest. It is Calvero whom the girl will always love—"of course."

Only among the minor characters is the color of reality allowed to emerge: in the frowzy, small-minded landlady, and in her dreadful friend who appears for just a few seconds and says nothing; in an armless music-hall performer encountered in a bar (later cut out of the film); and most of all in the self-contained, almost grotesquely prosaic street musicians who keep reappearing through the movie as representatives both of the hard everyday world where one must make a living as one can and of the "universal" world of art. In his treatment of these marginal figures Chaplin comes closest to a free and disinterested feeling for others; he could not have made such honest and simple use of them without a certain kind of love, even if this love is expressed sometimes only in the pitilessness of his observation.

The peculiarly stilted quality that troubles one in *Limelight* comes, then, not from any failure of sensibility but from a further narrowing of the field of associations and sympathies in which Chaplin's sensibility can operate, and from a consequent suppression of drama. The Tramp, despite his ultimate frigidity, at least maintained an active flirtation with the world, always escaping in the end but keeping up the excitement of the chase and even hinting strongly that he might like to be caught if only he did not like more to get away. Verdoux, having turned his frigidity into a means of making a living, is necessarily involved with the world from the start, though he tries hard to claim he is not; and he does get caught, to have his head cut off—which is possibly the kind of thing the Tramp was afraid might happen. Calvero is too self-contained either to commit murder like Verdoux or to run away like the Tramp; it would be undignified. He simply does not let anyone approach him. Certainly the five wives have left no traces; the pictures on Calvero's walls are pictures of himself. When the girl is practically forced on him, he hastens to proclaim his detachment ("... one more or less doesn't bother me") and to lay down the terms of their relation, which is to "platonic." It does not appear that this prescription is ever violated.

This Calvero stands alone on the stage—in the fading "lime-light"—and does not so much play out his personal drama as expound it. In the very tones of his voice one can feel his refusal to communicate dramatically. The girl, to whom he does most of his talking, is often little more than a point in space toward which he may orient himself; his words pass over and beyond her—they are not really intended for her at all. At bottom they are probably not even intended for us in the audience—the "monster without a head"—though, like the girl, we are allowed to listen and expected to admire. It is as if the whole movie were one of those dreams in which Calvero, trying to reassert his identity, dreams not of *being* on the stage but of *seeing* himself on the stage. He is his own audience, and his "inside," even to him, is only a mirror image of the outside. When he speaks, it is to hear his voice re-echoing within the isolation of his own being. How could he possibly have learned to sense when his words and postures begin to be false?—he has never watched the faces of those he has pretended to be talking to.

But I am not willing to leave it at that. It is not at all necessary that a clown should be in a true relation with others, or even that he should always be funny; the only necessity is that he should fail and that there should be moments when we are able to imagine that his failure is, "after all," a kind of success. Calvero's failure is clear enough: he cannot get us to take him seriously in the way he wants to be taken. We believe as much as he does in "Life" and the "miracle of consciousness"; it is an impertinence for him to lecture us about these things unless he can be eloquent, and eloquence is beyond him: all he can do is suggest the need for eloquence without ever really attaining it. Even his jokes are too often labored and stuffy. "What can the stars do?" he asks in his discourse on consciousness. "Nothing!—sit around on their axes." To hear this from the greatest comedian in the world!

But is his failure also a kind of success? I can only say it is possible to see it that way. I have no convincing argument to advance against those who see *Limelight* as no more than a crude structure of self-pity and banal "philosophy" interspersed here and there with glimpses of a past greatness. But the crudities of a great artist always have an extra dimension; Chaplin cannot so easily divest himself of his talent no matter how he may blunder. Nor can we divest ourselves of the sense of his presence, perhaps one might say his "tradition": the face and body that move before us on the screen have belonged also for all these years to the Tramp, and then to Verdoux; even the voice and the words come somehow not unexpected. This is an extra-aesthetic element, maybe, but there it is. One way or another, the movies are always forcing us outside the boundaries of art; this is one source of their special power. And of Chaplin perhaps it could even be said that in some sense he has never been an artist at all—though he is full of arts—but always and only a presence.

Calvero's failure has at least this in common with the Tramp's failure and Verdoux's: he fails in dead earnest and with a straight face, intelligently prepared for failure, it is true, but not for the particular kind of failure that comes to him, and never dreaming that his essential worth can be called into doubt. He is an honest bankrupt, so to speak, doing his best to the very end and concealing no assets; it just happens that the money in his vault is in some way devalued—not exactly counterfeit, but not altogether sound either. And yet there is something in the confidence with which he hands it over that makes one hesitate to examine it closely, at least in his presence. Suppose he should demand to see what money *we* are paying our debts with? "We're all grubbing for a living, the best of us," Calvero says once, and he is right as usual, though uninspired. For he does manage in spite of everything to implicate us in his failure. He does it not by detachment and true insight—as he might do if he were the projection of a "real" artist instead of a clown—but, on the contrary, by the hopeless depth of his own involvement; by his suspicious eagerness to have us look into his messy, unilluminating, and amateurishly doctored account books; and above all by the irresistible, brilliant purity of his egotism.

Nothing escapes the deflecting force of this uncompromising self-absorption. When Calvero philosophizes, he puts all philosophy under a cloud. Falling miles short of the kind of profundity he wants, he achieves instead a clown's profundity: we are moved not by what he says, but by his desire to speak. If he ends up with nothing but a worn-out "enigma"—well, so do the real philosophers. Supposing he were to ask us how one enigma can be better than another, could we give him a clear answer? The gap between Calvero and the philosophers is enormous, but in such gaps a clown has his victories: as Calvero gropes confidently in his darkness, it occurs to one finally that this gap between him and the philosophers is nothing compared to the gap between the philosophers and the truth. Again, when Calvero rhapsodizes on the "miracle of consciousness," he manages to suggest not only that we are all responding to life inadequately, but at the same time, by his aggressive "sincerity," that consciousness may be some kind of fake—and also that the possibility of its being a fake does not matter. And when he speaks with his most genuine emotion about love while demonstrating his own impenetrable isolation, and in his "secondary" role as a performer deflates his own sentiment with a savage little song consisting only of a meaningless repetition of the word "love," then he is striking at us very deeply, for at bottom we all fear we are incapable of love, and that what we call love is only something we wish to receive from others. That Chaplin himself is as much a "victim" in all this as we who watch him is only the completion of the irony. A clown's function is to be ridiculous and to make the world ridiculous with him. In this, Calvero has his success.

It remains to be said, nevertheless, that the famous scene near the end of the movie when Calvero performs on the stage as a comic violinist, with Buster Keaton as his accompanist, represents a kind of success far beyond the complex and unsteady ironies of the earlier parts. In this there is no longer any problem of interpretation and choice, no "victims" and no victories, no shifting of involvements back and forth between the performer and his role and his audience, no society, no egotism, no love or not-love, no ideas—only a perfect unity of the absolutely ridiculous. Perhaps the Tramp's adventure with the automatic feeding machine in *Modern Times* is as funny, but there it is still possible to say that something is being satirized and something else, therefore, upheld. The difficulties that confront Calvero and Keaton in their gentle attempt to give a concert are beyond satire. The universe stands in their way, and not because the universe is imperfect, either, but just because it exists; God himself could not conceive a universe in which these two could accomplish the simplest thing without mishap. It is not enough that the music will not stay on its rack, that the violin cannot be tuned, that the piano develops a kind of malignant disease—the violinist cannot even depend on a minimal consistency in the behavior of his own body. When, on top of all the other misfortunes that can possibly come upon a performer humbly anxious to make an impression, it can happen also that one or both of his legs may capriciously grow shorter while he is on the stage, then he is at the last extreme: nothing is left. Nothing except the deep, sweet patience with which the two unhappy musicians accept these difficulties, somehow confident—out of God knows what reservoir of awful experience—that the moment will come at last when they will be able to play their piece. When that moment does come, it is as happy a moment as one can hope for in the theater. And it comes to us out of that profundity where art, having become perfect, seems no longer to have any implications. The scene is unendurably funny, but the analogies that occur to me are tragic: Lear's "Never, never, never, never, never!" or Kafka's "It is enough that the arrows fit exactly in the wounds they have made."

WALTER KERR

The Lineage of Limelight

Witty and worldly, Walter Kerr (1913–1996) was the Pulitzer Prize–winning drama critic first for the New York Herald Tribune, *then for the* New York Times. *He was also a theater professional, writing and directing many Broadway productions. His deepest passion, however, was silent film comedy, and his masterwork as a critic was* The Silent Clowns, *a lavishly illustrated, magnificently detailed study not merely of the immortals (Chaplin, Keaton, Lloyd) but of many less well-remembered figures as well. This essay might well have stood as a coda to that distinguished work.*

One of the marks of homage we pay to a major artist is that we follow his best, his middling, and his poorest appearances with equal curiosity, if not with equal satisfaction. We do not make the production of a masterpiece the condition of our attendance upon his newest work; it is enough that he is working. Thus, for me—now that *Limelight* is here—it as ample satisfaction simply to *see* Chaplin again. Though the film runs a good two-and-a-half hours, I would have no great difficulty in sticking out another two-and-a-half without flinching. If I bring an excess of affection and respect with me, the affection and respect have

From *Focus on Chaplin* by Walter Kerr (New York, 1971), by permission of the Estate of Walter Kerr, Christopher D. Kerr, executor.

287

been earned a thousand times; if the new film tends to draw on these things in order to sustain it, I am happy enough to hand them over. Chaplin *can* do wrong; but he cannot be uninteresting.

And *Limelight* contains a good many things which carry their own weight. The climactic vaudeville sketch in which Chaplin is assisted by Buster Keaton is very funny. Chaplin has a delightful passage-at-arms with a hobgoblin landlady. Again and again the actor rescues a scene headed for bathos with a tart flash of honesty. And, perhaps most of all, he has made the interior excitement of succeeding in the theater seem real and moving: when a ballerina takes her first trial spin across a deserted stage some mysterious insight asserts itself and you know why you love this absurd profession.

But the fascination which these fragments hold for someone who is long since committed to Chaplin is quite different from the cool objectivity which must be pursued by the practicing critic. And—though no reviews have appeared at this writing—it is fairly clear that *Limelight* is in for trouble.

At first sight the difficulties which may be in store for Chaplin would seem to stem from his decision to produce an essentially serious, predominantly pathetic film in which there are—quite intentionally—only isolated bits of comedy. The old dream of Hamlet has come home to roost, we are tempted to think; the great clown has betrayed himself into an overambitious exercise in self-pity. And there are certainly moments in *Limelight* which smack so strongly of the confessional as to give support to this view.

I don't believe, though, that the problem of *Limelight* can be resolved so simply, or that the film can be distinguished from the main body of Chaplin's work in terms of seriousness, its "artiness," or its sentimentality. The sentimentality has always been there, though in the past it was usually balanced by a last-minute, face-saving comic shock; the comparative artiness of some of the photography is preferable to the harsh, flat, and old-fashioned grays which marked his last few films; and there is nothing here to say conclusively that Chaplin is incapable of a first-rate serious performance.

In spite of a certain uncomfortable coziness between Chaplin and Chaplin which runs through the film, there are many well-acted moments: the candid shame with which he accepts a loan from an old friend; the sharp tongue which he cannot still when he is offered a job he needs; the half-happy, half-stunned bewilderment of his discovery that his protégé is a better dancer than he had quite anticipated; the mocking, incredulous shrug with which he accepts an ironic dismissal from a ballet company. He has, in addition, directed the other actors well: Claire Bloom, Nigel Bruce, and son Sidney Chaplin give firm, confident, plausible performances.

What sets *Limelight* completely apart from the Chaplin tradition, and what damages it most seriously, is not its pretentious flirtation with weight, but its hopeless capitulation to words. The man who originally fought the coming of sound, who dared to produce at least two silent films long after sound had triumphed, and who, even when be began to speak, still struggled to keep the mobile image dominant over the sound track, has changed his mind. He has not only gone over to what he once considered the enemy; he has gone over with love.

From the first reel of *Limelight* it is perfectly clear that Chaplin now wants to talk, that he *loves* to talk, that in this film he intends to do little *but* talk. Where a development in the story line might easily be conveyed by a small visual effect, he prefers to make a speech about it. Where the 1917 music-hall background obviously opens the door to extensive onstage pantomime, he prefers to stand still and sing a song. This is not a compromise between the old and the new, an adjustment to inevitable and necessary change; it is a disturbing rejection of the nature of the medium itself.

Limelight has to do with a fading old vaudevillian who prevents a young dancer's suicide, who nurses the hysterically paralytic girl back to health in his own room, and who finally gives her the self-confidence she needs to work again. In an earlier Chaplin film we might have been sure of at least two scenes: one in which the unskillful and embarrassed Samaritan attempts to set up the sort of light housekeeping which will take care of the girl's needs, at first making a glorious mess of it and then suddenly and ingeniously making it all come out right (*The Kid, Modern Times*); and another in which he attempts to cheer her up with an inspirational little homily, *acted out* (David and Goliath in *The Pilgrim*, the effort to entertain the girls in *The Gold Rush*). Sound does not preclude the possibility of dramatizing these situations; it simply adds a dimension to be used or dismissed at will. In *Limelight* it is the drama-tization which has been dismissed. Mr. Chaplin simply lectures the girl, out loud and at great length. The content is entirely verbal.

Nor need the fact that this is no longer the little tramp necessarily inhibit the use of pantomime. Mr. Chaplin is playing a seedy and im-poverished former music-hall entertainer with a reputation for clown-ing; the realistic preparation is all there. Nor, finally, would the in-evitably comic quality of such improvisation in any way undercut the pathos which Mr. Chaplin is after; the pathos would be intensified at every turn (*City Lights*).

Take another, less extensive example. Chaplin tells the girl he is about to have an interview with a man who may employ him. He does not know what attitude to take: the condescending manner of a man who is regularly employed, or the supplicating manner of one who hasn't eaten in weeks. It is inconceivable that Chaplin should have been able to resist the impulse to act out both attitudes for the girl; but he has resisted it. There is, to be sure, some faint facial play as he talks out the problem, some hint of mimicry. But we are denied anything more graphic than this. The burden of the scene must rest on the di-alogue, and the impulse to illustration is forever chilled.

From being that genius who brought the form of the motion pic-ture to its purest realization, Mr. Chaplin has moved to the logical op-posite: he is no longer a man interested in making a *motion* picture at all. An inspired visual scenarist has become an indifferent playwright. There is nothing in *Limelight* which might not have been written for the stage, though it might better have been written in the heyday of the late Austin Strong.

Since Chaplin was, from the outset, painfully aware of the pitfalls of sound, how is it that he has now fallen so wholeheartedly into its deepest trap, its final excess? I think the answer lies in Chaplin's im-age of himself as philosopher.

It has always been known that the great Charlie fancied his talents as a speculative thinker. Nearly every study of Chaplin—from Sam Goldwyn's cursory *The Real Chaplin* of 1932 to Theodore Huff's ex-tended *Charlie Chaplin* of last year—remarks on his enthusiasm for "intellectual" conversation, his passionate pursuit of minds reputed to be superior in one way or another, his anxiety to meet them on their own level and, what is more, on their own subjects. Most such studies also manage to imply, in however roundabout terms, that the artist's enthusiasm tends to exceed his equipment.

Chaplin was perfectly able to resist the inroads of sound on his work as a comedian. (He didn't make an actual talking film until twelve or thirteen years after the sound revolution, and he was much praised for the manner in which he originally subordinated sound track to image.) What he apparently can no longer resist is the opportunity presented by sound to display the other, and hitherto hidden, side to his personality—his desire to be known as a thinker. He was undoubtedly encouraged in this by the vocabulary which his most ardent admirers had long used to describe his best work, a vocabulary which held the little tramp "profound," the tramp's adventures "shot through with significance," and the tramp's creator a "multiple genius."

But the difference between a visual profundity and a verbal one is very great. One is achieved intuitively, by implying layers of *unspoken* meaning behind a simple picture. The other speaks out its meaning in a series of logical equations which require no picture at all. (Thus, what Chaplin does *not* say at the end of *City Lights* is dazzling with meaning; all that he does say throughout the first half of *Limelight* is literal, explicit, and without esthetic life.)

The intuitive and the rational methods of getting at truth are antithetical methods which tend to fight one another. Rarely—very rarely—do we find the two highly developed, side by side, in a single personality. For Chaplin the switch-over was bound to be dangerous; in a predominantly pictorial medium it was almost sure to be disastrous.

The split between the artist and the thinker began with the closing moments of *The Great Dictator*. Throughout the first three quarters of that film the content—whether purposefully satirical or merely antic—is conveyed in mobile, lifelike images. The dictator does not make a speech to say that he covets the world: he dances with the globe in his hands. No one announces that the great new world order is somehow defective: a train persistently stops at the wrong place. Meanwhile an anonymous little barber shaves his customer to the rhythms of a Hungarian dance.

As the film progresses, the illiterate little barber is mistaken for the paranoid leader. At its climax, after a few preliminary comic misadventures, he is called upon to address the assembled nation. He hesitates. Then, looking directly into the camera, the figure before us launches into a long, literate harangue on the merits of political democracy. The figure is no longer anyone we recognize. It is patently not that of the barber we have fondly followed all evening; no pretense is made that the barber might be capable of such a speech. No explanation is offered because none is possible. We have simply and suddenly been introduced to the other Chaplin—Chaplin the thinker—in the intimacy of his living room. As though this first shock were not enough, another is in store for us: the speech is dreadful. It is a hoary collection of disorganized platitudes, belligerently delivered. Not only the barber has disappeared. Chaplin the artist has disappeared. The film has disappeared.

The Great Dictator need not have ended in this way, not even to make its point. The old Charlie would at least have given us an enemy plane dumping a bundle of propaganda leaflets onto Charlie's head; Charlie's girl friend Hannah laboriously spelling out words and phrases for him; and a final speech—halting, helpless, heartfelt—in which the little barber does his desperate best to reconstruct this beautiful dream, filling out in gesture which he cannot force into words. A speech in character might have been comic in its confusion and infinitely more touching in its earnest simplicity.

Chaplin's subsequent work stems directly from the last five minutes, and the worst five minutes, of *The Great Dictator*. The actor announced that *Monsieur Verdoux* was to have moral value: "Von Clausewitz said that war is the logical extension of diplomacy; M. Verdoux feels that murder is the logical extension of business." Given the intellectual posturing of this premise, it was no surprise to find the film degenerating into a thesis-piece whose point was "stated verbally by Chaplin in the bluntest possible terms and with a bitterness of intonation carrying with it, astonishingly enough, a grain or two of smugness" (Parker Tyler in *The Kenyon Review*).

Limelight has not the thesis structure of *Verdoux*, but it is ripe with random observations on Freud, life, love, nature, and fame. The language is—especially during the long first half—uncomfortably cosmic; the camera is steadily focused on Chaplin's mind. And there is finally a long of dialogue which summarizes the actor's whole latter-day development.

At one point the adoring dancer turns to the philosophical clown and says:

"To hear you talk no one would ever think you were a comedian."

Now this isn't just one of those unlucky lines that offers the reviewers an opening for sarcasm. It is much more than that, because Chaplin is ahead of the reviewers. He knows that the line is a dangerous one. He anticipates its dangers by reacting to it with mock dismay, with irony. Yet he will not part with it. He secretly hopes that, once he has made light of the whole business, the audience will still be impressed with the things a comedian can say when he puts his mind to it. He wants a disclaimer of intellectuality and an insistence upon intellectuality at one and the same moment. He is conscious of his present course, self-conscious about his present course, and determined upon his present course.

There are wheels within wheels here, but it might have been better had they never been set turning. A profound clown—the greatest, most beloved we have—is seeking a second reputation as a sage. It is not likely to equal his first.

VI

In Conclusion

J. HOBERMAN

After the Gold Rush: Chaplin at One Hundred

J. (for James) Hoberman has been a film critic at The Village Voice *since the 1980s. More than most of the mainstream critics, he has devoted much space and energy to the avant garde and the exotic. He is also the author or co-author of books about the Yiddish cinema, about the Jewish influence on the formation of modern mass culture, and, most intriguingly,* Lost Atlantis, *a fascinating study of European culture in the aftermath of the Soviet Union's collapse. This essay is a smart and affectionate appreciation of Chaplin's enduring legacy.*

He sleeps in the gutter and uses a rope to hold up his pants. He is frequently homeless and at best marginally employed. When he does work, his disorderly conduct often wrecks his employer's business, injuring innocent bystanders and bringing the police down. His world is filled with cops, to whom his instinctive response is instant flight — a madly determined, arm-flailing dash.

He is sneaky and sometimes violent. He desecrates public property. A petty thief when need be, he has no respect for authority. He

From the *Village Voice*, April 18, 1989, courtesy of the *Village Voice*.

is, of course, Charlie Chaplin's "Little Tramp," and if we stepped over him today on the streets of New York, we might scarcely recognize the prototype for the world's greatest film star, once the most popular man on earth, the icon of the 20th century, Jesus Christ's rival as the best-known person who ever lived.

Charlie Chaplin, born in London a century ago and the subject of a modest fete at the Museum of Modern Art, enjoyed sustained popularity on a scale that is difficult to imagine and may never be duplicated. He was not exactly a plaster saint, although if we judge him by the quality of his enemies (Hedda Hopper, Howard Hughes, HUAC, Hitler), his luster could hardly be greater. Scarcely a corporation man, Chaplin used his power to defy Hollywood mores and go his own way—ignoring the conventions of talking pictures, making highly personal political tracts, reinventing his image in a way no studio would have permitted.

Chaplin wasn't simply the first mass cultural icon, the embodiment of mass man, he *was* mass culture—vulgar, repetitive, shameless, addictive, utopian. In his disdain for language, he personified the universality of silent movies. As Charles Silver points out in his new monograph, Chaplin's two-reelers were immediately apprehendable: "No particular level of sophistication or even literacy was necessary . . . to see that he was special: you only had to *see*." As ancient as these artifacts are, children don't have to be educated to find them funny. His love of play and passion for disorder mirrors their own, although Chaplin's uncanny appeal is perhaps innate. (Is it that toddler walk and those spaniel eyes that, like Mickey Mouse's outsized, infantlike head, push the love button in our brains?)

Although Chaplin has been encrusted with sentimentality (much of it his own doing) and relegated to the realm of the timeless, he is and was a historical being. In the late '60s, when I came of age as a self-conscious moviegoer, Chaplin was being displaced by a revisionist reappreciation of Buster Keaton. Back then, Keaton's formalism and reflexiveness, his stylized cool and absence of sentiment seemed far more interesting than Chaplin's puppy dog, in-your-face humanism and crude theatricality. The icon obscured the artist: Chaplin's well-worn divinity concealed the radical nature of his enterprise, the degree to which his pre-1919 two-reelers thrive on urban chaos and visceral class awareness, the Wobbly esprit de corps that infuses his hatred of work, which he continually subverts and transforms into sport.

The subject and object of mechanical reproduction, Chaplin was the original parody automaton. In a recent issue of *Radical History*, Charles Musser contextualizes him in terms of Henry Ford's newfangled assembly line and the industrial efficiency technique known as "Taylorism." Indeed, reeking of class hostility, the baldly titled *Work* (released in 1915, four months after *The Birth of a Nation*) features Charlie as an assistant paperhanger employed by a bourgeois family called the Fords. *Modern Times* (1936), Chaplin's most elaborate production, is a virtual anthology of such slapstick two-reelers, every skit revolving around the struggle for survival at its most primal level. (Few movies have ever been more obsessed with the act of acquiring food.) "I came away stunned at the thought that such a film had been made and was being distributed," the critic for *New Masses* wrote. "*Modern Times* is not so much a fine motion picture as a historical event."

A historical event but not, relatively speaking, a hit. Today, *Modern Times* (which, among other things, allegorizes the process of studio filmmaking) seems Chaplin's definitive statement. Contrary to the five-year run of IBM commercials that have been spun off it, *Modern Times* criticizes not just industrial capitalism but work itself—as well as authority, the family, and the very nature of adult behavior.

He knew his audience. One thing he never sentimentalized was the rich. "No comedian before or after him has spent more energy depicting people in their working lives," writes Robert Sklar in *Movie Made America* of the star whose first film—a Keystone two-reeler released in February 1914—was aptly called *Making a Living*.

Chaplin exploded out of the Keystone ensemble at a time when the movies had again become rowdy, shaking off the five or six years of defensive gentility that followed the antinickelodeon crusades of 1908. Fittingly, the revolt against the new decorum was led by Mack Sennett, who had apprenticed with order's architect, D. W. Griffith. Although Chaplin perfected his supreme creation several months after leaving Keystone, it was there that he had his first and most extensive contact with the American people, that he mastered his timing and internalized Sennett's grotesque assault on the social order.

Within a year of leaving Sennett, Chaplin was considered the essence of laughter—although not everyone was amused. After *Work* was released, Sime Silverman, the founding editor of *Variety*, complained that "the Censor Board is passing matter in the Chaplin films that could not possibly get by in other pictures. Never anything dirtier was placed on the screen than Chaplin's 'Tramp.'" The association of Chaplin with impurity—sexual, racial, political—was something that would dog him for the next 40 years.

That spring, however, Chaplinitis swept the English-speaking world. By now Chaplin was his own trademark; the tramp was totally industrialized. There were Chaplin songs, Chaplin dances, Chaplin sketches in theatrical revues, Chaplin cocktails, Chaplin dolls, Chaplin shirts, Chaplin ties, Chaplin postcards, Chaplin animated cartoons, and a Chaplin comic strip. It was as if a new religion had been born and everyone wanted a piece of the cross. Placed beneath a marquee, the cardboard image of the little man with the skimpy mustache—his silhouette rendered indelible by bowler hat, baggy pants, and outsized shoes—was sufficient in itself to fill a theater. Demand far outstripped supply. The 26-year-old actor could not produce movies quickly enough to satisfy his fans.

Imitators were legion. "Among the happy youths of the slums, or the dandies of clubdom or college, an imitation of a Chaplin flirt of the coat, or the funny waddle of the comedian, is considered the last word in humour. To be Chaplinesque is to be funny; to waddle a few steps and then look naïvely at your audience," *Motion Picture Magazine* reported in a 1915 article simply called "Chaplinitis." Soon Chaplin look-alike contests were being held in amusement parks all over the U.S. Leslie T. (later Bob) Hope won one such in Cleveland. So many comedians were impersonating Chaplin on the screen—among them, Stan Jefferson (subsequently Laurel)—that Charlie had to file suit. It was said that for a time costume balls were ruined, because 90 per cent of the men appeared dressed as the Little Tramp. (In *The Idle Class*, Chaplin attended one such ball dressed as himself.)

America definitely had Chaplin on the brain. In Cincinnati, a holdup man used a Charlie Chaplin disguise. In a mysterious occurrence on November 12, 1916, the actor was simultaneously paged in 800 hotels. Chaplinitis spread to Europe and raged throughout the Great War. According to the British film historian Kevin Brownlow, Chaplin cut-outs were kidnapped from the lobbies of British movie theaters and born off to the trenches: "These life-sized models were popular with the troops, who would stand them on the parapet during an attack. The appearance of a crudely painted tramp, with baggy trousers and a bowler hat, must have bewildered the Germans, who had no idea who he was. To add to the confusion, British officers with a sense of humor would cultivate Chaplin mustaches, and in prison camps, every hut had its Chaplin impersonator." Nor were the French immune. "Charlot was born at the Front," wrote Blaise Cendrars. "The Germans lost the war because they didn't get to know Charlot in time."

Just as the war ended, Chaplin released his own vision of the trenches, the totally apatriotic *Shoulder Arms*, a spiritual precursor of *Catch*-22 whose bits include a fantasy of shelling the Germans with Limburger cheese and, an even more visceral evocation of combat, sleeping in a bunk that's virtually under water.

He was taken seriously almost immediately. The author of "Chaplinitis" called him a "genius" and boldly stated that "once in every century, a man is born who is able to color and influence his world. . . . Charles Chaplin is doing it with pantomime and personality." In May 1916, *Harper's Weekly* published "The Art of Charles Chaplin," an appreciation by a well-known stage actress that bracketed "the young English buffoon" with Aristophanes, Shakespeare, and Rabelais.

In France, Charlot was the subject of the first monograph on an individual film artist. In the Soviet Union, archformalist Viktor Shklovsky published a book on Chaplin in 1923. Chaplin was the movies' first *esque*, the only mass culture figure one could bracket with high modernists Eliot and Joyce, a fitting subject for a Cubist collage. (Later, Léger featured him in *Ballet Mécanique*.) It's easy to imagine Chaplin as a character in a Brecht play or Kafka novel, but in America, he was seen as the ultimate Horatio Alger hero. He arrived here a penniless immigrant—bona fide wretched refuse—and, within 24 months, became the highest paid actor in the world. (That

Chaplin refused to consummate the myth by becoming an American citizen would be held against him later.)

As an artist, he infused the pathos of the British proletariat—Dickens and the music hall—with the jazz rhythms and streamlined optimism of the newer, American variety, absorbing by osmosis French aestheticism and Jewish soul. (Feckless *Luftmensch* that Chaplin played, he was perceived as Jewish by both Jews and anti-Semites.) In a sense, Chaplin was the mascot of Western democracy. He was mobbed in Paris and London during his 1921 European tour, but ignored in Berlin, where—although some hipster had included his photograph among the Heartfields and Picabias of the 1920 Berlin Dada Fair—his films had not yet been released. Of course, the Germans would soon get their own Little Tramp/Hero of the Trenches/Man of the Century.

In *Modern Times*, Chaplin bid his greatest creation farewell. For the first time, the tramp's voice was heard (singing a nonsense song in a routine that contains in embryo all early Fellini), while the movie's last shot showed the tramp walking off down the road—no longer alone, but hand-in-hand with Paulette Goddard. "It is an ironical thought that the mustached face of Adolf Hitler will be the only living reminder of the little clown," *The New York Times* nostalgically editorialized shortly after the film's release. The thought bothered Chaplin as well. Before Hitler took power, he had been attacked by the Nazi press as "a little Jewish acrobat, as disgusting as he is tedious." (In fact, Chaplin wasn't Jewish, but, as a matter of principle, he never contradicted such accusations.) During Hitler's rule, Chaplin's movies were banned and all mention of his name proscribed. It was inevitable that this pair would go one on one.

Like twin gods in some fertile-crescent myth, the two most compelling personalities of the 20th century were born four days apart, in April 1889. They were both raised in poverty and domestic disorder, both lived as vagabonds, both dreamed of being artists, both captivated the masses, both sought absolute control over their worlds. Many, including Chaplin, believed that Hitler even borrowed his mustache from the Little Tramp. What was the secret of the atom compared to the source of Chaplin's power? Chaplin thought he understood the origin of Hitler's. In *The Great Dictator* he once and for all broke the speech barrier with a full-fledged Hitler rant in gibber-ish German. Thus did the Little Tramp acknowledge the tyranny of sound.

His reputation has had violent ups and downs. In 1919 *Theatre Maga-zine* published an article, hopefully entitled "Is the Charlie Chaplin Vogue Passing?" which scored "the appeal of every Chaplin picture to the lowest human instincts." Even when his artistic reputation was at its highest, Chaplin carried intimations of the underclass. "You have to go to squalid streets and disreputable neighborhoods if you want to see Chaplin regularly," Gilbert Seldes advised his readers on the eve of *The Gold Rush.*

No doubt Ronald Reagan would have pieties to mouth on Chap-lin's birthday, but there were periods in Chaplin's career when his most passionate defenders were Surrealists or Communists, and not even the mature success of *The Gold Rush* prevented American women's clubs from organizing a boycott of his pictures because Lita Grey divorced him. As movie-phobe H. L. Mencken noted with no small satisfaction, "The very morons who worshipped Charlie Chap-lin six weeks ago now prepare to dance around his stake while he is burned." A quarter of a century later, he suffered the most dramatic fall of any star. Small wonder that he would ultimately cast himself as the genteel mass murderer in *Monsieur Verdoux.*

Once a tramp, always a tramp: The subversion of public order, the potential for anarchy, was inextricably bound up in the Chaplin per-sona. He always found a way up authority's nose. Chaplin was at-tacked as a draft dodger during World War I, spuriously indicted for violating the Mann Act during World War II, threatened with depor-tation, and ultimately red-baited out of the United States at the height of the McCarthy period. But all that is forgotten now. On the 100th anniversary of Chaplin's birth, his progeny are everywhere and nowhere—as Garry Wills pointed out, Ronnie and Nancy mimed the last shot of *Modern Times* (embellished with an affectionately Chap-linesque kick in the butt), in *New Morning in America,* the movie shown to the world at the 1984 Republican convention.

Chaplin at 100 has become a free-floating image and an all-purpose *esque*—familiar now because he was familiar then. He is a neutral symbol of the information age, a million dollar trademark licensed to IBM to make their personal computers seem user-friendly. Leasing the Little Tramp's image from his heirs, IBM upgraded his wardrobe and occupational status: a floppy Little Yuppie for the Age of Reagan. (To approximate the full flavor of what in better days we called co-optation, one has to imagine a blue-chip corporation entrusting their $25 million advertising campaign to Richard Pryor in his "Bicentennial Nigger" heyday.)

Welcome to postmodern times: Released from the assembly line, transmuted into the pure being of empty signifier, the Little Tramp has been put back to work; he's making a living once more, earning his keep, sentenced in his afterlife to labor as a flack for the corporate order. But remember that *Modern Times* is set in Brazil and *The Kid* on Lafayette Street; that *City Lights* is a film about Donald Trump and Billie Boggs. Look at the early movies and then look around you. See if you can't find Chaplin—our contemporary—out there on the street.

Index

A NOTE ON THE EDITOR

Best known as a film critic for *Time* magazine, Richard Schickel is also the maker of an award-winning documentary film about Charlie Chaplin and the author or co-author of more than thirty books, most of them about the movies. They include major biographies of Elia Kazan, D. W. Griffith, and Clint Eastwood, and shorter books about Marlon Brando, Cary Grant, Douglas Fairbanks, Sr., James Cagney, and Woody Allen; a definitive study of Walt Disney; and a pioneering consideration of the celebrity system. His *Good Morning, Mr. Zip Zip Zip* is a memoir of growing up with the movies in the World War II years. Mr. Schickel has also written, directed, and produced a great many television programs, most of them documentaries about film and filmmakers. He received many awards for his reconstruction of Samuel Fuller's *The Big Red One.* He has held a Guggenheim Fellowship and has received the British Film Institute book prize and the Maurice Bessey award for film criticism. He lives in Los Angeles.